ENGLISH FUNDAMENTALS

ENGLISH FUNDAMENTALS

Eighth Edition   Form A

Donald W. Emery
University of Washington

John M. Kierzek
Late of Oregon State University

Peter Lindblom
Miami-Dade Community College

MACMILLAN PUBLISHING COMPANY
New York
COLLIER MACMILLAN PUBLISHERS
London

English Fundamentals copyright © 1933, 1941, 1950, and 1958 by
Macmillan Publishing Co., Inc. Earlier editions of *English
Fundamentals, Form A*, copyright © 1968, 1976, 1980 by Macmillan
Publishing Co., Inc.

MACMILLAN PUBLISHING COMPANY
866 Third Avenue, New York, New York 10022

COLLIER MACMILLAN CANADA, INC.

ISBN 0-02-333080-5

Printing: 1 2 3 4 5 6 7 8   Year: 5 6 7 8 9 0 1 2 3

ISBN 0-02-333080-5

PREFACE

As with the previous editions, the eighth edition of *English Fundamentals* required revisions done with a very fine sense of balance. The tendency to make changes simply for the sake of a new look or new materials was very strong. The opposite tendency, retaining material simply because it occurred in the previous editions, was equally strong. To avoid errors both of omission and commission, we followed the best evaluative practices available. We sent questionnaires to a large number of teachers who have used the book in previous editions, and we reviewed the professional literature that we have read since the previous edition. In all of this review work, we tried to keep uppermost in our minds the needs of students in basic composition courses and the needs of the teachers of those students. We engaged in serious discussion and debate in order to produce an eighth edition suited to the times and to the needs of composition students.

This new work, *English Fundamentals*, eighth edition, does not differ markedly from the previous edition—just as the seventh edition was much like earlier editions. The general organization, the sequence of lessons, and the clearly worded instructions and exercises will be familiar to those who have used the book in earlier editions. The instruction still begins with an analysis of the basic patterns of the sentence. On this foundation of basic sentence structure, the book builds students' knowledge of sentence formation and combining, punctuation, and usage. From these elements, the book moves finally to a section on writing, surveying college writing from paragraphs to longer essays.

The first few lessons use elementary sentences containing one-word subjects and, for the most part, one-word verbs to explain basic structure and the relationships between subjects and verbs. This simplified presentation of basic language patterns provides a useful review for more accomplished students, and it also provides manageable first-time instruction for those who are just beginning formal studies of the language. Thus the book can be used in remedial and first-semester classes and can serve as a review text in more advanced classes.

After thorough explanation and extensive practice on fundamentals, we deal with more advanced and complex matters. Techniques for building well-developed sentences, including the use of subordinate clauses, phrases, and appositives, are taught first by analysis and example and then by development. Special attention is given to writing techniques such as sentence combining. Exercises require the student to practice strategies of sentence formation that use all the resources of the language. The aim here is twofold: to develop the ability to write with flexibility and sophistication, and to develop the ability to recognize correct patterns and usage in material that is under revision.

The sections on paragraphs and essays provide an overview of most of the types of writing required at the college level. The discussions begin with an explanation of the writing process and some work in invention. The work then moves to practical applications of the writing process to essay tests, paragraphs, and essays. The examples and assignments are taken from a wide variety of disciplines, including science and business, so as to hold the interest of as many students as possible.

Two appendixes complete the book. The first is an extensive discussion of study skills that presents plans for reading and taking notes and provides a discussion of study habits and time management. This first appendix also includes a section on dictionary usage, complete with actual excerpts from several widely used desk dictionaries. The second appendix provides a set of diagnostic tests as a compact, easily graded check on knowledge of spelling, punctuation, sentence structure, and usage.

As always, the eighth edition of *English Fundamentals* will be available in three forms: A, B, and C. Each form provides a completely new set of exercises for the instructional content, which remains the same in all forms. Work on the exercises can be done in the text and detached without damaging the instructional materials.

We would like to offer our special thanks to all who assisted us in assessing the seventh edition and developing the eighth. The following people offered us valuable suggestions that we considered while developing the text, which is of course our responsibility and not theirs. Our thanks then to Victor Aquino Jr. of Green River Community College, Robert B. Bland of Gulf-Coast Bible College, Marion Bratt of Phoenix College, Irene Brenalvirez of Nassau Community College, Gerald L. Brown of the University of Pittsburgh at Johnstown, Dr. Trent Busch of Valdosta State College, Linda M. Comerford of Indiana University—Purdue University at Indianapolis, Sister Mary Colleen Dillon of Thomas More College, Robert Doak of Wingate College, Elizabeth F. Duke of Virginia Commonwealth University, Lucille M. Johnson of Pacific Lutheran University, W. Grayson Lappert of Baldwin-Wallace College, Eugenie C. Mann of The College of Charleston, David A. McMurrey of the University of Texas at Austin, Lynn R. Neil of Northwest Nazarene College, Adrian S. Palmer of the University of Utah, Charles Rankin of Georgia College, Agnes Elizabeth Robertson of Georgia Institute of Technology, and Richard F. Thompson of Northern Virginia Community College. We also acknowledge a debt of gratitude to Eben Ludlow of Macmillan for valuable advice and assistance.

D. W. E.
P. L.

CONTENTS

LESSON

1 The Simple Sentence;
Subjects and Verbs

O NE WAY of defining a **sentence** is to say that it is an orderly arrangement of words that makes sense. If we wish to be more technical, we can say that a sentence is a self-contained grammatical unit, usually containing a subject and a verb, that conveys to the listener or the reader a meaningful assertion, question, command, or exclamation.

Despite the difficulty of producing a satisfying definition, we must acknowledge the importance of the sentence as a basic unit of written or oral expression. In the first few lessons of this book, we shall examine the parts that make up a sentence and the distinctive characteristics of a few basic types of sentences that are the underlying structures of more complicated grammatical units.

To begin our work, we must be sure that we can recognize the two indispensable parts of a sentence, the **subject** (the unit about which something is said) and the **verb** (the unit that says something about the subject). Here are a few things to remember about the subject–verb relationship:

1. When the sentence is one that reports a specific action taking place, the verb usually displays itself prominently and is easily recognized. For instance, in "The rusty bumper on the front of my truck *rattles* noisily," the verb tells what happens—it is, unmistakably, *rattles*. Then, by asking the question, "Who or what rattles?" we come up with the subject, *bumper*; notice that neither "Front rattles" nor "Truck rattles" tells us what the sentence really means.

2. The function of many sentences, however, is not to report that the subject *does* something. Instead, the purpose is to say something about the *condition* of the subject: to point out a descriptive quality of it or to say that something else resembles or is the same thing as the subject. In this kind of sentence you must look for verbs like *am, are, is, was, were, seem,* and *become*, words that are almost impossible to define because they lack the concrete exactness and action of verbs like *rattle, throw, injure,* and *explode*. In the descriptive type of sentence, the subject usually reveals itself easily. For example, in "The long first *chapter* seemed particularly difficult," the *who* or *what* about which the statement is being made—in other words, the subject—is *chapter*. "Chapter particularly" or "Chapter difficult" in no way resembles a statement. But "Chapter seemed," although incomplete, does sound like a statement, or at least the nucleus of a statement; therefore the verb is *seemed*.

3. Very often the true subject has material intervening between it and its verb:

The *cost* of these items *rose*. [The subject is *cost*, not *items*.]
Only *one* of my friends *called* me. [The subject is *one*, not *friends*.]
Each of the cars *is* in the garage. [The subject is *each*, not *cars*.]

1

4. The normal order of the modern English sentence places the subject before the verb. We sometimes use sentences, however, beginning with some kind of adverbial modification, in which the verb precedes the subject:

Behind the house *stood* [verb] an old *mill* [subject].

5. A very common type of sentence with the inverted subject–verb arrangement uses *here* or *there* preceding the verb:

Here *is* [verb] my late *theme* [subject].
There *are* [verb] ten *chairs* [subject] in this room.
Suddenly there *came* [verb] a *cry* [subject] for help.

For our first practice work we shall use only one-word subjects. With this limitation the subject is always a noun or a pronoun. We should now remind ourselves of a few facts about the *form* of nouns, pronouns, and verbs, so that we can easily recognize them.

A **noun** is a word that names something, such as a person, a place, a thing, a quality, or an idea. A noun is called a *common noun* and is not capitalized if it names just any member of a group or class (*man, city, school, relative*); it is called a *proper noun* and is capitalized if it names a particular individual in a group or class (*Albert Lawson, Toledo, Horace Mann Junior High School, Aunt Louise*).

Most nouns have two forms; they show whether the noun is naming one thing (singular number) or more than one thing (plural number, which adds *s* or *es* to the singular): one *coat*, two *coats*; a *lunch*, several *lunches*. Proper nouns are rarely pluralized, and some common nouns have no plural form, for example, *honesty, courage, ease*, and *hardness*. (Lesson 28 examines in detail the special spelling problems of plural nouns.)

Nouns often follow *the, a*, or *an*, which are called **articles**. A descriptive word (an adjective) may come between the article and the noun. But the word that answers the question "What?" after an article is a noun:

A (*or* The) happy ——————— (The space must be filled with a noun.)

Another aid in identifying nouns is the recognition of certain suffixes. (See Supplement 1.)* Here are some of the common suffixes we find on hundreds of nouns:

age [break*age*]; ance, ence [resist*ance*, insist*ence*]; dom [king*dom*]; hood [child*hood*]; ion [prevent*ion*]; ism [national*ism*]; ment [move*ment*]; ness [firm*ness*]; or, er [invest*or*, los*er*]; ure [expos*ure*]

A **pronoun** is a word that substitutes for a noun. There are several classes of pronouns. (See Supplement 2.) The following classes can function as subjects in the basic sentences that we will be examining in these early lessons:

• Personal, used to substitute for definite persons or things: *I, you, he, she, it, we, they*.

* In some lessons of this book you will find notations referring you to a supplement that is appended at the end of the lesson. Read the supplement *after* you have thoroughly studied the lesson. The lesson contains the essential information that is vital to your understanding of subsequent lessons and exercises. The supplement presents material that has relevance to some points of the lesson but has only incidental application to the lessons and exercises that follow. The supplements at the end of this lesson are found on p. 3.

- Demonstrative, used to substitute for things being pointed out: *this, that, these, those.*
- Indefinite, used to substitute for unknown or unspecified things: *each, either, neither, one, anyone, somebody, everything, all, few, many,* and so on.
- Possessive, used to substitute for things that are possessed: *mine, yours, his, hers, its, ours, theirs.*

A **verb** is a word that expresses action, existence, or occurrence by combining with a subject to make a statement, to ask a question, or to give a command. One easy way for you to identify a word as a verb is to use the following slot test:

Let's _____ [something].

Any word that will function in this position to complete the command is a verb: "Let's *leave.*" "Let's *buy* some popcorn." "Let's *be* quiet." This test works only with the basic present form of the verb, not with forms that have endings added to them or that show action taking place in the past: "Let's *paint* the car" (not "Let's *painted* the car").

Supplement 1

A **suffix** is a unit added to the end of a word or base, making a derived form. A similar unit added to the beginning of a word is called a **prefix.** Thus, to the adjective *kind,* we add a prefix to derive another adjective, *unkind,* and a suffix to derive the nouns *kindness* and *unkindness.* An awareness of how suffixes are used will do far more than aid you in your ability to recognize parts of speech: Your spelling will improve and your vocabulary will expand as well.

Hundreds of nouns have distinctive suffix endings. The definitions of some of these suffixes are rather difficult to formulate, but you can quite readily figure out the meanings of most of them: *ness,* for instance, means "quality or state of" (thus *firmness* means "the state or quality of being firm"); *or* and *er* show the agent or doer of something (an *investor* is "one who invests").

Supplement 2

Two classes of pronouns, the **interrogative** and the **relative,** are not listed here. Because they are used in questions and subordinate clauses but not in simple basic sentences, they will not be discussed until later lessons.

Another type of pronoun that you use regularly (but not as a true subject) is the **intensive** or **reflexive** pronoun, the "self" words used to add emphasis:

You *yourself* made the decision.

or to name the receiver of an action when the doer is the same as the receiver:

The boy fell and hurt *himself.*

The first example is the intensive use; the second is the reflexive. Pronouns used this way are *myself, yourself, himself* (not *hisself*), *herself, itself, ourselves, yourselves,* and *themselves* (not *themself, theirself,* or *theirselves*).

The "self" pronouns are properly used only for these two purposes. They should not be substituted for regular personal pronouns:

Jean and I [not *myself*] received invitations.
The coach sent Tom and *me* [not *myself*] in near the end of the game.

EXERCISE 1
Subjects and Verbs

NAME _____ SCORE _____

DIRECTIONS: In the space at the left, copy the word that is the verb of the italicized subject.

_____ 1. The *reason* for the senator's refusal soon became clear to all of us.

_____ 2. *Several* of the new students misinterpreted the instructions.

_____ 3. The temporary *chairman* quickly tabled my resolution.

_____ 4. *One* of the defense attorneys cross-examined the witness.

_____ 5. *This* is our most popular inexpensive lawnmower.

_____ 6. Here is our most popular inexpensive *lawnmower*.

_____ 7. A home *computer* with a word processor lightened his work.

_____ 8. Only *two* of our salespeople work on Saturdays.

_____ 9. Not far from our apartment is a well-equipped *playground*.

_____ 10. A *series* of mishaps delayed the completion of the spaceship.

_____ 11. From deep in the abandoned well came a faint *cry* for help.

_____ 12. *All* except one of my classes this semester meet in Clark Hall.

_____ 13. In the outer office there's an extra *typewriter* for student use.

_____ 14. The revised *schedule* for this year's concerts is now available.

_____ 15. *Neither* of the two treaties pleased the midwestern lawmakers.

_____ 16. Only a few *chances* on this exciting raffle remain unsold.

_____ 17. A few withered *apples* still hang from the branches of the tree.

_____ 18. At the end of the book is a detailed *index*.

_____ 19. A 747 on its way to London roared down the runway.

_____ 20. *Some* of these stories offended a few members of the audience.

DIRECTIONS: In the space at the left, copy the word that is the subject of the italicized verb.

_____ 1. The view from my office window *is* not very inspirational.

_____ 2. One of the Australian runners soon *outdistanced* the champion.

_____ 3. At the entrance to the embassy *stood* a six-foot-tall U.S. Marine.

_____ 4. Lowered supplies of strategic metals *worry* many military experts.

_____ 5. Most of these sheepherders *came* originally from Spain.

_____ 6. Here *comes* that tiresome Mr. Lowe with his two mischievous sons.

_____ 7. An infestation of locusts *brought* famine to the area.

_____ 8. Nearly all of the children in the audience *listened* attentively to the speaker.

_____ 9. The displeasure of the presiding judge *was* apparent to all of us.

_____ 10. Only a small part of the new evidence *proved* usable.

_____ 11. The sale of 600 acres of the original plantation *gave* Uncle Talmadge the necessary capital.

_____ 12. There *were*, of course, other reasons for my refusal.

_____ 13. Not one of his so-called friends *came* forward with an offer of help.

_____ 14. Barely discernible through the thick fog over the river *were* the towers of lower Manhattan.

_____ 15. The end of the bargaining sessions between labor and management *is* now in sight.

_____ 16. The greenhouse, in addition to the garage, *received* heavy damage during the flood.

_____ 17. One of the lugs on the left rear wheel *worked* loose.

_____ 18. Early the next morning a small party of young hikers *appeared* at our camp.

_____ 19. The sudden appearance of the principal *quieted* the noisy students.

_____ 20. Here *are* three complimentary tickets for the next home game.

EXERCISE 2
Subjects and Verbs

NAME _____   SCORE _____

DIRECTIONS: In the first space at the left, copy the subject of the sentence. In the second space, copy the verb.

_____ 1. The possibility of your uncle's election is remote.

_____
_____ 2. Rumors of a revolt against the military leaders spread throughout the villages.

_____ 3. They're two of my father's oldest friends.

_____
_____ 4. On the western horizon loomed the jagged peaks of the Rockies.

_____
_____ 5. Three of my high-school classmates work during the summer as lifeguards.

_____
_____ 6. The chances of misunderstandings among the foreign delegates are great.

_____
_____ 7. Another of his annoying traits is his exaggerated self-pity.

_____
_____ 8. The lack of first-aid equipment in the factory shocked the inspectors.

_____ 9. Most of the vacationers leave the island after Labor Day.

_____
_____ 10. He's without question the best qualified of the five applicants.

_____ 11. Here is an extra copy of the class schedule.

_____
_____ 12. A layer of heavy, ominous clouds blocked out the sun.

_____
_____ 13. There I sat, miserable and self-conscious.

_____
_____ 14. There were three other equally apprehensive freshmen in the waiting room.

_____ 15. Out of the dense fog appeared the dim figure of a camel.

_____
_____ 16. A feeling of frustration and resentment overcame me.

_____
_____ 17. The teacher's dismay over our son's study habits is understandable.

_____
_____ 18. Many of Joyce's coworkers in the Peace Corps attended her wedding.

_____
_____ 19. On the fifth floor are offices for our graduate teaching fellows.

_____
_____ 20. One of the real heroes of the uprising was Sergeant Lewis.

_____
_____ 21. Your bill for purchases during March is payable on May 15.

_____ 22. I've enough money for only three tickets to the movie.

_____ 23. To his loyal friends and patient family, he dedicated his first volume of essays.

_____ 24. From somewhere in the dark basement came the faint squeaking of mice.

_____ 25. Ugly stories of police brutality occasionally slipped by the dictator's censors.

_____ 26. Next in the procession was the fife-and-drum corps from Central High School.

_____ 27. For breakfast he sometimes has a small steak with three fried eggs.

_____ 28. There's no excuse for such carelessness.

_____ 29. Two thirds of our students support themselves.

_____ 30. The presence of a neutral mediator prevented further outbreaks.

_____ 31. Onto the rolling plains of Oklahoma surged the eager throngs of homeseekers.

_____ 32. Between the house and the swimming pool is a partially covered patio.

_____ 33. The last of our long procession of summer guests left for home yesterday.

_____ 34. Only three of our large group of tourists spoke German.

_____ 35. Fear of exposure, rather than any sense of wrongdoing, sent Charles to his counselor.

_____ 36. A series of minor mishaps and awkward reverses embarrassed the candidate.

_____ 37. Above the gains of either political party is the welfare of our country.

_____ 38. And now, ladies and gentlemen, here is our distinguished speaker for this evening.

_____ 39. Enrollment in my adult-education class exceeds that in my regular day class.

_____ 40. After that humiliating incident, they're no longer welcome here.

LESSON

2 Verbs, Adjectives, Adverbs, and Prepositions

IN LESSON 1 you learned how to recognize a verb. The verb form that you examined then is called the **base** or **infinitive;** it is the form that "names" the verb. In the English sentence, verbs change their form according to three conditions: person, number, and tense. You should learn the most important of these forms, the ones that occur in nearly every sentence that you speak or write.

Person distinguishes the person(s) speaking (first person: *I, we*), the person(s) spoken to (second person: *you*), and the person(s) or thing(s) spoken about (third person: *he, she, it, they*). **Number** shows whether the reference is to one thing (singular number) or to more than one thing (plural number). **Tense** refers to the time represented in the utterance, whether it applies to the present moment (I *believe* him) or to some other time (I *believed* him, I *will believe* him). (See Supplement 1.)

To demonstrate these changes in form, we can use a chart or arrangement called a *conjugation*. In the partial conjugation that follows, three verbs are used: *earn, grow,* and *be*. The personal pronoun subjects are included to show how the person and number of the subject affect the form of the verb.

SINGULAR	PLURAL

Present Tense

I earn, grow, am	We earn, grow, are
You earn, grow, are	You earn, grow, are
He earns, grows, is	They earn, grow, are

Past Tense

I earned, grew, was	We earned, grew, were
You earned, grew, were	You earned, grew, were
He earned, grew, was	They earned, grew, were

Future Tense

I shall earn, grow, be	We shall earn, grow, be
You will earn, grow, be	You will earn, grow, be
He will earn, grow, be	They will earn, grow, be

Present Perfect Tense

I have earned, grown, been	We have earned, grown, been
You have earned, grown, been	You have earned, grown, been
He has earned, grown, been	They have earned, grown, been

Past Perfect Tense

I had earned, grown, been	We had earned, grown, been
You had earned, grown, been	You had earned, grown, been
He had earned, grown, been	They had earned, grown, been

Future Perfect Tense

I shall have earned, grown, been	We shall have earned, grown, been
You will have earned, grown, been	You will have earned, grown, been
He will have earned, grown, been	They will have earned, grown, been

Notice that in the past tense *earn* adds an *ed* ending but *grow* changes to *grew*. This difference illustrates regular and irregular verbs, the two groups into which all English verbs are classed. *Earn* is a regular verb and *grow* is an irregular verb. Lesson 20 lists many irregular verbs and examines certain usage problems that come from confusion between regular and irregular verbs. Notice also that some of the verb forms consist of more than one word *(will earn, have grown, will have been)*. In such uses, *will* and *have* are called **auxiliary verbs**. More auxiliary verbs are examined in Lesson 5.

With the "naming" words (nouns and pronouns) and the "action" words (verbs), we can construct true sentences:

Harriet arrived.
He laughed.
Power corrupts.

But for the production of more varied and complete sentences we rely on the "describing" words (adjectives and adverbs) and on prepositional phrases.

An **adjective** is a word that describes or limits—that is, gives qualities to—a noun. The positions in which adjectives are found within the sentence are (1) preceding a noun that is in any of the noun positions within the sentence (The *small* child left. He is a *small* child. I saw the *small* child. I gave it to the *small* child); (2) following a describing (linking) verb and modifying the subject (The child is *small*. Mary looked *unhappy*. We became *upset*); and, less often, (3) directly following the noun (He provided the money *necessary* for the trip. The hostess, *calm* and *serene*, entered the hall).

Certain characteristics of form and function help us to recognize adjectives. There are several suffixes that, when added to other words or roots of other words, form adjectives. Here again, an understanding of the meaning of a suffix can save trips to the dictionary. For instance, in the hundreds of adjectives ending in *able (ible)*, the suffix means "capable of" or "tending to"; thus *usable* means "capable of being used" and *changeable* means "tending to change."

able, ible [read*able*, irresist*ible*]; al [internation*al*]; ant, ent [resist*ant*, diverg*ent*]; ar [lun*ar*]; ary [budget*ary*]; ful [meaning*ful*], ic, ical [cosm*ic*, hyster*ical*]; ish [fool*ish*]; ive [invent*ive*]; less [blame*less*]; ous [glamor*ous*]; y [greas*y*]

(One word of warning: Many other words in English *end* with these letters, but you can easily see that they are not employing the suffix. T*able*, ferm*ent*, arr*ive*, d*ish*, and pon*y*, for instance, are not adjectives.)

Nearly all adjectives, when they are used in comparisons, can be strengthened or can show degree by changing form or by using *more* and *most*:

great trust, *greater* trust, *greatest* trust
sensible answer, *more sensible* answer, *most sensible* answer

The second of these forms (*greater* trust, *more sensible* answer) is the **comparative degree**. It compares two things. The third (*greatest* trust, *most sensible* answer) is the **superlative degree** and distinguishes among three or more things. (See Supplement 2.)

Another modifier is the **adverb,** a word that modifies anything except a noun or a pronoun. Most adverbs modify verbs (He returned *soon*); others modify adjectives and other adverbs (The *very* old man walked *quite* slowly); and some modify whole sentences (*Consequently*, we refused the offer).

Adverbs tell certain things about the verb, the most common being

1. Manner: John performed *well*. We worked *hard*. The child laughed *happily*. *Gladly* would I change places with you.

2. Time: I must leave *now*. I'll see you *later*. *Soon* we shall meet *again*.

3. Frequency: We *often* go on picnics, *sometimes* at the lake but *usually* in the city park.

4. Place: *There* he sat, alone and silent. *Somewhere* we shall find peace and quiet.

5. Direction: The police officer turned *away*. I moved *forward* in the bus.

6. Degree: I could *scarcely* hear the speaker. I *absolutely* refuse to believe that story.

This classification gives a helpful clue to the recognition of the most frequently used adverbs, which supply the answers to such questions as "How?" (manner), "When?" (time or frequency), and "Where?" (place).

Adverbs of a subclass called **intensifiers** modify adjectives or adverbs but not verbs: a *very* good meal, his *quite* surprising reply, *too* often, *somewhat* reluctantly, and so on.

A **preposition** is a word that introduces a phrase and shows the relationship between its object and some other word in the sentence. Notice that many prepositions show a relationship of space or time. Here are some common prepositions; those in the last column are called *group prepositions:*

about	beside	inside	through	according to
above	besides	into	throughout	because of
across	between	like	till	by way of
after	beyond	near	to	in addition to
against	by	of	toward	in front of
around	down	off	under	in place of
at	during	on	until	in regard to
before	except	out	up	in spite of
behind	for	outside	upon	instead of
below	from	over	with	on account of
beneath	in	since	without	out of

Every preposition has an object; with its object and any modifiers, the preposition makes a prepositional phrase. You can easily illustrate the function of prepositions by constructing sentences like the following:

After lunch I conferred *with* the owner *of* the building. [Objects: *lunch, owner, building.*]

Two *of* the motions were seconded *by* a delegate *from* Detroit. [Objects: *motions, delegate, Detroit.*]

Because of the noise made *by* the workers *in* the room *above* my office, I usually go *into* one *of* the other offices when I talk *on* the telephone. [Objects: *noise, workers, room, office, one, offices, telephone.*]

In spite of my warning, the boy rushed *out of* the house and stood *in front of* the parked truck. [Objects: *warning, house, truck.*]

11

Supplement 1

An awareness of the changes in verb forms is necessary before you can understand why certain of these forms are preferred over others in given sentences, why a careful speaker is expected to say, for instance, "The price of eggs *is* (not *are*) rising" or "I *saw* (not *seen*) him recently." Usage problems of this type are examined in Lessons 20 and 21.

Supplement 2

There are other classes of words that modify nouns but differ somewhat in form and use from the true adjectives. But when we concentrate on the *functions* of the various kinds of words, we can safely classify as adjectives all words that precede nouns and limit their meaning, including articles, numerals, and possessives (*an* apple, *the* weather, *my three* roommates); modifiers that can be used also as pronouns (*these* people, *some* friends, *all* workers); and nouns that modify other nouns (*basketball* players, *summer* days, *crop* failures).

Many words can be used as adjectives or as pronouns; the position of a word within the sentence determines which part of speech it is:

Many [*adj.*] friends of mine [*pron.*] believed this [*adj.*] story.
Many [*pron.*] of my [*adj.*] friends believed this [*pron.*].

EXERCISE 3
Parts of Speech

NAME _____ SCORE _____

DIRECTIONS: In each space at the left, write one of the following numbers to identify the part of speech of each italicized word:

1. Noun	3. Verb	5. Adverb
2. Pronoun	4. Adjective	6. Preposition

_____ 1. Most of us freshmen are *envious* of Carol's athletic *skills*.

_____ 2. The young *athlete skillfully* avoided the tackler.

_____ 3. *Without* a doubt, the accident was *avoidable*.

_____ 4. My roommate's return from Italy *before* the end of the month is *doubtful*.

_____ 5. We arrived *late* and missed the *introduction* of the speaker.

_____ 6. The vice-president's *arrival* at some *later* date is expected.

_____ 7. You should use *this* tennis racket; *mine* is too heavy for you.

_____ 8. *This* is my violin case; the one leaning *against* the wall is yours.

_____ 9. Her youthful mistakes *now* weigh *heavily* on her conscience.

_____ 10. On his month-long diet, Bob *conscientiously* recorded his *weight* every day.

_____ 11. *Until* the end of the year the payments will be made *monthly*.

_____ 12. *Each monthly* payment should arrive by the fifth of the month.

_____ 13. All of *these* bills are *payable* by the end of this week.

_____ 14. *These* are my *favorite* flowers.

_____ 15. Some players *accused* the coach of *favoritism*.

_____ 16. The *accusations* were *easily* proved false.

_____ 17. *Everyone* expected you to have *proof* of your story.

_____ 18. She sang *noticeably better* after only a few lessons.

_____ 19. He built a *better* mousetrap, but no one *noticed* it.

_____ 20. *During* the lawyer's plea, Doris *seemed* quite uninterested.

_____ 21. *Either* of these plans will hasten the *completion* of the merger.

_____ 22. In their *haste* the planners *overlooked* one important problem.

_____ 23. *Without* your good *advice* I would never have entered college.

_____ 24. I *advise* you to return to the reception room and sit *down*.

_____ 25. *One* of our speedy ends *downed* the football in the end zone.

_____ 26. We soon *grew weary* of Thatcher's juvenile jokes.

_____ 27. The three *juveniles wearily* trudged back to Kamp Karefree.

_____ 28. *Behind* the farmhouse is a very *deep* well.

_____ 29. If you dig *deep* enough, you are *certain* to find water.

_____ 30. One of his grandfathers had found a *watery* grave in the *depths* of the Indian Ocean.

_____ 31. The new man works *well* but seems *painfully* shy.

_____ 32. *Many* people find Sylvia's *shyness* quite attractive.

_____ 33. *Many* of the *attractions* at the county fair are inexpensive.

_____ 34. Drastic economies *lowered* the *original* expenses.

_____ 35. Mary had *originally* planned to get a degree in *economics*.

_____ 36. The car parked next to *ours* had a *flat* tire.

_____ 37. The taxi driver *flatly* refused to go *beyond* the city limits.

_____ 38. The possibilities of financial gain in this job are *almost limitless*.

_____ 39. Her nephew had *never* been *gainfully* employed.

_____ 40. My *employer* is often cranky, but *yours* seems quite mild.

EXERCISE 4
Subjects and Verbs

NAME _____ SCORE _____

DIRECTIONS: In the first space at the left, copy the word that is the subject of the sentence. In the second space copy the verb. Many of the verbs consist of more than one word.

_____   1. Wide reading will most certainly extend your vocabulary.

_____   2. The sight of the crossroads store brought back memories of my first job.

_____   3. There is no really easy way to the mastery of language.

_____   4. The selection of worthwhile reading materials is one of the teacher's greatest challenges.

_____   5. On a shelf near the rear of the store stood a keg of pungent dill pickles.

_____   6. No longer will the wicked dragon imperil the villagers.

_____   7. One of the best exhibits at the fairgrounds was a model dairy.

_____   8. Membership in a high-school sorority or rally squad rarely impresses a college admissions officer.

_____   9. Complaints about the unfairness of life will not win you much sympathy.

_____   10. We will, at some more convenient time, examine your proposal in more detail.

_____   11. Registration of all new voters will have ended by July 15.

_____   12. Never before has there been such an extensive use of television in an election.

_____   13. Not one of my answers on the personality profile test agreed with the correction chart.

_____   14. This will be Jenny's first trip beyond the borders of the state of Texas.

_____   15. We're really unhappy with next fall's football schedule.

_____   16. A few months later, the presidency of the largest campus in the state system became available.

_____   17. She's known my mother ever since college days.

_____   18. At my age the discomforts of airports, airplanes, and motels have made travel a real bore.

_____   19. There's been a noticeable improvement lately in the behavior of this class.

_____   20. With luck we will have finished these tiresome interviews by lunchtime.

21. Never again will you find high-quality ski jackets at these amazing prices.
22. We've already had three tornado warnings this month.
23. Only a few of the distinguished graduates attended the meeting.
24. Yours was the only entry with correct answers to every one of the problems.
25. Vital to a successful season for the Vikings will be the health of Sherman, our star quarterback.
26. Perhaps one of the county road crews will bulldoze a road to the lakeshore.
27. With Taylor's fumble on the last play went our chance for a tie score.
28. Lack of rainfall had a disastrous effect on our region last year.
29. In the row ahead of us sat a group of noisy, gum-chewing youngsters.
30. Neither of these two copiers really fits our needs.
31. Beyond stretched the seemingly endless expanse of the Manitoba prairie.
32. During the second semester of my sophomore year, my expenses rose alarmingly.
33. There were only two unoccupied seats on the bus.
34. Along the south wall of the balcony are three copying machines.
35. The drop in the property tax rate for next year will come as a pleasant surprise.
36. Some of the speaker's attempts at humor were in questionable taste.
37. Among the thousands of worthless papers were two valuable letters from Abraham Lincoln.
38. A few days at the quiet, secluded beach resort will revive your spirits.
39. There is a serious misprint on the last page of the third chapter.
40. Few of my classmates seemed interested in the debate.

3 Basic Sentence Patterns with Intransitive Verbs

YOU MAY be surprised to learn that, in spite of the apparent complexity of English sentences, there are only a few *basic* patterns into which words can be arranged and still make sense. In this lesson and the following lesson, we shall examine five basic sentence patterns, which you should think of as the simplest units of communication. If you learn to recognize these five basic patterns, you will feel more secure later in your study of more complicated sentences, most of which are combinations of basic sentences or well-defined and orderly alterations of them.

Each of the five basic sentence types is distinguished from the others by the nature of the verb, that is, (1) whether a complement ("completer") must be added, and (2) the kind of complement that must be added if the subject–verb combination by itself does not make a complete statement. The first determination must be whether a verb use is transitive or intransitive.

A **transitive** verb names an activity performed by the subject *upon* something. A transitive verb requires the addition of a direct object, the receiver of the action:

Yesterday I *wrecked* _____. (A "something" is required.)
The banker *demanded* _____. (A "something" is required.)
All of us *appreciate* _____. (A "something" is required.)

As we shall learn in the next lesson, where we examine the direct object in detail, these subject–verb combinations make sense only when some noun is added to show what received the action:

Yesterday I wrecked my *car*.
The banker demanded three *references*.
All of us appreciate your *kindness*.

An **intransitive** verb does not require a direct object; in other words, an intransitive verb does not name an activity that is carried over to or performed upon something. In this lesson we shall study the two basic sentence patterns that use intransitive verbs.

Sentence Pattern 1 contains an intransitive verb and is the only basic sentence that does not require a complement.

SAMPLE SENTENCE: Children run.

This pattern can be represented as follows:

$$S.—V.i.,$$

with the *V.i.* standing for "intransitive verb," the kind of verb in which no action is performed on or transferred to anything. Pattern 1 sentences nearly always contain modifiers:

Sometimes the neighborhood children run happily down the street.

Notice that the material associated with the verb is all adverbial: *sometimes* (When?), *happily* (How?), *down the street* (Where?). All of these additions, of course, augment the total meaning of the verb, but the important characteristic of a Pattern 1 sentence is that there is no noun answering the question "What?" after the verb. Spotting the lack of a noun answering the question "What?" after the verb is the best way to recognize an intransitive verb.

In some Pattern 1 sentences, the purpose of the statement is to say no more than that the subject exists. Usually some adverbial material is added to show the place or the time of the existence:

> Your friends *are* in the front hall.
> The dedication *occurred* much later.
> There *were* several refusals.

In most Pattern 1 sentences, however, some activity takes place, but no completer is needed because the action is not transferred to anything:

> The boat *sank.*
> My roommate *sings* beautifully.
> Jackson Creek *flows* into the Platte River.

Sentence Pattern 2 includes two closely related kinds of sentences. The purpose of the first type is to say that the subject is the same thing as something else, in other words, to rename the subject:

SAMPLE SENTENCE: The child is a genius.

The noun or pronoun that renames the subject is called a **subjective complement,** because it completes the verb and renames the subject. The special type of intransitive verb that is used in Pattern 2 sentences is called the **link** or **linking verb.**

$$\text{S.} \; - \; \text{V.lk.} \; - \; \text{S.C.}$$
$$\text{(child)} \quad \text{(is)} \quad \text{(genius)}$$

Or we can also represent this sentence as follows:

$$N_x - V.lk. - N_x$$

This kind of representation can be helpful; it shows that both of the noun units (*child* and *genius*) refer to the same thing.

In the second type of Pattern 2 sentence, the subjective complement is an adjective; it relates to the subject as a describer rather than as a renamer:

SAMPLE SENTENCE: The child is clever.

$$\text{S.} \; - \; \text{V.lk.} \; - \; \text{S.C.}$$
$$\text{(child)} \quad \text{(is)} \quad \text{(clever)}$$
$$\text{N.} \; - \; \text{V.lk.} \; - \; \text{Adj.}$$

There are comparatively few verbs that have the linking function. We can conveniently think of them in three closely related groups:

1. *Be,* the most commonly used linking verb, and a few others meaning essentially the same thing: *seem, appear, prove, remain, continue,* and so forth.

> My roommate *is* a very good student.
> The speaker *seemed* unhappy.
> He *remained* a rebel.
> The weather *continued* warm.

2. *Become*, and a few others like it: *turn, grow, work, get, wear*, and so forth.

Later she *became* an accountant.
The weather *turned* colder.
I *grew* weary of his talking.

3. A few verbs referring to the senses *(look, smell, taste, feel, sound)*, which can be followed by adjective subjective complements that describe the condition of the subject. Ability to recognize this kind of N.—V.lk.—Adj. sentence pattern will help you understand a few troublesome usage problems that will be examined in a later lesson—to understand why, for instance, careful writers use "feel bad" rather than "feel badly."

Mr. Smith now *looks* better.
These cookies *taste* good.
I *feel* bad about the election results.

EXERCISE 5
Sentence Pattern 2

NAME _____ SCORE _____

DIRECTIONS: Each of the following sentences is a Pattern 2 sentence containing a noun (or pronoun) subjective complement. Circle the subject and underline the verb. In the space at the left, copy the subjective complement.

_____ 1. Our annual sale of home furnishings was a great success.

_____ 2. Jenkins is undoubtedly the best woman for the job.

_____ 3. With further practice, Janet will become a very good cellist.

_____ 4. The most convenient rehearsal time will be next Tuesday.

_____ 5. In spite of our opposing political views, we still remain good friends.

_____ 6. These revelations proved an embarrassment to our candidate.

_____ 7. After a hard-fought game, Central High emerged the winner.

_____ 8. This old town was, for a short time during the eighties, the territorial capital.

_____ 9. Senator Billings has always been an advocate of equal rights.

_____ 10. History remains the greatest teacher of all.

_____ 11. This treaty will prove a strong deterrent to war.

_____ 12. Mr. Hale's five cats have become a neighborhood nuisance.

_____ 13. The yellow raincoat on the chair is mine.

_____ 14. The revelation of this misconduct in office will prove an incentive to reform.

_____ 15. During the bitterly cold winter some of the mercenaries turned traitor.

_____ 16. This seems the only possible solution to our problem.

_____ 17. A useless old shoe became Fido's favorite plaything.

_____ 18. He's been a good friend since college days.

_____ 19. My trip to the state high-school basketball tournament was one of the highlights of my senior year.

_____ 20. In ten years Burke will probably be a powerful figure in state government.

DIRECTIONS: Each of the following sentences is a Pattern 2 sentence containing an adjective subjective complement. Circle the subject and underline the verb. In the space at the left, copy the subjective complement.

_____ 1. By the end of March our annual report will be ready.

_____ 2. The judge's displeasure was immediately apparent.

_____ 3. Any one of these three chain saws will prove satisfactory.

_____ 4. Some of the younger team members felt guilty about the defeat.

_____ 5. An increase in taxes seems inevitable.

_____ 6. I've always been deathly afraid of snakes.

_____ 7. None of the three suggested candidates will be acceptable to the farmers.

_____ 8. The community's response to the fund drive was excellent.

_____ 9. A few of the tenor's high notes sounded flat to me.

_____ 10. I'm happy about your recent promotion.

_____ 11. Those black clouds over the foothills look ominous.

_____ 12. By late afternoon the weather had turned unpleasantly hot.

_____ 13. Some of the local foodstuffs will probably taste strange to you.

_____ 14. After a short rest Tim felt strong again.

_____ 15. Unfortunately all of the remaining butter had turned rancid.

_____ 16. Eventually the rest of the family became convinced of my innocence.

_____ 17. The children will feel bad about your leaving.

_____ 18. A person will never get really rich in this highly competitive business.

_____ 19. In spite of his quiet reply, the parole officer looked really angry.

_____ 20. Over the telephone Ms. Swift's secretary sounded upset.

Sentence Patterns with Intransitive Verbs

NAME _____ SCORE _____

DIRECTIONS: Circle the subject and underline the verb in each of the following sentences. If the sentence is a Pattern 2 sentence, copy the subjective complement in the space at the left. If the sentence is a Pattern 1 sentence, leave the space blank.

_____ 1. In two more years Mr. Crate will be eligible for a pension.

_____ 2. The shed will look better with a new coat of paint.

_____ 3. Your car will run better after this tune-up.

_____ 4. In front of us sat a group of talkative youngsters.

_____ 5. The bowling alley is the most popular gathering place in town.

_____ 6. One of the bolts in the undercarriage had worked loose.

_____ 7. Grandmother had worked hard all of her life on the farm.

_____ 8. Three of the local managers resigned in protest.

_____ 9. To me your plan sounds workable.

_____ 10. Luke is one of the most sought-after high-school athletes in the country.

_____ 11. Mike's customary lunch is some kind of junk food.

_____ 12. Mike's customary lunch consists of junk food.

_____ 13. Edith had never felt really comfortable in the dreary old mansion.

_____ 14. Without the garlic and herbs, this pasta will taste insipid.

_____ 15. A high point of every morning in the village is the arrival of the bus from Centerville.

_____ 16. Yesterday the bus arrived late in the afternoon.

_____ 17. Here is a list of the necessary cooking utensils for the camping trip.

_____ 18. A dozen students remained in the hall after the lecture.

_____ 19. Fran's unusual behavior remains a puzzle to us.

_____ 20. I'm too old for such vigorous pastimes.

_____ 21. After our cleaning and polishing, the living room looked spotless.

_____ 22. From the top of the bluff we looked across the bay.

_____ 23. The noise from the construction work in the neighboring building became almost unbearable.

_____ 24. Jason's career as an engineer had been only partially successful.

_____ 25. My next project is a tour of the Greek islands.

_____ 26. The three students in the principal's office appeared apprehensive.

_____ 27. The three students waited apprehensively in the principal's office.

_____ 28. There's enough room for all of us in the front seat.

_____ 29. After three days the cream had turned sour.

_____ 30. Beyond the north boundary of the state park, the highway turns to the west.

_____ 31. All of the suggested remedies sound rather extreme to me.

_____ 32. Unquestionably the delegate to the national convention will be you.

_____ 33. Here is enough money for your taxi fare to the airport.

_____ 34. Of all the hundreds of Christmas presents, Lenny's favorite was a small music box.

_____ 35. The embarrassed young man's face reddened noticeably.

_____ 36. The embarrassed young man's face turned bright red.

_____ 37. There was no explanation for the postponement.

_____ 38. This morning's paper is full of alarming news from Africa.

_____ 39. After a short rest you'll feel ready for the climb to the summit.

_____ 40. The family became more and more critical of my plans for a career.

LESSON
4

Basic Sentence Patterns
with Transitive Verbs

IN SENTENCE PATTERN 3 sentences the verb names some activity and the subject is, of course, the doer of that activity, as it is in many Pattern 1 sentences. But in a Pattern 3 sentence, the subject and the verb, even with the addition of adverbial material, do not give a complete statement because the activity named in the verb is performed *on* something. This kind of verb is a transitive verb, for which we shall use the symbol *V.tr.*

SAMPLE SENTENCE: Children play games.

The complement (completer) required with a transitive verb is the **direct object.** It names the receiver of the action; in other words, a transitive verb *trans*fers the action to an object. The direct object is always a noun or a noun equivalent, such as a pronoun, and we find it by asking the question "What?" of the transitive verb:

I broke my *glasses.* [What names the activity? *Broke* is the verb. Who did the action? *I* is the subject. What was broken? *Glasses* is the direct object.]
Someone threw *stones* at us. [What was thrown? *Stones* is the direct object.]

(See Supplement 1.)

We can represent this sentence pattern as follows:

$$\text{S.} \quad - \text{V.tr.} - \text{D.O.}$$
$$\text{(Children)} \quad \text{(play)} \quad \text{(games)}$$

Another helpful representation is as follows: N_x—$V.tr.$—N_y. N stands for a noun or for a noun equivalent such as a pronoun. The small letters x and y show that the nouns refer to separate things: *I* and *glasses* are obviously not one and the same, nor are *someone* and *stones.* Contrast this formula with the formula for a Pattern 2 sentence with a noun subjective complement (The child is a genius: N_x—$V.lk.$—N_x). The Pattern 2 formula shows that the two noun units refer to the same thing.

Sentence Patterns 4 and 5 are alike in that both patterns require two complements to give meaning to the subject–verb unit. They differ quite distinctly, however, in the functional nature of the verb and the resultant structure of the sentences.

Pattern 4 sentences contain two complements, the indirect object and the direct object. The direct object, the receiver of the action, answers the question "Who?" or "What?" after the transitive verb. The **indirect object** answers a question such as "To whom (or which)?"or "For whom (or which)?" Thus, in the sentence "She sang a lullaby," we have a Pattern 3 sentence, but in "She sang the children a lullaby," we have a Pattern 4 sentence:

SAMPLE SENTENCE: The child gives the parents pleasure.

$$\text{S.}—\text{V.tr.}—\text{I.O.}—\text{D.O.}$$

We can also chart this pattern as follows:

$$N_x \quad \text{—V.tr.—} \quad N_y \quad \text{—} \quad N_z$$
(child) (gives) (parents) (pleasure)

By this method we get a very important structural clue: all three of the noun elements refer to different things. (See Supplement 2.)

A typical verb for Pattern 4 is *give*, as in "The clerk gave me a refund." You can easily see why the two complements are used here: The sentence mentions the thing that is given (*refund*, the D.O.) and also the person to whom the D.O. is given (*me*, the I.O.). Although the I.O. usually names a person, it can name a nonhuman thing, as in "We gave your *application* a careful reading."

Other verbs that are commonly used this way and therefore produce a Pattern 4 structure are *allow, assign, ask, tell, write, send, show, pay, grant*, and so on. Nearly all sentences using such verbs can make essentially the same statement by using a prepositional phrase, the preposition usually being *to* or *for*. When the prepositional phrase is actually present in the sentence, it is a Pattern 3 sentence.

> I sent him the money. [Pattern 4; *him* is an indirect object.]
> I sent the money to him. [Pattern 3; *him* is the object of a preposition.]
> Mother bought us some taffy. [Pattern 4.]
> Mother bought some taffy for us. [Pattern 3.]

Pattern 5 consists of two closely related types of sentences. There are two complements in Pattern 5 sentences. The one closer to the verb is the direct object, and the second one is the **objective complement,** which we can define as a noun that *renames* the direct object or an adjective that *describes* the direct object:

> SAMPLE SENTENCES: The parents consider the child a genius.
> The parents consider the child clever.
> S.—V.tr.—D.O.—O.C.

In our method of representing sentences to show the parts of speech and the reference of the noun elements, these sentences would appear this way:

$$N_x \quad \text{—} \quad \text{V.tr.} \quad \text{—} \quad N_y \quad \text{—} \quad N_y$$
(parents) (consider) (child) (genius)
$$N_x \quad \text{—} \quad \text{V.tr.} \quad \text{—} \quad N_y \quad \text{—} \quad \text{Adj.}$$
(parents) (consider) (child) (clever)

The reference of the two nouns following the verb is a key to the difference between this type of sentence and a Pattern 4 sentence: In a Pattern 4 sentence the two noun complements refer to separate things, but in a Pattern 5 sentence they refer to the same thing.

> Mother made us some fudge. [Pattern 4; *us* and *fudge* refer to separate things.]
> This experience made John an activist. [Pattern 5; *John* and *activist* refer to the same thing.]

Because the objective complement renames or describes the direct object, we can use a handy ear test to help us recognize this pattern: The insertion of *to be* between the complements will give us acceptable English idiom:

> We appointed Jones [to be] our representative.
> I thought this action [to be] unnecessary.

Sometimes the word *as* is used between the direct object and the objective complement:

We appointed Jones as our representative.

Some adjective objective complements are very important to the meaning of the verb. It is sometimes effective to place these objective complements immediately after the verb and before the direct object:

He set free [O.C.] the caged animals [D.O.].

USUAL ORDER: He set the caged animals free.

The following verbs are among those most commonly used in Pattern 5 sentences: *elect, appoint, name, call, consider, find, make,* and *think.*

Supplement 1

With one special kind of verb, there is a problem of distinguishing between a direct object and the object of a preposition. Here are two examples:

Harry jumped off the box.
Harry took off his raincoat.

The first sentence is Pattern 1. *Off* is a preposition, *box* is the object of the preposition, and the prepositional phrase is used as an adverbial modifier, because it tells *where* Harry jumped. The second sentence is Pattern 3. The verb, with its adverbial modifier *off*, is the equivalent of the transitive verb *remove. Raincoat* is the direct object.

There is another way to distinguish between the adverbial use and the prepositional use of such a word as *off* in the preceding examples. When the word is a vital adverbial modifier of the verb, it can, in most cases, be used in either of two positions: immediately following the verb or following the direct object:

Harry took off his raincoat.
Harry took his raincoat off.

But when the word is a preposition, the alternate position is not possible: "Harry jumped the box off" is not an English sentence.

Here are some other examples of this kind of verb with adverbial modifier. Notice that in each case you can easily find a transitive verb synonym for the combination:

. . . give up [relinquish] her rights.
. . . leave out [omit] the second chapter.
. . . put out [extinguish] the fire.
. . . make over [alter] an old dress.
. . . make up [invent] an excuse.*

Supplement 2

Noun reference symbols like N_x, N_y, and N_z are useful tools in distinguishing one sentence pattern from another. "John (N_x) met the senator (N_y)" is a Pattern 3 sentence: The two nouns represent separate, distinct persons. But "John (N_x)

---

* You might try to recall as many meanings for *to make up* as you can. One modern desk dictionary gives seventeen.

became a senator (N_x)" is Pattern 2 because the nouns refer to the same person.

These noun reference distinctions cannot be applied, however, in those occasional sentences that include a reflexive pronoun, one of the pronouns ending in *self*. Compare, for example, "John hurt the puppy" and "John hurt himself." In the second sentence, although *John* and *himself* are one and the same, the sentence is clearly Pattern 3: the verb is transitive and the action of the verb is transferred to *himself*, a direct object. This same irregularity—of noun reference, not of basic patterning—can also occur in Pattern 4 and Pattern 5 sentences:

Mrs. Lewis bought her *daughter* a bicycle. [S.—V.tr.—I.O.—D.O.]
Mrs. Lewis bought *herself* a bicycle. [S.—V.tr.—I.O.—D.O.]

Eric considers his *father* a genius. [S.—V.tr.—D.O.—O.C.]
Eric considers *himself* a genius. [S.—V.tr.—D.O.—O.C.]

Complements of Transitive Verbs

NAME _____ SCORE _____

DIRECTIONS: Each of these sentences is a Pattern 3 sentence. Circle each subject and underline each verb. In the space at the left, copy the direct object.

_____ 1. We enjoyed the second half of the concert very much.

_____ 2. The sergeant understood only a few of the old man's mumbled words.

_____ 3. My friend handed over his wallet to the officer.

_____ 4. Modernization of the transit system will require the expenditure of millions of dollars.

_____ 5. Unfortunately, you filled out only a part of the questionnaire.

_____ 6. One of the intruders had left fingerprints on the window ledge.

_____ 7. By the end of the semester, our class will have read most of Wharton's novels.

_____ 8. Each of the judges then sampled Mrs. Wood's justly famous watermelon pickles.

_____ 9. After the trial the judge received dozens of abusive letters.

_____ 10. Within a few weeks the boss's nephew had taken over several of my duties.

_____ 11. We finally bought the cheaper one of the two home computers.

_____ 12. The drama department will sponsor a series of poetry readings.

_____ 13. On the next play our fullback made up the lost yardage.

_____ 14. A row of thorny bushes around the huts keeps out predatory animals.

_____ 15. For this recipe you will need a variety of Oriental vegetables.

_____ 16. Our committee looks over hundreds of applications each year.

_____ 17. The chairwoman then brought up the matter of the increase in parking fees.

_____ 18. The new edition of this dictionary contains hundreds of new words.

_____ 19. Some of us in the office blame the supervisor for this costly delay.

_____ 20. Lloyd regularly points out the weaknesses in my golf game.

COMPLEMENTS OF TRANSITIVE VERBS

DIRECTIONS: The following sentences are Pattern 3, 4, or 5 sentences. Circle each subject and underline each verb. Identify the italicized complement by writing one of the following in the space at the left:

D.O. (direct object)   I.O. (indirect object)   O.C. (objective complement)

_____ 1. The next day he sent *all* of his tax records to his lawyer.

_____ 2. He also gave the tax *officer* a copy.

_____ 3. Some of you probably think my decision a foolish *one*.

_____ 4. The hotel will have a car *ready* for you at ten o'clock.

_____ 5. Mr. Lewis assigned the *class* a challenging research project.

_____ 6. The personnel officer will ask *you* some questions about your previous experience.

_____ 7. After dinner Ted showed his guests *dozens* of boring pictures of his three poodles.

_____ 8. None of Bert's teachers had ever called him a dedicated *scholar*.

_____ 9. Mr. Carlson made *us* one of his famous chocolate pies.

_____ 10. The old man's ridiculous political beliefs made him the *laughingstock* of the community.

_____ 11. The mill owner recently laid off every *one* of the part-time workers.

_____ 12. Regular use of this fertilizer will keep your lawn *green* all summer.

_____ 13. The trustees named Dean Grafton *chairwoman* of the search committee.

_____ 14. For a graduation gift Mr. Lowe bought his *niece* a motorcycle.

_____ 15. A pinch of salt will give this *sauce* added flavor.

_____ 16. A pinch of salt will make this sauce more *flavorful*.

_____ 17. The salesman allowed me only two hundred *dollars* on my old car.

_____ 18. You'll find the weather here most *agreeable*.

_____ 19. Judge Adair always gives a first *offender* a stern lecture.

_____ 20. Marge brought us a *box* of pralines from New Orleans.

EXERCISE 8
Complements

NAME _____ SCORE _____

DIRECTIONS: Circle the subject and underline the verb in each of the following sentences. Identify the italicized word by writing in the space at the left one of the following:

      S.C. (subjective complement)   D.O. (direct object)

      I.O. (indirect object)   O.C. (objective complement)

If the italicized word is *not* used as one of these complements, leave the space blank.

_____ 1. Our stay in Majorca will always remain *one* of my most pleasant memories.

_____ 2. A panel of home economists pronounced yours the most *original* of the menus.

_____ 3. All of the youngsters feel *excited* about the camping trip.

_____ 4. This stock will pay *you* a substantial dividend each quarter.

_____ 5. During my stopover in Atlanta, I looked up two old college *friends*.

_____ 6. The parole officer obviously considered my explanation *unsatisfactory*.

_____ 7. Fortunately for us, the foreman of the jury was one of Dale's *ex-roommates*.

_____ 8. Ms. Lerner had left *Ireland* forty years ago.

_____ 9. In her will, Ms. Lerner left the town *library* a substantial bequest.

_____ 10. Your remark left me *speechless*.

_____ 11. Mrs. Woodruff still looks surprisingly *youthful*.

_____ 12. On my way home I'll pick up your *laundry*.

_____ 13. Some of the leaves on my philodendron have turned *brown*.

_____ 14. The storekeeper paid his two delivery *boys* a minimum wage.

_____ 15. The lawyer read *us* the last paragraph of the will.

_____ 16. There will be a repeat *performance* of the operetta next Tuesday.

_____ 17. Regular use of the lubricant will keep your car repair bills *low*.

_____ 18. Surprisingly all of the children kept *quiet* during the lengthy sermon.

_____ 19. The inspectors called the housing facilities a *disgrace*.

_____ 20. Their pilot had never before flown a *helicopter*.

_____ 21. High above, two hawks flew in wide *circles*.

_____ 22. After your two-week vacation, you look much *better*.

_____ 23. With your new glasses you will see much *better*.

_____ 24. The violent pitching of the small boat made some of the crew *seasick*.

_____ 25. In those days Mr. Lucas made a good *salary*.

_____ 26. Every fall Mother made *each* of the boys a stocking cap.

_____ 27. Jason is probably one of the wealthiest *men* in town.

_____ 28. The trip to the hospital through the heavy afternoon traffic seemed an *eternity*.

_____ 29. The colonel granted the two condemned *men* their last request.

_____ 30. The governor has declared Clay County a disaster *area*.

_____ 31. NBC will bring *you* live coverage of the tournament.

_____ 32. Dr. Stevens's lecture seemed unnecessarily *long*.

_____ 33. The escapee had dyed her hair jet *black*.

_____ 34. Lately there has been little *communication* between the two sisters.

_____ 35. The manager offered *me* a refund for the damaged stereo.

_____ 36. Las Vegas odds-makers consider the *Dolphins* a ten-point favorite.

_____ 37. The court appointed *Herb Kane* as my legal adviser.

_____ 38. After dinner the distinguished guest paid the *cook* a fine compliment.

_____ 39. Betty has not yet made out her *schedule* for next term.

_____ 40. The senior class voted Ms. Allen their class *adviser*.

LESSON 5

Forms of the Verb; Auxiliary Verbs

I N THIS lesson we shall call attention to a few more forms and uses of verbs, including some additional auxiliary verbs. With these forms and those that you have already examined, you will be acquainted with nearly all verb forms that the average speaker and writer will ever use.

In Lesson 2 you examined a partial conjugation of three verbs, *earn, grow,* and *be.* Some of you may want to refer to that conjugation (pages 9, 10) as we take note of a few more points about changes in form in verbs.

1. All verbs except *be* have in the third-person singular of the present tense and of the present perfect tense the distinguishing *s* (or *es*) ending, the present tense having it on the verb form and the present perfect tense on the auxiliary *has.* Notice that on nouns the *s(es)* ending shows a plural form, whereas on verbs it shows a singular form.

2. The verb *be* is completely irregular. The conjugation shows you that, unlike any other verb in the language, it has three forms *(am, is,* and *are)* in the present tense and two forms *(was* and *were)* in the past tense.

3. In general, the tenses are used as follows:

- Present: Action occurring at the present moment: He *earns* a good salary.
- Past: Action occurring at a definite time before the present moment: Last year he *earned* a good salary.
- Future: Action occurring at some time beyond the present moment: Next year he *will earn* a good salary.
- Present perfect: Action continuing to the present moment: So far this year he *has earned* ten thousand dollars.
- Past perfect: Action continuing to a fixed moment in the past: Before leaving for college, he *had earned* ten thousand dollars.
- Future perfect: Action continuing to a fixed moment in the future: By next Christmas he *will have earned* ten thousand dollars.

4. The conjugation shows you that the two verbs *earn* and *grow* differ in form in all tenses except the present tense and the future tense. *Earn* is a regular verb and *grow* is an irregular verb.

We customarily make use of three distinctive forms, called the **principal parts** of the verb, to show the difference between the two classes of verbs. The principal parts are (a) the *base* or infinitive, the "name" of the verb, used in the present tense with *(e)s* added in the third-person singular; (b) the *past,* the form used in the simple past tense; and (c) the *past participle,* the form used in the three perfect tenses.

On the basis of these three forms, we classify verbs as being regular or irregular. In all regular verbs the past and the past participle are alike, formed simply by the addition of *ed* to the base form (or only *d* if the base word ends in *e*). The irregular verbs are more complicated because for nearly all of them the past tense and the participle are not spelled alike. Following are the three forms of several irregular verbs, illustrating some spelling changes and endings that are found:

BASE	PAST	PAST PARTICIPLE
be	was, were	been
become	became	become
bite	bit	bitten
break	broke	broken
catch	caught	caught
do	did	done
eat	ate	eaten
put	put	put
ring	rang	rung
run	ran	run
see	saw	seen

(You will study more principal parts of verbs and the usage problems associated with them in Lesson 20.)

Another change in form for both regular and irregular verbs—the addition of *ing* to the base form—produces the **present participle.** One of its important uses is explained in the next paragraph.

In the sample conjugation, you observed the use of *shall/will* and *have* as auxiliary verbs in the future tense and the perfect tenses. Another important auxiliary is *be*, used with the *ing* form (the present participle) of the main verb to produce what is called the progressive form. As an example of its use, if someone asks about the assignment in your English class, you would probably not reply, "Right now, we *review* parts of speech." Instead, you would say, "Right now, we *are reviewing* parts of speech," to show that the action is not fixed in an exact moment of time but is a continuing activity. This very useful type of verb occurs in all six tenses:

We *are reviewing.*
We *were reviewing.*
We *shall be reviewing.*
We *have been reviewing.*
We *had been reviewing.*
We *shall have been reviewing.*

Another type of auxiliary verb includes *may, might, must, can, could, would,* and *should.* These words are called *modal auxiliaries*, and they are used the way *will* and *shall* are used:

I *should study* this weekend.
I *should have studied* last weekend.

(See Supplement 1.)

Do as an auxiliary verb combines with the base form of a main verb to make a rarely used "emphatic" form (But I *did pay* that bill last month). In Lesson 6 you will examine the much more common use of the *do* auxiliary, in questions and negatives.

Here are a few other points to remember about auxiliary verbs:

1. *Have, be,* and *do* are not used exclusively as auxiliaries; they are three of our most commonly used main verbs:

I *have* a new car. [Main verb.]
I *have* bought a new car. [Auxiliary.]

He *is* a good speaker. [Main verb.]
He *is* becoming a good speaker. [Auxiliary.]
He always *does* a good job for us. [Main verb.]
Yes, I *did* embellish the story somewhat. [Auxiliary.]

2. When the verb unit contains auxiliaries, there may be short adverbial modifiers separating parts of the whole verb phrase:

We *have* certainly *been studying* hard.
Students *have,* in certain cases, *registered* late.

3. In a few set expressions following introductory adverbs, usually adverbs of time, we place the subject within the verb phrase between an auxiliary and the main verb:

Never *have I experienced* such embarrassment.
Only rarely *has she returned* to Toledo.

Supplement 1

Variations of some modals and "time" auxiliaries make use of *to* in the verb phrase. Here are examples of some that you use and hear regularly:

I *have to leave* [= *must leave*] early.
You *ought to apologize* [= *should apologize*].
Mr. Bright *used to be* a teacher.
You *were supposed to be* here on time.
I *am to leave* soon for Chicago.
I *am going to leave* soon for Chicago.

EXERCISE 9
Auxiliary Verbs; Basic Sentence Patterns

NAME _____ SCORE _____

DIRECTIONS: Each of these sentences contains at least one auxiliary verb. (Some have two; some have three.) Copy the auxiliary verb(s) in the first space at the left. In the second space, write 1, 2, 3, 4, or 5 to identify the sentence pattern.

_____ 1. Resistance to Councilwoman Poynter's proposal has
____ been growing.

_____ 2. Someone must have tampered with the smoke detector.
____

_____ 3. Some of you should have been paying closer attention.
____

_____ 4. This could very well be our last meeting of the year.
____

_____ 5. Grandfather has been telling the children some wild
____ tales of his seafaring days.

_____ 6. Only then did we realize the extent of the damage.
____

_____ 7. All of my friends are being helpful.
____

_____ 8. The market for these illegal painkillers has been expand-
____ ing alarmingly.

_____ 9. We've always been happy with the service at this restau-
____ rant.

_____ 10. Applicants must send us their résumés before August 1.
____

_____ 11. The failure of the tax levy has left our schools danger-
____ ously vulnerable.

_____ 12. By this time the manager should have worked out a ro-
____ tation system for overtime help.

_____ 13. The officer had already handed Mike a traffic citation.
____

_____ 14. The attendant should have had the car ready for us by
____ noon.

_____ 15. In my opinion you're being unfairly critical of the apart-
____ ment manager.

_____ 16. Three realtors have already made Ms. Strong attractive
____ offers for her waterfront property.

_____ 17. No one with half a mind would believe your ridiculous
____ story.

_____ 18. Next year I'll paint the fence white.
____

_____ 19. I should have bought myself some good snow tires ear-
____ lier in the season.

_____ 20. The addition of some applesauce would have made this
____ cake moister.

37

_____

——————

_____

——————

_____

——————

_____

——————

_____

——————

_____

——————

_____

——————

_____

——————

_____

——————

_____

——————

_____

——————

_____

——————

_____

——————

_____

——————

21. I could have shown you a shorter route to the ski resort.

22. Never before have I heard a more thrilling concert.

23. There must be some good reason for Harry's decision.

24. Laura's car has been giving her some trouble lately.

25. By this time tomorrow you will have finished all of your final exams.

26. The preceding year's drought had kept the price of wheat high.

27. No one had ever told Bob the news about Sue's new job.

28. This class has been making excellent progress since the first of the year.

29. Perhaps we should have bought the children less bulky presents.

30. Seldom does a car owner find a bargain like this.

31. The persistent spring rains have made further work on the access road impossible.

32. There should have been more time for discussion after Dean Allen's lecture.

33. The champion has been training hard for his next fight.

34. This food processor can make cooking a real pleasure.

35. The attachments will save the cook hours of tedious work.

36. You should be feeling rested in a few hours.

37. One of the robbers must have been waiting in the stolen truck.

38. Dad will never willingly give up his noisy old manual typewriter.

39. We'll be waiting in the car for you.

40. Paul has just recently mailed Ms. Benham his letter of resignation.

EXERCISE 10
Complements

NAME _____ SCORE _____

DIRECTIONS: In the space at the left, write one of the following to identify the italicized word:

      S.C. (subjective complement)   I.O. (indirect object)

      D.O. (direct object)   O.C. (objective complement)

If the italicized word is not used as a complement, leave the space blank.

_____ 1. In time, the crotchety old man grew quite *fond* of the stray cat.

_____ 2. The Bon Marché store is calling their clearance sale a *blockbuster*.

_____ 3. Surprisingly the beautiful blossom of this plant smells unpleasantly *rancid*.

_____ 4. Mom indignantly turned off the television *set*.

_____ 5. At Cooper's Corner you should turn off the *thruway* and onto the county road.

_____ 6. In this relatively short time Marie's hair had turned *gray*.

_____ 7. In seven innings Dawson allowed the *Yankees* only three hits.

_____ 8. Some of you might consider yesterday a completely wasted *day*.

_____ 9. One of the apprentices had taken over Mr. Terry's *duties* in the library.

_____ 10. Experiences like these will give *people* a new conception of public duty.

_____ 11. In a world of stress and strain, the scholar must become a *person* of action.

_____ 12. A two-run homer by Lawson gave the *Braves* a three-point lead.

_____ 13. The Joneses are packing their *camper* for a vacation trip to British Columbia.

_____ 14. A mysterious black car has stood in front of my neighbor's *house* all day.

_____ 15. Mr. Bryant rarely talks about his war *experiences*.

_____ 16. Mr. Bryant rarely talks to *any* of his classmates.

_____ 17. During the power outage the milk in our refrigerator turned *sour*.

_____ 18. The suggestions from the union's headquarters proved *helpful*.

_____ 19. The FDA pronounced the new drug *safe*.

_____ 20. Mr. Blume made his *grandchild* a trapeze in the backyard.

_____ 21. This kind of gift makes the child's parents *nervous*.

_____ 22. Jake's part-time job, along with his full schedule of classes, keeps him really *busy*.

_____ 23. The realtor found *us* a small but comfortable apartment.

_____ 24. You'll find life in this village quite *dull*.

_____ 25. One of the officers found the murder *weapon*.

_____ 26. The carpenter carefully felt the *surface* of my newly completed desk.

_____ 27. According to him, the surface felt rather *rough*.

_____ 28. There will very likely be a thorough *investigation* of the affair.

_____ 29. The heavy wind damaged a few of the deck *chairs*.

_____ 30. A short rest period right now would be most *welcome*.

_____ 31. For the junior class party, Maybelle cleverly made over *one* of her mother's dresses.

_____ 32. Through the dense fog we could barely make out the ferry landing *slip*.

_____ 33. Mr. Thorpe had promised his *workers* a year-end bonus.

_____ 34. Those fresh strawberries in the display case surely look *inviting*.

_____ 35. The union members appointed Jeff Burke their *delegate* to the national convention.

_____ 36. She's one of the top *scorers* on our team.

_____ 37. The farmer told the *reporter* a rambling story about flying saucers.

_____ 38. You should not cut your *grass* really short during this extremely hot period.

_____ 39. Carstairs knows the botanical *name* for every flower in his huge garden.

_____ 40. All of us feel *bad* about the results of the election.

LESSON
6 Alterations of Basic Sentence Patterns

A NY LONG piece of writing made up exclusively of basic sentences would be too monotonous to read. You should think of the basic sentences not as models for your writing but as elementary units, important because they are the structures from which amplified sentences develop.

In this lesson we shall look at two alterations of basic sentence patterns resulting in sentences that use passive verbs and sentences that are in the form of a question. Lessons 7 through 11 then show how basic sentences can be combined and reduced to subordinate clauses and phrases to produce varied, well-developed sentences.

Passive Voice

In Lesson 2 you examined a partial conjugation of the verb *earn*. The forms listed there are in the active voice, which means that the subject is the doer of the action. A more complete conjugation would include the passive verb forms. These make use of the auxiliary verb *be* combined with the past participle of the verb, as shown in the following illustration of the third-person plural in the six tenses:

They *are earned.*
They *were earned.*
They *will be earned.*
They *have been earned.*
They *had been earned.*
They *will have been earned.*

The present and past tenses of progressive verbs can also be shifted to the passive voice, giving us forms in which *be* is used in two auxiliary capacities in the same verb form:

These cars *are being sold* at a loss.
These cars *were being sold* at a loss.

(See Supplement 1.)

Because only transitive verbs have passive forms, the basic patterns that can be altered to passive versions are Patterns 3, 4, and 5. When the idea of a Pattern 3 sentence is expressed with a passive verb, there is no complement in the sentence:

ACTIVE VOICE: Children play games.
PASSIVE VOICE: Games are played [by children].

If the doer of the action is expressed in a sentence using a passive verb, the doer must occur as the object of the preposition *by*.

When a Pattern 4 sentence is altered to form a passive construction, the indirect object that followed the active verb becomes the subject of the passive verb:

> ACTIVE VOICE: Children give the parents pleasure.
> PASSIVE VOICE: The parents are given pleasure [by the children].

Here the passive verb is followed by a complement, *pleasure*, which we can continue to call a direct object in spite of the fact that it follows a passive verb.

Notice also how a Pattern 5 sentence can be given a different kind of expression by means of a passive verb, with the direct object becoming the subject:

> ACTIVE VOICE: The parents consider the child a genius.
> The parents consider the child clever.
> PASSIVE VOICE: The child is considered a genius [by the parents].
> The child is considered clever [by the parents].

Here also the passive verb requires a complement (*genius, clever*), which, because it renames or describes the subject, should be called a subjective complement.

Questions

People who grow up using the English language are usually not aware that most questions are quite different from statements in the grammatical arrangement of their sentence parts. We should note these differences, particularly because they are basic to understanding certain usage problems that you will study later.

In the sentence types that you examined in earlier lessons, you noted the normal positioning of the main sentence parts: subject first, followed by the verb, followed by the complement, if any. In questions, however, other arrangements are possible. The most effective method of showing these structures is to contrast the structure of a statement with that of a question. First of all, we must recognize that there are two kinds of questions: (1) the question answered by "Yes" or "No" and (2) the question answered by information.

QUESTION ANSWERED BY "YES" OR "NO"

The best way to demonstrate the altered arrangement of sentence parts in a question is by reference to a four-part classification of verbs. (See Supplement 2.)

1. If the verb is *be* in the present tense or in the past tense, used either as the main verb or as an auxiliary verb, the subject and the *be* form (*am, is, are, was,* or *were*) reverse positions:

John is happy. Is John happy?
The passengers were injured. Were the passengers injured?
My proposal is being considered. Is my proposal being considered?

2. With other one-word verbs in the present or past tense, the proper form of the auxiliary *do* is used, followed by the subject and the base form of the main verb:

You see Ms. Locke often. Do you see Ms. Locke often?
You heard the announcement. Did you hear the announcement?

42

3. If the verb already has an auxiliary, the subject follows the auxiliary. When there are two or more auxiliaries, the subject follows the first one:

I may carry your books. May I carry your books?
You have seen the movie. Have you seen the movie?
They will arrive tomorrow. Will they arrive tomorrow?
You have been studying all day. Have you been studying all day?
The child should have been told. Should the child have been told?

4. When *have* in the present tense is the main verb, two versions of the question are possible:

You have enough money. Have you enough money?
                       Do you have enough money?

QUESTION ANSWERED BY INFORMATION

Some questions ask for information instead of a "Yes" or a "No." They use words called **interrogatives,** words standing for unknown persons, things, or descriptive qualities: pronouns *(who, what, which, whoever, whatever)*; adjectives *(what, which, whose, whatever, whichever)*; and adverbs *(when, where, why, how).* The interrogative pronoun *who* has two forms: *who* when it functions as a subject or a subjective complement and *whom* when it serves as an object.

In questions using these words, the normal arrangement of sentence parts is retained only if the interrogative is the subject or modifies the subject:

My *brother* [S.] paid the bill.
Who [S.] paid the bill?

Ten sophomores [S.] were chosen.
How many sophomores [S.] were chosen?

In all other situations (1) the subject–verb positioning is altered as it is in "Yes"/"No" questions, and (2) the interrogative word, or the unit modified by the interrogative, stands at the beginning of the sentence, to signal the fact that a question, not a statement, is forthcoming:

You studied *geometry* [D.O.] last night.
What [D.O.] did you study last night?

You saw *Martha* [D.O.] at the party.
Whom [D.O.] did you see at the party?

My brother is forty years *old* [S.C.].
How old [S.C.] is your brother?

She is Mother's *cousin* [S.C.].
Who [S.C.] is she?

She bought a sports *car* [D.O.].
What kind [D.O.] of car did she buy?

You [S.] called *Bob* [D.O.] a *thief* [O.C.].
Who [S.] called Bob a thief?
Whom [D.O.] did you call a thief?
What [O.C.] did you call Bob?

When the interrogative unit is the object of a preposition, two versions of the question are often possible: the entire prepositional phrase may stand at the beginning, or the interrogative may stand at the beginning with the preposition in its usual position:

The speaker was referring *to the mayor*.
To whom was the speaker referring? [*Whom* is the object of the preposition.]
Whom was the speaker referring *to?* [*Whom* is still the object of the preposition.]

(See Supplement 3.)

Supplement 1

The passive voice serves a real purpose in effective communication: it should be used when the *doer* of the action is unknown or is of secondary interest in the statement. In such a situation the writer, wishing to focus attention on the *receiver* of the action, places that unit in the emphatic subject position. The passive verb form makes this arrangement possible. Thus, instead of some vague expression such as "Some unknown person had tampered with the carburetor," we can say, "The carburetor *had been tampered* with."

Some of you may have heard the passive voice called "weak." Admittedly some writers do get into the habit of using the passive form when there is little justification. In most narrative writing, the doer of the action is logically the subject of the verb. "The fullback crossed the goal line" would certainly be preferred to "The goal line was crossed by the fullback," a version that gives the same information but tends to retard the narrative flow.

You should practice with passive constructions so that you can use this important device when it is called for. Equally important, if a criticism of your writing mentions doubtful uses of the passive, you can hardly be expected to do much effective rewriting if you can't recognize the passive verb.

Supplement 2

The four-part classification of the verb also determines the structuring of sentences that are negative rather than positive. The positioning of the negator *not* (or its contraction *n't*) depends on the presence or absence of an auxiliary verb. Sentences using *be* or *have* must be considered special cases.

1. If the verb is *be* in the present tense or in the past tense, used either as the main verb or as an auxiliary verb, the *not* follows the *be* form:

I am *not* happy about this.
They were *not* [*weren't*] able to attend.
He was *not* [*wasn't*] paying attention.

2. With other one-word verbs in the present or past tense, the proper form of the auxiliary *do* is used, followed by the negator and the base form of the main verb:

I do *not* [*don't*] consider him reliable.
She does *not* [*doesn't*] play golf.
They did *not* [*didn't*] reply.

3. If the verb already has an auxiliary, the negator follows the auxiliary. When there are two or more auxiliaries, the *not* follows the first one:

We could *not* [*couldn't*] be happier.
You may *not* have heard her correctly.
They will *not* [*won't*] return this week.
This light ought *not* to have been left on.

4. When *have* in the present tense is the main verb, two negative forms are possible:

I have *not* [*haven't*] enough money with me.
I do *not* [*don't*] have enough money with me.

Supplement 3

At the informal language level another version—"*Who* was the speaker referring to?"—is often found, despite the traditional demand for the objective case for the object of a preposition. The formal level of both spoken and written English would call for the first version: "*To whom* was the speaker referring?"

Alterations of Basic Sentences: Passive Verbs

NAME _____ SCORE _____

DIRECTIONS: These sentences are Pattern 3, 4, or 5 sentences. In the first space at the left, write the pattern number. In the second space, write the verb form that is used when the italicized word in the sentence is made the subject.

EXAMPLE:

_4_
will be sent

Later I will send *you* a copy of the bulletin.

_____ 1. Nearly everyone in town heard the *explosion*.
_____

_____ 2. We'll give your *application* careful thought.
_____

_____ 3. Some of Bill's neighbors have harvested his *crops* during his illness.
_____

_____ 4. The firefighters keep the aid *cars* ready for any emergency.
_____

_____ 5. You should return this *questionnaire* not later than July 1.
_____

_____ 6. The supervisor allows our *crew* only a half hour for lunch.
_____

_____ 7. The voters obviously considered *Ms. Turner* the best-qualified candidate.
_____

_____ 8. Local gossips are busily talking about the Jackmans' marital *difficulties*.
_____

_____ 9. Jake has not told the *judge* everything about the plot.
_____

_____ 10. Someone should have notified the *sentry* at the main gate.
_____

DIRECTIONS: A passive verb has a direct object, a subjective complement, or no complement. Each of these sentences uses a passive verb. Underline the verb. If there is a complement in the sentence, copy it in the first space at the left. In the second space, identify it by writing D.O. for direct object or S.C. for subjective complement. If the sentence has no complement, leave both spaces blank.

_____ _____	1.	Many farm families were left homeless by the flood.
_____ _____	2.	The graduate students were not told the reason for the increased tuition.
_____ _____	3.	By a wide margin Sherwood was elected secretary.
_____ _____	4.	Portage Bay can be easily seen from our front yard.
_____ _____	5.	These boots can be made practically waterproof.
_____ _____	6.	The mayor had never been shown the revised building plans.
_____ _____	7.	Some disinterested person should be appointed arbitrator.
_____ _____	8.	The jam should then be sealed in leak-proof jars.
_____ _____	9.	The prime minister was asked a few rather impertinent questions by the young reporter.
_____ _____	10.	Laura's eldest son has been offered a good job in Newark.
_____ _____	11.	You will be sent the test results within two weeks.
_____ _____	12.	The warehouse door should never be left unlocked overnight.
_____ _____	13.	The interest rate is calculated weekly.
_____ _____	14.	The information about the king's health cannot be kept a secret much longer.
_____ _____	15.	The Lockwood children had been taught good manners by their stern grandmother.
_____ _____	16.	Shawn's car has been painted bright red.
_____ _____	17.	Some poor underling will probably be made the scapegoat in this unsavory affair.
_____ _____	18.	Mark's manuscript was returned promptly with no comment.
_____ _____	19.	For this tedious work Mimi was paid a barely livable wage.
_____ _____	20.	We've been told nothing about the merger.

Alterations of Basic Sentences: Questions

NAME _____ SCORE _____

DIRECTIONS: The purpose of this exercise is to contrast the structure of a question with that of a statement. In the space at the left, copy the word from the question that serves the function indicated:

      D.O. (direct object)   O.P. (object of preposition)

      S.C. (subjective complement)

The statement following the question has the same basic structure as that of the question.

_____ (D.O.)
1. What will we serve for dessert?
We will serve apple *pie* (D.O.) for dessert.

_____ (S.C.)
2. What will our dessert be?
Our dessert will be apple *pie* (S.C.).

_____ (D.O.)
3. How many people does the county employ?
The county employs nearly three hundred *people* (D.O.).

_____ (O.P.)
4. Which of the two guides can we rely on?
We can rely on the *older* (O.P.) of the two guides.

_____ (D.O.)
5. Whom has Martha selected as her maid of honor?
Martha has selected her *sister* (D.O.) as her maid of honor.

_____ (D.O.)
6. How much money did you spend on your trip?
I spent four hundred *dollars* (D.O.) on my trip.

_____ (S.C.)
7. How old is your grandfather?
My grandfather is sixty-five years *old* (S.C.).

_____ (D.O.)
8. Whom will you invite to the party?
I'll invite my *neighbors* (D.O.) to the party.

_____ (S.C.)
9. Who will the guests at the party be?
The guests at the party will be my *neighbors* (S.C.).

_____ (D.O.)
10. How many fish did you catch?
I caught four *fish* (D.O.).

_____ (D.O.)
11. Whose car did you borrow?
I borrowed Joan's *car* (D.O.).

_____ (D.O.)
12. Whom has the chancellor appointed as chairwoman?
The chancellor has appointed *Dr. Lewis* (D.O.) as chairwoman.

_____ (O.P.)
13. What have you two been arguing about?
We have been arguing about *politics* (O.P.).

_____ (O.P.)
14. To whom should I address this last card?
You should address this last card to *Aunt Letty* (O.P.).

_____ (D.O.)
15. How much did the old man pay you?
The old man paid me twenty *dollars* (D.O.).

DIRECTIONS: This exercise contains twenty-five questions. The italicized word in each question is a complement or the object of a preposition. In the space at the left, write one of the following to identify the italicized word:

     D.O. (direct object)   O.C. (objective complement)
     S.C. (subjective complement)   O.P. (object of preposition)
     I.O. (indirect object)

_____ 1. Which *one* of these watches should I buy for my sister?

_____ 2. When will the college authorities make this information *available* to the student body?

_____ 3. *Whom* do the police suspect?

_____ 4. *What* will the withholding tax on my new salary be?

_____ 5. How *hot* do the August days get here on the desert?

_____ 6. How much money does your nephew owe *you?*

_____ 7. How much *money* does your nephew owe you?

_____ 8. *Whom* should our union send to the regional meeting?

_____ 9. *Which* of these amendments did you vote for?

_____ 10. How *tall* will this bush grow?

_____ 11. *Who* will the supervisor's replacement be?

_____ 12. *Whom* will the boss name as the supervisor's replacement?

_____ 13. How *deep* should we make this ditch?

_____ 14. How *deep* should this ditch be made?

_____ 15. How many *people* have you told this ridiculous story to?

_____ 16. What *salary* did the old man promise you?

_____ 17. What salary did the old man promise *you?*

_____ 18. *Whom* in the chain of command do you report to?

_____ 19. What will you allow *me* on my old Chevrolet?

_____ 20. *Whom* do you consider the best manager in the league?

_____ 21. Whom do you consider the best *manager* in the league?

_____ 22. How *accurate* are the weather forecasts on TV?

_____ 23. To *whom* am I indebted for this doubtful honor?

_____ 24. What *kind* of student has your oldest son become?

_____ 25. How much has your group leader told *you* about the campaign?

7 Coordination:
The Compound Sentence

To BEGIN our study of sentences that build on the simple patterns we have limited ourselves to in previous lessons and exercises, let us examine this student writer's description of a snowstorm:

(1) The first really serious snowfall began at dusk and had already spread a treacherous powdering over the roads by the time the homeward-bound crowds reached their peak. (2) As the evening deepened, porch and street lights glowed in tight circles through semisolid air. (3) The snow did not fall in a mass of fat, jovial flakes; it squalled in a writhing mist of tiny particles and seemed less snow than a dense, animated fog. (4) Through the night the wind rose, worrying the trees as a puppy shakes a slipper. (5) It rushed round the corners of buildings and tumbled over roofs, from which it snatched armfuls of snow to scatter in the streets. (6) Save for the occasional grumble of a sanitation truck sullenly pushing its plow, all sound stopped. (7) Even the wind was more sensible than audible. (8) Day did not dawn. (9) The world changed from charcoal gray to lead between six and seven, but the change was one from night to lesser night. (10) The snow still whirled. (11) Drifts had altered the neat symmetry of peaked roofs into irregular mountain ranges ending in sheer cliffs four or five feet above the leeward eaves. (12) The downwind side of every solid object cast a snow shadow that tapered away from a sharp hump until it merged into the surrounding flat pallor. (13) Along the street, windshield wipers, odd bits of chrome, startling blanks of black glass, and isolated headlights decorated large white mounds. (14) Men and women shut off their alarm clocks, stretched, yawned, looked out of their windows, paused in a moment of guilt, and went back to bed. (15) Snow had taken the day for its own, and there was no point in arguing with it.

The sentences of this paragraph are made up of groups of related words: clauses and phrases. The word group that is basic to all communication is the **clause,** which contains at least one subject and one verb. (In a later lesson we shall study the **phrase,** a group of related words *not* containing a subject and verb in combination.)

The writer of the paragraph may not have consciously considered the fact, but the entire passage is based on short, simple sentences of the patterns studied in the preceding lessons. Recalling or inventing the scenes, actions, and responses associated with the event, the author projected a series of subject–verb combinations, in other words, clauses: the snowfall began, the snowfall had spread a powdering, the homeward-bound crowds reached their peak, the evening deepened, lights glowed, and so on.

The writer's problem was to combine or alter these short statements and put them into their most pleasing and effective form. Presenting all of them as basic sentences would communicate the author's ideas but in a form that, in addition to being monotonous, would not give proper emphasis to the most important ideas. Only two sentences (8 and 10) are retained as one-subject, one-verb basic sentences. Some of the sentences (3, 9, and 15) combine two basic sentences, giving each clause equal force. Some (1 and 5) join more than one verb to the same subject. Sentence 13 joins more than one subject to the same verb, and Sentence 14 has two subjects joined to six verbs.

In the next several lessons we shall be examining the word groups—independent clauses, subordinate clauses, and phrases—that are the language tools allowing a writer to apply various strategies to produce effective sentences.

A sentence, as you learned in Lesson 1, is a word group containing a subject and a verb. From this definition, and from the one already given for a clause, it would seem that a sentence and a clause are identical. And this is true for one kind of clause, the **independent clause** (also called the *main clause* or *principal clause*). The independent clause can stand by itself as a sentence. Every example sentence and every exercise sentence that you have worked with thus far in this book has been made up of one independent clause. We call a sentence consisting of only one independent clause a **simple sentence.**

One means of combining or altering short statements is compounding, or joining grammatically equal parts so that they function together. A compound may be formed of equal parts within the independent clause of a simple sentence. If, however, entire independent clauses are joined, or compounded, the result is a new kind of sentence altogether.

All of the sentence units you have studied can be compounded; that is, a sentence may contain two or more subjects, verbs, complements, or modifiers joined by a coordinating conjunction. The three common coordinating conjunctions for this use are *and, but,* and *or;* other coordinators are *nor, for,* and *yet.* Sometimes the equal grammatical relationship is pointed out by the use of pairs of words, called *correlatives: not (only) . . . but (also), either . . . or, neither . . . nor:*

> You *and* I know the answer. [Compound subjects.]
> My favorite desserts are cake *and* pie. [Compound subjective complements.]
> I studied long *and* hard *but* failed the test. [Compound verbs and adverbs.]
> I found the lecture *and* the discussion neither interesting *nor* instructive. [Compound direct objects and objective complements.]
> I can see you either during the lunch hour *or* after 5 P.M. [Compound prepositional phrases.]

Compounding is often used with two (sometimes more than two) independent clauses; the result is a common type of sentence called the **compound sentence.** Any of the coordinating conjunctions and any of the correlatives mentioned already can be used to join two independent clauses. In the compound sentence, the presence or absence of one of these coordinators is the basis for a decision in punctuation, a decision so important that you must be able to recognize the compound sentence and must know that it can occur in either of two patterns:

1. The two clauses are joined by a coordinating conjunction. The normal punctuation is a comma before the conjunction:

> I had reviewed the material, but I did poorly on the test.

It is important to distinguish this sentence from a nearly synonymous version using a compound verb:

> I had reviewed the material but did poorly on the test.

In this second version the sentence is not a compound sentence because there is no separate subject for the second verb. It is a simple sentence and in usual practice would be written without a comma.

2. The two independent clauses are *not* joined by a coordinating conjunction. The normal punctuation is a semicolon between the two clauses. (See Supplement 1.) Sometimes, in this kind of compound sentence, the two independent clauses stand side by side with no word tying them together:

No one had warned me; I was completely unaware of the difficulty.

Often the second clause begins with an adverbial unit that serves as a kind of tie between the clauses. This adverbial unit may be
a. A simple adverb:

For the time being I use a motorcycle; later I plan to buy a car.
These were last year's highlights; now we must look at plans for next year.

b. A short phrase:

I cannot comment on the whole concert; in fact, I slept through the last part of it.

c. A conjunctive adverb. The commonest conjunctive adverbs are *therefore, however, nevertheless, consequently, moreover, otherwise, besides, furthermore,* and *accordingly.* These words, often followed by a comma, should be used cautiously; they usually contribute to a heavy, formal tone. To lessen this effect, writers often place them, set off by commas, within the second clause:

The evidences of perjury are conclusive; therefore we find you guilty.
Your arguments were well presented; however, we feel that the plan is too expensive.
Your arguments were well presented; we feel, however, that the plan is too expensive.

Because adverbial units like *later* and *therefore* are not coordinating conjunctions, the use of a comma in this type of sentence is inappropriate. The important thing to remember is that when the independent clauses are joined by a coordinating conjunction, the use of a comma is the custom. When there is no coordinating conjunction, the comma will not suffice; the customary mark is the semicolon.

Supplement 1

The serious error that results when a writer uses a comma—or no mark at all—in a compound sentence whose clauses are not joined by a coordinating conjunction is called the **comma fault** or the **run-on sentence.**

Remember that the punctuation suggestions made in this lesson apply only to the compound sentence. At this point in your study of the English sentence, your natural fear of *under*punctuation between clauses may lead you to produce sentences like these:

I have written to John Barlow; from whom I hope to get a letter of recommendation.
Although union delegates and management have met several times; little progress can be reported.

These semicolons are inappropriate. These sentences are *not* compound sentences; in each case the sentence is made up of one independent clause and one dependent or subordinate clause. You should be able to avoid this kind of overpunctuating after your examination of dependent clauses (Lessons 8–10).

EXERCISE 13

Coordination: The Compound Sentence

NAME _____ SCORE _____

DIRECTIONS: The twenty-five sentences here illustrate three types of sentences:

(1) The sentence is a simple sentence with the subject having two verbs joined by a coordinating conjunction. Normal punctuation within the sentence: none.

We worked all day on the car but could not find the trouble.

(2) The sentence is a compound sentence with the two independent clauses joined by a coordinating conjunction: *and, but, or, nor, yet,* or *for.* Normal punctuation: comma before the conjunction.

We worked all day on the car, and now it runs well.

(3) The sentence is a compound sentence without one of the coordinating conjunctions joining the independent clauses. (The second clause often begins with an adverbial unit.) Normal punctuation: a semicolon.

We worked all day on the car; now it runs well.

In each of the following sentences, a ^ marks a point of coordination. If the sentence is Type 1, write 0 in the space at the left. If the sentence is Type 2, write C (for comma) in the space. If the sentence is Type 3, write S (for semicolon) in the space.

_____ 1. Most of this emerging country's riches are in reserve ^ their development will require careful management.

_____ 2. Thousands of people ski every winter in the Whitlock area ^ but ignore it as a hiking area in the summer.

_____ 3. It is not a matter of hunters' rights ^ it is a matter of the survival of a rare and endangered species.

_____ 4. Currently we consider the situation critical ^ but before long we'll probably laugh at our worries.

_____ 5. Two of the new transfer students didn't pay the lab fees ^ and had to postpone the course till next year.

_____ 6. The materials in our local library are not cataloged properly ^ obviously we should hire a librarian.

_____ 7. The lottery winners either accept the money now ^ or take a chance on the mystery jackpot in December.

_____ 8. To this point I've reported on the company's finances ^ now I'd like to tell you about our two new directors.

_____ 9. Columnists in the newspapers dropped a few hints ^ and soon rumors were afloat.

_____ 10. The stereos in the crates are to go to the warehouse ^ those in the cardboard cartons will be used in the display.

_____ 11. The tires on the truck should be alternated periodically ^ otherwise the wear on the tread will be uneven.

_____ 12. A banker could be trusted only if he wore a vest and carried a cane ^ or at least we peasants thought so.

_____ 13. The price for this demonstration model is $9,500 ^ if you want the cruise control, the price is $9,700.

_____ 14. This model sells for $9,700 ^ but is available without the cruise-control feature for $9,500.

_____ 15. For $9,500 you can have this demonstrator ^ or for $200 extra you can have it with the cruise-control feature.

_____ 16. The price of the demonstrator is $8,700 ⌢ however, you can have it without cruise control for $8,500.

_____ 17. The union delegates flatly refused our offer ⌢ and with that refusal the friendly negotiating ended.

_____ 18. Jacoby's last-minute field-goal attempt was straight as an arrow ⌢ but lacked about ten feet in length.

_____ 19. The executors would not allow an extra payment ⌢ nor did they seem sympathetic to my needs.

_____ 20. For the police, the blizzard meant traffic problems ⌢ for the youngsters, it meant a school holiday.

_____ 21. The Shermans must have left town in a hurry ⌢ for there's a five-day accumulation of papers on the porch.

_____ 22. Federal agents picked up the smugglers and the contraband ⌢ and the town resumed its usual sleepy existence.

_____ 23. Some people magnify slight pauses in their sentences ⌢ and consequently tend to overpunctuate.

_____ 24. Ordinarily my newspaper is delivered by four o'clock ⌢ it's never been this late before.

_____ 25. The undergraduates will be affected by these rules ⌢ therefore they should be represented on the committee.

LESSON

8 Subordination: The Adverb Clause

To this point you have had practice with the simple sentence (one independent clause) and the compound sentence (two or more independent clauses). Basic as these sentences are to our thinking and writing, too much reliance on them can produce a deadening monotony in writing. Worse, the reader is often left to figure out what the writer has in mind but hasn't managed to express in the independent clauses.

"Rain began to fall, and we stopped our ball game" is a perfectly correct sentence. But notice these slightly altered versions:

> When rain began to fall, we stopped our ball game.
> After rain began to fall, we stopped our ball game.
> Because rain began to fall, we stopped our ball game.

These three, in addition to lessening the singsong tone of the compound sentence, are more informative. The first two tell the time at which the game was stopped—and notice that *when* and *after* point out slightly different time elements. The third version gives a different relation between the two statements; it tells not the time of but the reason for stopping the game.

If, instead of writing the compound sentence "Rain was falling, and we continued our ball game," you write "Although rain was falling, we continued our ball game," you have refined your thinking and your expression. Your readers now interpret the sentence exactly as you want them to: They now know that the ball game was continued in spite of the fact that rain was falling.

The process by which a statement is reduced to a secondary form to show its relation to the main idea is **subordination.** The very important grammatical unit that expresses a secondary idea in relation to a main idea is the **subordinate,** or **dependent, clause,** which we define as a subject–verb combination that cannot stand alone as a sentence. Rather, it functions *within* a sentence as a single part of speech: an adverb, an adjective, or a noun. A sentence made up of one independent clause and at least one dependent clause is a **complex sentence.**

The **adverb clause** can be distinguished from other dependent clauses because, like the simple adverb, it describes the action or state of being by telling something about the action: the time it took place, the reason for or the result of its taking place, and so on. The most common types of adverb clauses, in fact, answer direct questions about the action: "When?" (clause of time); "Where?" (clause of place); and "Why?" (clause of reason).

The relationship between an adverb clause and the main clause is shown by the conjunction that introduces the adverb clause. Remember that the conjunction—the structural signal of subordination—is not an isolated word standing between the two clauses. It is part of the subordinate clause. In such a sentence as "We waited until the police arrived," the unit "the police arrived" could stand alone as an independent clause. But the clause is made dependent by the inclusion of *until,* which signals the dependence of the clause on something else in the sentence for its total meaning.

57

Various types of adverb clauses, together with their most common conjunctions, are listed for you here, with examples:

Time (*when, whenever, before, after, since, while, until, as, as soon as*)

> She left *before I could recognize her.*
> You must not talk *while you eat.*
> You may leave *when I tell you to.*
> *After the bell rings,* no one enters.
> I haven't seen him *since we left school.*
> He shouted *as I drove by.*

Place (*where, wherever*)

> We parted *where the paths separated.*
> I shall meet you *wherever you want me to.*

Cause or Purpose (*because, since, as, that, in order that*)

> She quit school *because her mother was ill.*
> *Since we could not pay the fine,* we could not drive the car.
> *As you are the senior member,* you should lead the procession.
> They died *that their nation might live.*
> They came to America *in order that they might have freedom of speech.*

Manner (*as, as if, as though*)

> Stan acted *as if the party was boring him.*
> Please do the work *as you have been instructed.*

Result (*that, so that*)

> He was so late *that he missed the lecture.*
> It rained all night, *so that the garden flowers were ruined.*

Condition (*if, unless, provided that, in case, on condition that*). This kind of adverb clause gives a condition under which the main clause is true:

> Stop me *if you have heard this before.*
> He will not give his talk *unless we pay his expenses.*
> I shall go *provided that you drive carefully.*
> *If I were you,* I would accept the offer.
> *If you had told me earlier,* I could have helped.

Certain kinds of conditional clauses can occur in an alternate arrangement. The *if* is not used; instead, a subject–verb inversion signals the subordination. Sentences like the last two preceding examples sometimes take this form:

> *Were I you,* I would accept the offer.
> *Had you told me earlier,* I could have helped.

Concession (*although, though, even if, even though*). This clause concedes or admits a fact in spite of which the main idea is true:

> *Although he is quite small,* he plays basketball well.
> Our car is dependable *even though it is old.*

Comparison (*than, as*). Two distinctive characteristics of the adverb clause of comparison should be noted: (1) Part or all of the verb, although it is needed grammatically, is usually not expressed; and (2) when an action verb is not expressed in the subordinate clause, the appropriate form of the auxiliary *do* is often used even though the *do* does not occur in the main clause:

Gold is heavier *than iron* [*is*].
Your dress is as new *as hers* [*is*].
Her theme was better *than any other student's in the class* [*was*].
Ellen sold more tickets *than Mary did*.

Your attention was directed in the preceding discussion to the omission of parts of the adverb clause of comparison. **Ellipsis** is the term used for this omission, and a clause that leaves some parts understood or unexpressed is called an **elliptical clause.** (See Supplement 1.) In addition to clauses of comparison, other kinds of adverb clauses may be elliptical. You should be aware of them; not only are they structures that can lend variety to your writing, but also some of them must be used with caution if you are to avoid an awkward error (the dangling modifier) that you will study in a later lesson.

In the following examples, brackets enclose the parts of the clauses that may be unexpressed:

While [*I was*] *walking home*, I met Mr. Jones.
When [*he is*] *in New York*, he stays at the Plaza.
Call your office *as soon as* [*it is*] *possible*.
Repairs will be made *wherever* [*they are*] *needed*.
Mary, *although* [*she is*] *a talented girl*, is quite lazy.
If [*you are*] *delayed*, call my secretary.
Your ticket, *unless* [*it is*] *stamped*, is invalid.

Adverb clauses may modify adjectives and adverbs:

We are sorry *that we were delayed*. [Modifies the adjective *sorry*.]
The test was so difficult *that I could not finish it*. [Modifies the adverb *so*.]

A Note on Sentence Variety

Although some adverb clauses—those of comparison, for instance—have a fixed position within the sentence, many adverb clauses may be placed before, inside, or following the main clause. The beginning writer should practice various arrangements to relieve the monotony that comes from reliance on too many "main-subject-plus-main-verb" sentences:

When they deal with the unknown, Greek myths are usually somber.
Greek myths, *when they deal with the unknown*, are usually somber.
Greek myths are usually somber *when they deal with the unknown*.
[NOTE: Usually a comma is not needed when the adverbial clause is the final element of the sentence.]
Although he did not have authority from Congress, President Theodore Roosevelt ordered construction of the Panama Canal.
President Theodore Roosevelt, *although he did not have authority from Congress*, ordered construction of the Panama Canal.
President Theodore Roosevelt ordered construction of the Panama Canal *although he did not have authority from Congress*.

Supplement 1

Occasionally an elliptical adverb clause of comparison must be recast because the exact meaning is unclear when parts of the clause are unexpressed. Here are two sentences that are ambiguous in the shortened forms of the clauses:

Mr. Alton will pay you more *than Stan.*

PROBABLE MEANING: Mr. Alton will pay you more than [he will pay] Stan.

POSSIBLE MEANING: Mr. Alton will pay you more than Stan [will pay you].

Parents dislike homework as much *as their offspring.*

PROBABLE MEANING: Parents dislike homework as much as their offspring [dislike homework].

POSSIBLE MEANING: Parents dislike homework as much as [they dislike] their offspring.

EXERCISE 14
Adverb Clauses

NAME _____   SCORE _____

DIRECTIONS: Identify each of the italicized adverb clauses by writing one of the following numbers in the space at the left:

1. Time	3. Manner	5. Result	7. Concession
2. Place	4. Cause	6. Condition	8. Comparison

_____ 1. The shortstop doffed his cap to the crowd *as he walked to the dugout*.

_____ 2. *Unless this rain stops soon,* most of the county will be flooded.

_____ 3. *Though every club member worked hard,* we sold only two hundred lottery tickets.

_____ 4. *When the moon is full,* strange things happen in our town.

_____ 5. The flight was diverted to Denver *because our airport was fogged in*.

_____ 6. Both parents worked *in order that the children could attend private schools*.

_____ 7. We can get reserved seats *if we send in our money before Friday*.

_____ 8. *Wherever I go nowadays,* people worry about inflation.

_____ 9. I carefully checked every one of the electrical connections, *exactly as you had told me to*.

_____ 10. Sue Ellen sold more Girl Scout cookies *than anyone else in her troop*.

_____ 11. *While looking for a parking spot,* Dad had a rather mild temper tantrum.

_____ 12. *As none of the campers had volunteered,* the overnight hike was canceled.

_____ 13. I wouldn't lend you my motorbike *even if you paid me for it*.

_____ 14. Tom's new office isn't as comfortable *as his old one*.

_____ 15. Libby often studied by candlelight *after the dorm lights had been turned off*.

_____ 16. Lately Mr. Allen has been acting *as if his job bores him*.

_____ 17. *Although exhausted from the tennis matches,* Lillian danced every dance at the party.

_____ 18. You should have turned off the motor *as soon as the red light flashed*.

_____ 19. *Were I you,* I'd leave town in a hurry.

_____ 20. After Dean Jones's remark Jack was so amused *that he giggled*.

ADVERB CLAUSES

DIRECTIONS: Each sentence contains one adverb clause. Underline each adverb clause. In the space at the left, write one of the following numbers to identify the type of clause:

1. Time	3. Manner	5. Result	7. Concession
2. Place	4. Cause	6. Condition	8. Comparison

_____ 1. The tenor sang so poorly that the audience hissed him.

_____ 2. The guard at the gate will admit you if you have a membership sticker on your windshield.

_____ 3. Jane went home early because the bright sun had given her a headache.

_____ 4. We stayed at the airport until Marie's plane had left.

_____ 5. Mr. Reeves recognized his old basketball coach though he had not seen him in thirty years.

_____ 6. Has any one of you team members seen Terry since he returned?

_____ 7. Since our funds were running low, we hitchhiked to the basketball tournament.

_____ 8. Although he has never had a lesson, Jerry plays the piano quite well.

_____ 9. The family stopped their traveling wherever the men could find work.

_____ 10. No one worked harder at the picnic than Alice Dow.

_____ 11. I certainly would accept Dean Liston's offer if I were you.

_____ 12. We can have our picnic wherever you want to.

_____ 13. Before we left, our host served us a light lunch.

_____ 14. Jack is now as tall as his older brother was two years ago.

_____ 15. Had we spent less time at the museum, we could have returned home in time for dinner.

_____ 16. While driving to work this morning, I planned my next vacation trip.

_____ 17. Recently Terry has been behaving as if he resented our presence.

_____ 18. In her new job Rachel made more money in four months than she made all year at her old job.

_____ 19. Ben complains so much that people don't enjoy his company.

_____ 20. All the petty problems of everyday life fade away when I am skiing.

LESSON

9 Subordination: The Adjective Clause

A N **ADJECTIVE CLAUSE** modifies a noun or a pronoun by giving information that points out, identifies, describes, or limits the meaning of the noun or the pronoun. The normal position of an adjective clause is immediately following the noun or the pronoun that it modifies.

Nearly all of the adjective clauses you read, write, or speak use *that, which, who(m), whose, when,* or *where* to tie the adjective clause to the noun or the pronoun it modifies. These subordinators are called **relatives.** Unlike the simple conjunctions that introduce adverb clauses, the relatives function *within* the adjective clause as pronouns (used as subjects, direct objects, or objects of prepositions), adjectives, or adverbs.

It is helpful to think of an adjective clause as a reduced simple sentence that is incorporated within another sentence. This combining is possible when the second clause repeats, directly or by reference, a noun or a pronoun in the first clause. The relative word, by substituting for the repeated noun or pronoun, refers ("relates") directly to the word being modified. Notice that the relative, because it is the word signaling the subordination, always begins the adjective clause.

The following paired units illustrate this process. Every "A" unit has two simple sentences, the second of which repeats a noun in the first. The "B" sentence shows how the second idea has been reduced to a subordinate clause and has become part of the first sentence:

A. This is a well-built truck. *The truck* will save you money.

B. This is a well-built truck *that* will save you money. [The clause modifies *truck.* *That*, the relative pronoun, is the subject of the adjective clause.]

A. Alice has a new boyfriend. *The new boyfriend* [or He] sings in a rock group.

B. Alice has a new boyfriend *who* sings in a rock group. [*Who* is the subject in the clause that modifies *boyfriend.*]

A. Here is the book. I borrowed *the book* [or it] yesterday.

B. Here is the book *that* I borrowed yesterday. [*That* is the direct object in the adjective clause.]

A. The firm hired Chet Brown. The boss had known *Chet Brown* [or him] in Omaha.

B. The firm hired Chet Brown, *whom* the boss had known in Omaha. [*Whom* is the direct object in the adjective clause.]

A. May I introduce Dick Hart? I went to college with *Dick Hart* [or him].

B. May I introduce Dick Hart, with *whom* I went to college? [The clause modifies *Dick Hart*. Notice that the preposition *with* stands at the beginning of the clause with its object *whom*. At the informal level of language usage, the preposition in this structure is sometimes found at the end of the clause. See also Supplement 3 of Lesson 6.]

A. She is a young artist. I admire *the young artist's* [or her] work.

B. She is a young artist *whose* work I admire. [*Work* is in this position because, although it is the direct object of *admire*, it cannot be separated from its modifier, the relative adjective *whose*, which must be placed at the beginning of the adjective clause.]

The relative adverbs *when* and *where* introduce adjective clauses in combinations meaning "time when" and "place where." The following examples show that the subordinator is really the equivalent of an adverbial prepositional phrase. (The "B" sentences are complex sentences combining the material of the two "A" sentences.)

A. I remember a time. You thought otherwise *at that time*.

B. I remember a time *when* you thought otherwise.

A. This is the spot. The wreck occurred *at this spot*.

B. This is the spot *where* the wreck occurred.

These clauses are logically considered adjective clauses because they immediately follow nouns that require identification, and the clauses give the identifying material. If you remember the "time-when" and "place-where" combinations, you will not confuse this type of adjective clause with other subordinate clauses that may use the same subordinators.

NOTE: In certain adjective clauses the relative word is often unexpressed; the meaning is instantly clear without it: the food *(that) we eat*, the house *(that) he lived in*, the man *(whom) you saw*, the time *(when) you fell down*, and so on.

Restrictive and Nonrestrictive Adjective Clauses

An adjective clause is either restrictive or nonrestrictive, and, as you will learn in Lesson 17, an important use of the comma requires that you understand the difference between the two types.

The restrictive adjective clause, the kind that is not set off by commas, *is essential to the identification of the word being modified:*

The grade *that I received on my report* pleased me.
Anyone *who saw the accident* should call the police.

You can see that without the modifying clauses ("The grade pleased me"; "Anyone should call the police"), the nouns are not identified. What grade and what anyone are we talking about? But when we add the modifiers, we identify the *particular* grade and the *particular* anyone. In other words, this kind of clause restricts the meaning of a general noun to one specific member of its class.

The nonrestrictive adjective clause, **which does require commas, supplies additional or incidental information about the word that it modifies,** *but the information is not needed for identifying purposes.* Don't, however, get into the habit of thinking that a nonrestrictive clause is unimportant; unless it has some importance to the meaning of the sentence, it has no right to be in the sentence. If the noun being modified does not require identification, the modifier following it is nonrestrictive and requires commas. It follows, then, that nonrestrictive modifiers are found following proper nouns (*Mount Everest, Philadelphia, Mr. Frank Lockwood*); nouns already identified (the oldest *boy* in her class, her only *grandchild*); and one-of-a-kind nouns (Alice's *mother*, the *provost* of the college, the *writer* of the editorial).

The following examples contrast restrictive and nonrestrictive adjective clauses. (See Supplement 1.)

I visited an old and close friend *who is retiring soon.* [Restrictive.]
I visited my oldest and closest friend, *who is retiring soon.* [Nonrestrictive.]

The man *whose car had been wrecked* asked us for a ride. [Restrictive.]
Mr. Ash, *whose car had been wrecked,* asked us for a ride. [Nonrestrictive.]

A small stream *that flows through the property* supplies an occasional trout. [Restrictive.]
Caldwell Creek, *which flows through the property,* supplies an occasional trout. [Nonrestrictive.]

She wants to retire to a place *where freezing weather is unknown.* [Restrictive.]
She wants to retire to Panama City, *where freezing weather is unknown.* [Nonrestrictive.]

Supplement 1

A few distinctions in the use of *who, which,* and *that* in adjective clauses are generally observed. *Which* refers only to things; *who* refers to people; and *that* refers to things or people. *That* is used only in restrictive clauses; in other words, a "that" adjective clause is not set off by commas. Because *which* is the relative pronoun that must be used in a nonrestrictive clause modifying a thing, a convention that *which* should not introduce a restrictive adjective clause is generally, but by no means always, observed.

EXERCISE 15
Adjective Clauses

NAME _____ SCORE _____

DIRECTIONS: Each italicized unit is an adjective clause. In the space at the left, copy the word the clause modifies. Be prepared to explain in class why some of the clauses are set off by commas (nonrestrictive) and some are not (restrictive).

_____ 1. Someone has already bought the antique bench *that I saw earlier.*

_____ 2. Can you suggest any vegetables *that might grow in this rocky soil?*

_____ 3. We looked for a quiet spot *where we could study.*

_____ 4. Luke then hitchhiked to Mobile, *where shipyard workers were being hired.*

_____ 5. The popular conductor will retire after next Wednesday's concert, *which is already sold out.*

_____ 6. The hat *she wore at the wedding* attracted much attention.

_____ 7. Jeff O'Neal is one old-timer *who will never be forgotten in this town.*

_____ 8. Jeff O'Neal is one old-timer *whom this town should honor.*

_____ 9. The park will be named for Jeff O'Neal, *who played an important role in the town's early days.*

_____ 10. Here is a picture of Jeff O'Neal, *whose granddaughter still lives in the family home.*

_____ 11. How do you like the tie *I'm wearing?*

_____ 12. Have you ever met the woman *against whom you will be playing in the semifinal round?*

_____ 13. Bert recently received a letter from Larry Benham, *with whom he had roomed at Dartmouth.*

_____ 14. He had received his degree in 1932, *when jobs in pharmacy were scarce.*

_____ 15. Unfortunately this happened to him at a time *when he should have been enjoying his retirement.*

_____ 16. Those *who arrive late* will not be seated until the first intermission.

_____ 17. Laura is one of those people *who are rarely on time.*

_____ 18. Laura is the only one of my friends *who is still going to college.*

_____ 19. Last year the only game *I saw* ended in a tie.

_____ 20. Cuthbert had been named after his maternal grandfather, *who had come to America from Scotland.*

ADJECTIVE CLAUSES

DIRECTIONS: Each sentence contains one adjective clause. Underline the adjective clause. In the space at the left, copy the word it modifies. These sentences also contain some adverb clauses. An adjective clause may be contained within an adverb clause, or an adverb clause may modify something within an adjective clause, in which case it should be considered part of the adjective clause.

_____ 1. The flight on which our party was booked was canceled at the last minute.

_____ 2. Uncle Theo, who is usually very cautious when money is involved, lent Edith the down payment.

_____ 3. The meat that was served to us was so tough that I could hardly cut it.

_____ 4. Can you give me one reason that our plan might fail?

_____ 5. I had known very little about meteors until I read the book you recommended.

_____ 6. I'm afraid that the person who told you that story imagined nine tenths of it.

_____ 7. Did you get the name of the person whose car ran into yours?

_____ 8. The police are looking for anyone who was in the area when the fire broke out.

_____ 9. In front of the theater was a block-long line, at the very end of which we saw our two friends.

_____ 10. These con men can always find someone who's trusting, greedy, and foolish.

_____ 11. Two police officers were stationed where they could observe everyone who went through the turnstile.

_____ 12. Although three couples whom she had invited did not show up, Sylvia considered her party a success.

_____ 13. Any contribution you can make will be appreciated.

_____ 14. The new senator offered four amendments, only one of which the committee accepted.

_____ 15. As director of personnel, you must often make decisions that are painful to you.

_____ 16. Sarah read us a poem she had written when she was in the sixth grade.

_____ 17. Reserved seats that have not been sold by Tuesday will be on general sale on Wednesday.

_____ 18. Samuel Johnson, who published his famous dictionary in 1755, defined a lexicographer as "a harmless drudge."

_____ 19. According to my teacher, my opening paragraph, which I had rewritten ten times, needed reworking.

_____ 20. Bud showed us a letter of recommendation from a druggist he'd worked for while he was in college.

10 Subordination: The Noun Clause

THE NOUN clause contains, of course, a subject–verb combination and some kind of subordinator that keeps the clause from being an independent clause. The noun clause, unlike most adverb and adjective clauses, is not an appendage detachable from the main clause. Rather, it functions *within* the main clause in one of the noun "slots": subject, direct object, renaming subjective complement, object of preposition, or appositive.

You will better understand the use of the noun clause if you think of it as a clause equivalent of a "something" or a "someone" in one of these noun slots:

Someone told a lie.
The *witness* told a lie. } [Single-word subjects.]
Whoever repeated that story told a lie. [Noun clause as subject.]

Mr. Allen announced *something*.
Mr. Allen announced his *resignation*. } [Single-word direct objects.]
Mr. Allen announced *that he would resign*. [Noun clause as direct object.]

Give the package to *someone*.
Give the package to the *janitor*. } [Single-word objects of preposition.]
Give the package to *whoever opens the door*. [Noun clause as object of preposition.]

His *story* is very convincing.
What he told us is very convincing. [Noun clause as subject.]

This is his *story*.
This is *what he told us*. [Noun clause as subjective complement.]

Can you tell me your *time* of arrival?
Can you tell me *when you will arrive*? [Noun clause as direct object.]

Most of the noun clauses that you read and write will be in the above-mentioned positions: subject, direct object (the commonest use), subjective complement, or object of preposition. Two other rather special uses should be noted, the "delayed" noun clause and the appositive noun clause.

One common use of a noun clause is as a delayed subject. The signal for this construction is the word *it* standing in subject position, with the meaningful subject being a noun clause following the verb:

It is unfortunate *that you were delayed*. [Although the clause follows the verb, it is the real subject and therefore is a noun clause. The meaning of the sentence is "That you were delayed is unfortunate."]

A related noun clause use puts *it* in the direct object slot with a noun clause following an objective complement. This use, which is encountered less frequently than the delayed subject, gives us a clause that we can call a delayed direct object:

I consider it unlikely *that he will resign*.

To understand the other special noun clause, we must know what an appositive is. The **appositive** is a noun unit inserted into a sentence to *rename* another noun that usually immediately precedes the appositive. A simple example occurs in the following sentence:

Senator Jones, *a dedicated environmentalist*, objected.

Because any noun unit can be used as an appositive, noun clauses sometimes function in this position. Some noun clause appositives are separated from the first noun by at least a comma, sometimes by a heavier mark:

There still remains one mystery: *how the thief knew your name.* [The noun clause renames the preceding noun, *mystery.*]

A rather special type of noun appositive clause, subordinated by *that* and following such nouns as *fact, belief, hope, statement, news,* and *argument,* is usually not set off by any mark of punctuation:

You cannot deny the fact *that you lied under oath.*
Your statement *that the boss is stupid* was undiplomatic.

(See Supplement 1.)

The subordinating words that serve to introduce noun clauses are conjunctions *(that, if, whether);* pronouns *(who, whom, what, which, whoever, whatever, whichever);* adjectives *(whose, which, what);* and adverbs *(when, where, why, how).* Remember that the subordinating word is part of the clause and always stands at or near the beginning of the clause. Remember also that in noun clauses used as direct objects the conjunction *that* is often unexpressed because the meaning is usually clear without it.

The supervisor suspects *that I lost the file.* [Noun clause subordinated by the conjunction *that.*]
I wonder *if you ever received my letter.* [Noun clause subordinated by the conjunction *if.*]
All of us hope *you'll feel better soon.* [Noun clause subordinated by the understood conjunction *that.*]
I do not know *who he is.* [Noun clause subordinated by the pronoun *who* used as the subjective complement within the clause.]
We wonder *what John will do now.* [Noun clause subordinated by the pronoun *what* used as the direct object within the clause.]
Tell me *whom Mary is feuding with now.* [Noun clause subordinated by the pronoun *whom* used as the object of the preposition *with.*]
I can't decide *which car I should buy.* [Noun clause subordinated by the adjective *which* modifying the direct object *car.*]
Why Jack left town is still a mystery. [Noun clause subordinated by the adverb *why.*]

(See Supplement 2.)

Supplement 1

Because an appositive is a renamer, it represents a reduced form of a Pattern 2 sentence in which a subject and a noun subjective complement are joined by a form of *be.* The writer of the sentence "Senator Jones, a dedicated environmentalist, objected" could have written two simple sentences, the second one repeating a noun used in the first:

Senator Jones objected.
Senator Jones [or He] is a dedicated environmentalist.

The adjective clause offers the writer one device for compressing this information into one sentence:

Senator Jones, *who is a dedicated environmentalist*, objected.

The appositive represents a further compression:

Senator Jones, *a dedicated environmentalist*, objected.

If you think of the appositive as a renamer of the preceding noun (the two nouns could be joined by a form of *be*), you have a handy test to help you recognize any noun appositive use:

There still remains one mystery: *how the thief knew your name.*
   [Test: The mystery *is* how the thief knew your name.]
You cannot deny the fact *that you lied under oath.*
   [Test: The fact *is* that you lied under oath.]
Your statement *that the boss is stupid* was undiplomatic.
   [Test: The statement *is* that the boss is stupid.]

If you remember a few points about the form, the function, and the positioning of adjective clauses and noun clauses, you should have little difficulty in distinguishing between them. Although certain kinds of noun clauses in apposition may, at first glance, look like adjective clauses, a few simple tests clearly show the difference:

The news *that you brought us* is welcome. [Adjective clause.]
The news *that Bob has recovered* is welcome. [Noun clause.]

If you remember that an adjective clause is a *describer* and that an appositive noun clause is a *renamer*, you can see that in the first sentence the clause describes—in fact, identifies—the noun *news*, but it does not actually tell us what the news is. In the second sentence the clause does more: It tells us what the news is. Remember the *be* test. "The news is *that you brought us* . . ." does not make sense, but "The news is *that Bob has recovered* . . ." does; therefore the second clause is a noun clause in apposition. Another test that can be applied to these two types of sentences is based on the fact that in adjective clauses, but not in noun clauses, *which* can be substituted for *that*. "The news *which* you brought us . . ." is acceptable English; the clause, in this case, is an adjective clause. But because we can't say "The news *which* Bob has recovered . . .," this time the clause is a noun clause; it cannot be an adjective clause.

Supplement 2

You have probably already noticed that the pronouns, adjectives, and adverbs that subordinate noun clauses are essentially the same words that are used in questions (Lesson 6). The two uses are alike in the important respect that they always stand at the beginning of the clause. The two uses differ in that as interrogatives the words bring about the subject–verb inversion, whereas in noun clauses the subject–verb positioning is the normal one:

Whom will the mayor appoint? [This sentence is a direct question; it calls for an answer. *Whom* is the direct object of the main verb.]

I wonder *whom* the mayor will appoint. [This sentence is a statement, not a direct question. Notice that a question mark is not required. *Whom* is the direct object within the noun clause.]

EXERCISE 16
Noun Clauses

NAME _____ SCORE _____

DIRECTIONS: Identify the use of each italicized noun clause by writing one of the following abbreviations in the space at the left:

S. (subject or delayed subject)   S.C. (subjective complement)
D.O. (direct object or delayed   O.P. (object of preposition)
    direct object)   Ap. (appositive)

_____ 1. The lawyers suspect *that Dobbyns would be a hostile witness.*

_____ 2. Delbert's main worry right now is *that he will be replaced at the office by a computer.*

_____ 3. You certainly should have told Ms. Sherwood *why you were absent.*

_____ 4. Most commentators think it unlikely *that the incumbent can be re-elected.*

_____ 5. *How your sister-in-law spends her money* should be no concern of yours.

_____ 6. Lapham always agrees enthusiastically and loudly with *whatever the boss says.*

_____ 7. The mechanic showed us *how the wiring should have been done.*

_____ 8. It is unfortunate *that you bought your furniture before the big clearance sale.*

_____ 9. All of us should be worrying about *how fast the deficit is growing.*

_____ 10. *That the first witness was lying* is now clear to all of us.

_____ 11. Tom's excuse was *that his alarm clock did not function.*

_____ 12. Tom's excuse, *that his alarm clock did not function,* was not very convincing.

_____ 13. It is well known around town *that Mr. Carbury is a compulsive gambler.*

_____ 14. I knew *you'd enjoy the concert.*

_____ 15. The belief *that tomatoes are poisonous* was once widely held.

_____ 16. The jury was impressed by the fact *that the accused man had served with distinction in the Navy.*

_____ 17. Is that *what you truly believe?*

_____ 18. Can anyone tell me *where I can find a public telephone?*

_____ 19. *Whoever believes that wild story of yours* will believe anything.

_____ 20. These people will vote for *whoever promises them lower taxes.*

NOUN CLAUSES

DIRECTIONS: Each of the following sentences contains one noun clause. Put parentheses ( ) about each noun clause. In the space at the left, write one of the following to identify the use of the noun clause:

S. (subject or delayed subject)	S.C. (subjective complement)
D.O. (direct object or delayed direct object)	O.P. (object of preposition)
	Ap. (appositive)

_____ 1. If you agree with me that corrective measures must be taken, you'll vote for me in the primary election.

_____ 2. Our dog has been lost several times in the past; he'll walk away with whoever pets him.

_____ 3. We think it quite possible that our dog will come home as soon as he gets really hungry.

_____ 4. Was Thornton's reply what you had expected?

_____ 5. Panic spread throughout the rural areas after a fortune teller predicted that there would be an earthquake.

_____ 6. According to the manager, Cranwell's main problem is that he will not practice hard enough.

_____ 7. I'm sure that the committee liked your suggestion that the surplus funds should be put into government bonds.

_____ 8. It surprised all of us that the rookie pitcher lasted through eight innings.

_____ 9. Do you sometimes wonder if you have chosen the right profession?

_____ 10. If you knew she'd refuse, why did you make the offer?

_____ 11. Whatever amount you can pay now will be reflected in the interest rate we'll give you.

_____ 12. Our organization will provide food and shelter to whoever needs help.

_____ 13. It's still true that the wheel that squeaks the loudest gets the grease.

_____ 14. There is a remote possibility that the missing fishermen are waiting out the storm in some harbor.

_____ 15. Dr. Alton wouldn't tell the class when they would have their next test.

_____ 16. What you have just told me confirms a rumor that I heard yesterday.

_____ 17. What Mark received from his aunt's estate was much less than he had hoped for.

_____ 18. Many townspeople think it disgraceful that the mayor missed the welcoming ceremony at the airport.

_____ 19. The refugees had no food except what the Army gave them.

_____ 20. We marvel at how well Muriel plays the flute, even though she has had only a few lessons.

EXERCISE 17
Subordinate Clauses

NAME _____ SCORE _____

DIRECTIONS: The italicized material in each of these sentences is a subordinate clause. In the first space at the left, write Adv., Adj., or N. to identify the clause. Within the italicized clause the word printed in boldface type is a complement. Identify it by writing in the second space at the left one of the following:

S.C. (subjective complement)	D.O. (direct object)
I.O. (indirect object)	O.C. (objective complement)

_____
_____
1. The park ranger warned the group *that he would not be* **responsible** *for their safety if they continued the climb.*

_____
_____
2. Ms. Strom explained to the children that the birds *that they had spotted in the fir tree* were starlings.

_____
_____
3. *If you can tell* **us** *the name of the capital of Zimbabwe,* you'll win a year's supply of detergent.

_____
_____
4. Andy's poor grades in mathematics partially explain *why he never became an* **engineer.**

_____
_____
5. The car was registered in the name of a local entrepreneur *whom the FBI had been seeking.*

_____
_____
6. The evening celebration was not entirely successful *because the noisy fireworks made a few of the children almost* **hysterical.**

_____
_____
7. The advertisement reported that a handsome reward would go to *whoever finds the missing* **briefcase.**

_____
_____
8. Our governor is a forgiving man; he recently appointed to the Board of Regents a woman *who once called him* **incompetent.**

_____
_____
9. Mr. Benson beamed when the photographer told him *that he looked quite* **youthful** *for a man of sixty-five.*

_____
_____
10. Time relationships sometimes become confused for people *as they grow* **older.**

_____
_____
11. *As his hostess told* **Tim** *the Latin names for the flowers,* he busily wrote them in his notebook.

_____
_____
12. "Anyone can see *why experts call this painting a* **masterpiece,**" said the pompous guide.

_____
_____ 13. The food was greasy and overcooked, *although the half-starved hik-ers considered it very* **tasty.**

_____
_____ 14. The carpet *that your store sent me* is not what I ordered.

_____
_____ 15. The story *she told us* left us speechless.

_____
_____ 16. During "show-and-tell" time in the lower grades, children some-times report on family events *that should be kept* **secret.**

_____
_____ 17. After the trial period the boss and her three assistants will decide *what your salary will be.*

_____
_____ 18. "I think your concluding paragraph will be more effective *if you make it* **shorter** *by about half,*" said the teacher.

_____
_____ 19. Official announcements from the White House have been enthusias-tic, *although a few spokespersons remain* **cautious.**

_____
_____ 20. Home owners in the Mud Lake area worry about what could hap-pen if fire breaks out *while the water pressure is* **low.**

_____
_____ 21. The three children were discussing an important matter: *what kind of dessert their mother should serve* **them.**

_____
_____ 22. At a press conference tomorrow a representative of the search com-mittee will announce **who** *the five finalists are.*

_____
_____ 23. A recently hired night watchman is apparently the person *who had turned the burglar* **alarm** *off.*

_____
_____ 24. An accountant **whom** *Peter knew only casually* came forth with the bail money.

_____
_____ 25. We finally found a place *where we could store our* **goods.**

11 Subordination: Phrases

A PHRASE is a group of related words that does *not* contain a subject and a verb in combination. Like the subordinate clause, the phrase is used in the sentence as a single part of speech.

Many of the sentences that you have studied thus far have shown the common modifying uses of the **prepositional phrase,** which consists of a preposition (see Lesson 2), a noun or a pronoun used as its object, and any modifiers of the object. Most prepositional phrases are used as adjectives or adverbs:

> Most *of my friends* live *in the East.* [The first phrase is used as an adjective to modify the pronoun *most;* the second is used as an adverb to modify *live.*]

Much less commonly, a prepositional phrase is used as a noun:

> *Before lunch* is the best time for the meeting. [The phrase is the subject of the verb *is.*]
> She waved to us from *inside the phone booth.* [The phrase is the object of the preposition *from.*]

Another very important kind of phrase makes use of a verbal. A **verbal** is a word formed from a verb but used as a different part of speech. There are three kinds of verbals, the gerund, the participle, and the infinitive.

A **gerund** is recognized by the ending *ing,* either on the simple form *(studying)* or on an auxiliary *(having studied, being studied, having been studied).* Before one of these units can be called a gerund, however, it must be used as a *noun* within the sentence:

> *Studying* demands most of my time. [Subject.]
> I usually enjoy *studying.* [Direct object.]
> My main activity is *studying.* [Renaming subjective complement.]
> You won't pass the course without *studying.* [Object of preposition.]
> Might I suggest to you another activity: *studying?* [Appositive.]

Not all gerund uses are as simple as these. The single-word gerund use is uncomplicated. "He enjoys *studying*" and "He enjoys *football*" are alike in their structure; the only difference is that in one the direct object is a word formed from a verb and in the other it is a regular noun. But gerunds (like the participles and infinitives that we shall look at shortly) have a verb quality that nouns do not have: They can take their own adverbial modifiers *and complements.* A **gerund phrase,** therefore, is a gerund plus its modifiers and/or complements.

As was suggested about noun clauses, you might think of the gerund phrase as the equivalent of a "something" that fills one of the noun slots in the sentence: subject, direct object, renaming subjective complement, object of preposition, or (rarely) appositive.

As in basic sentences, the kind of complement in a verbal phrase is determined by the kind of verb from which the verbal is derived. Thus the gerund, participial, or infinitive form of a transitive verb must be followed by a direct object (sometimes used with an indirect object or an objective complement), and the verbal form of a linking verb must be followed by a subjective complement. The following examples will help to clarify this important point. In each of the examples, the phrase is a gerund phrase because it is used as the direct object of the main verb:

He enjoys *walking in the snow*. [The gerund has no complement. Compare "He walks in the snow."]

He enjoys *building model airplanes*. [*Airplanes* is the direct object of the gerund *building*. Compare "He builds model airplanes."]

He enjoys *being helpful*. He enjoyed *being elected treasurer*. [*Helpful* is the subjective complement of the gerund *being; treasurer* is the subjective complement of the passive gerund *being elected*. Compare "He is helpful" and "He was elected treasurer."]

He enjoyed *telling us the good news*. [*Us* is the indirect object and *news* the direct object of the gerund *telling*. Compare "He told us the good news."]

He enjoyed *making our vacation pleasant*. [*Vacation* is the direct object and *pleasant* the objective complement of the gerund *making*. Compare "He made our vacation pleasant."]

The **participle** is identical in form with the four gerund forms; in addition, there are the past participle (*studied*) and a progressive form (*having been studying*). The difference between the participle and the gerund is one of use: Whereas the gerund is always used as a noun (subject, direct object, renaming subjective complement, or object of preposition), the participle is used as an adjectival modifier:

The *injured* bird clung to the *swaying* branch. [The past participle *injured* modifies the noun *bird;* the present participle *swaying* modifies the noun *branch*.]

A **participial phrase** consists of a participle plus its modifiers and/or complements. Because the participial phrase, in addition to its value as a describing unit, shows its verb origin by naming an activity, it offers a possible substitute for a string of monotonous independent clauses, as the following example shows:

Jensen stood at home plate. He waggled his bat. He eyed the pitcher malevolently. He took a mighty swing at the first pitch. He hit the ball out of the park. [Five independent clauses.]

Standing at home plate, waggling his bat and eyeing the pitcher malevolently, Jensen took a mighty swing at the first pitch, hitting the ball out of the park. [One independent clause and four participial phrases.]

The similarity between an adjective clause and a participial phrase is obvious:

A man mounted the platform. The man [or He] was carrying a gun. [Two independent clauses.]

A man *who was carrying a gun* mounted the platform. [Adjective clause. *Gun* is a direct object of the verb.]

A man *carrying a gun* mounted the platform. [Participial phrase. *Gun* is a direct object of the participle.]

The Joneses left at intermission. They had found the play exceedingly dull. [Two independent clauses.]

The Joneses, *who had found the play exceedingly dull*, left at intermission. [Adjective clause. *Play* is a direct object and *dull* an objective complement of the verb.]

The Joneses, *having found the play exceedingly dull*, left at intermission. [Participial phrase. *Play* is a direct object and *dull* an objective complement of the participle.]

These two examples point out another similarity: Like the adjective clause, the participial phrase is either restrictive or nonrestrictive. The phrase in the first example is an identifier; it is restrictive and is not set off by commas. The phrase in the second example is not needed for identifying purposes. It requires commas because it is nonrestrictive.
(See Supplement 1.)

The **absolute phrase** is a special kind of participial phrase, different from the standard participial phrase in both form and function. Within the absolute phrase, the participle follows a noun or a pronoun that is part of the phrase. The phrase adds to the meaning of the whole sentence, but it does not directly modify any noun or pronoun in the sentence. The absolute phrase is a versatile structure capable of many variations and widely used in modern prose writing to point out subtle relationships underlying the ideas within a sentence:

> *The rain having started,* we abandoned our tents.
> The police recovered eight of the paintings, *three of them badly damaged.*
> The mob reached the palace gates, *the leader (being) a burly, redhaired sailor.* [Occasionally an absolute phrase having a noun plus a renamer or describer appears with the participle *being* unexpressed.]

A special kind of phrase using *with* to introduce one of these absolute phrases can add subtle modifying and narrative coloring to a sentence:

> *With the band playing and the crowd applauding furiously,* Jim Kinman was obviously uncomfortable.
> Sidney died *with his works unpublished.*
> They held the funeral on the second day, *with the town coming to look at Miss Emily beneath a mass of bought flowers.* (W. Faulkner)
> But we can't possibly have a garden party *with a dead man just outside the front gate.* (K. Mansfield)

Notice that the *with* in this construction is quite unlike *with* in its common prepositional use:

> The acquitted woman left the courtroom *with her lawyer.*
> The acquitted woman left the courtroom *with her head held high.*

An **infinitive** is a verbal consisting of the simple stem of the verb, generally preceded by *to* (*to* is called the sign of the infinitive). The infinitive uses auxiliaries to show tense and voice: *to study, to have studied, to be studying, to have been studying, to be studied, to have been studied.*

An **infinitive phrase** consists of an infinitive plus its modifiers and/or complements. Infinitive units are used as nouns, as adjectives, and as adverbs:

> *To leave the meeting before Nora's speech* would be tactless. [The infinitive phrase is used as the subject of the sentence. Within the phrase *meeting* is the direct object.]
> It would be tactless *to leave the meeting before Nora's speech.* [In this pattern the infinitive phrase is called a delayed subject; hence it serves a noun use. The signal word is *it;* although it stands in subject position, the infinitive phrase is the meaningful subject. Sometimes the *it* is in the direct object slot with the delayed infinitive phrase following an objective complement: "I would consider it tactless *to leave the meeting before Nora's speech.*" Compare a similar noun clause use in Lesson 10.]

I wanted *to give Chalmers another chance.* [The infinitive phrase is the direct object of *wanted.* Within the phrase *Chalmers* is the indirect object and *chance* the direct object of the infinitive. Compare "I gave Chalmers another chance."]

My plan is *to become an active precinct worker.* [The infinitive phrase is used as a noun; it is a subjective complement that renames the subject *plan.* Within the phrase *worker* is the subjective complement of the infinitive. Compare "I became an active precinct worker."]

The test *to be taken tomorrow* is not difficult. [The infinitive is used as an adjective modifying *test.*]

I am happy *to make your acquaintance.* [The infinitive phrase is used as an adverb modifying the adjective *happy.*]
To be sure of a good seat, you should arrive early. [The infinitive phrase is used as an adverb modifying *should arrive.*]

Infinitive phrases sometimes include their own subjects. Notice that a pronoun used as the subject is in the objective case:

We wanted *her to resign.*
We know *him to be a good referee.*

The infinitive without the *to* may form a phrase that is used as the direct object of such verbs as *let, help, make, see, hear,* and *watch:*

The teacher let *us leave early.*
I heard *the teacher mispronounce a word.*

The infinitive without *to* is also sometimes used as the object of a preposition, such as *except, but,* or *besides:*

He could do nothing except *resign gracefully.*

Supplement 1

The structural similarity between the adjective clause and the participial phrase carries another implication concerning sentence variety. The adjective clause has little freedom of movement within the sentence. It follows as closely as possible the word it modifies; even a few words intervening between the two units might confuse the reader. And the restrictive (identifying) participial phrase normally follows the noun it modifies (as in the "man carrying a gun . . ." sentence).

But the nonrestrictive participial phrase, unlike the nonrestrictive adjective clause it closely resembles, need not always follow immediately the word it modifies. Here we have an important device for achieving variety in sentence structure: Skilled writers often place a nonrestrictive participial phrase *before* the noun, to begin the sentence. Some phrases of this type also lend themselves effectively to placement at the end of the clause:

My oldest brother, *having squandered the inheritance,* declared himself bankrupt.
Having squandered the inheritance, my oldest brother declared himself bankrupt.
My oldest brother declared himself bankrupt, *having squandered the inheritance.*

EXERCISE **18**

Gerund Phrases

NAME _____ SCORE _____

DIRECTIONS: In the space at the left, write one of these numbers to identify the use of the italicized gerund phrase:

1. Subject
2. Direct object
3. Subjective complement
4. Object of preposition

_____ 1. By *leaving the office twenty minutes earlier,* you can get the 5:50 train home.

_____ 2. I wish that our neighbor's dog would stop *barking at every passing car.*

_____ 3. *Finding a good replacement for Jo Walters* will not be easy.

_____ 4. You might try *being more congenial with the people who work under you.*

_____ 5. After *watching television for three hours,* Brewster decided that he would study for the test.

_____ 6. Your first big mistake was *picking up the three hitchhikers.*

_____ 7. We hear that the governor is considering *vetoing the bill.*

_____ 8. Your main responsibility will be *keeping some semblance of order at the press conference.*

_____ 9. *Reading the minutes of the last meeting* seems a waste of time.

_____ 10. Janet's boyfriend was convicted of *leaving the scene of an accident.*

_____ 11. Many of the faculty believe that *lowering the admission requirements* will be necessary before long.

_____ 12. One member of Congress even suggested *sending an aircraft carrier to the region.*

_____ 13. We must guard against *dropping even a hint about the surprise birthday party.*

_____ 14. Our chance of *catching enough fish for a meal* is fast fading.

_____ 15. How much will *adding a new room to the cabin* increase my property tax?

_____ 16. Lucy maintains that no other household chore is as boring as *dusting the furniture.*

_____ 17. The highlight of the trip was *watching the launching of the spaceship.*

_____ 18. The speaker concluded her lecture by *pleading for help for her country's homeless.*

_____ 19. When may I begin *parking my car in the reserved lot?*

_____ 20. Upon *hearing this alarming news,* Mr. Allen had every lock in his house changed.

81

EXERCISE **18**

Participial Phrases

DIRECTIONS: Each of the following sentences contains one participial phrase. Use parentheses ( ) to mark the beginning and the end of each participial phrase. In the space at the left, copy the noun or the pronoun that the participial phrase modifies.

————————— 1. Bert's first job as an actor was in a TV commercial extolling the virtues of a new cat food.

————————— 2. Having been brought up properly, the children refused a third helping of dessert.

————————— 3. A short, fat man dressed in an outrageous clown outfit led the cheering.

————————— 4. Students maintaining a B-plus average are excused from taking the test.

————————— 5. Brownell intercepted a pass on the thirty-yard line, setting up the Cougars' tie-breaking touchdown.

————————— 6. Anyone knowing the whereabouts of the missing visitors should get in touch with the police.

————————— 7. Bernice did not recognize any of the dozen or so people sitting at the head table.

————————— 8. The watchman turned and walked away, obviously not much impressed by our tale of woe.

————————— 9. By restricting admission to those holding life-membership cards, the manager made some new enemies.

————————— 10. Careening wildly out of control, the car sheared off three fence posts.

————————— 11. Jean could barely read the note in the faint light coming through the dirty window.

————————— 12. Realizing that she had been duped, Barbara hurriedly left the fairgrounds.

————————— 13. Rose really enjoys showing guests the pictures taken by her son in Italy.

————————— 14. The librarian explained that an incunabulum is a book printed before 1501.

————————— 15. The ex-member of Congress terminated the interview, knowing full well that he had been caught in a lie.

————————— 16. Every spring the college raises money for charity by auctioning items left by students in classrooms.

————————— 17. On the day following the trial, the defense attorney was accused of offering a bribe to a witness.

————————— 18. Grandpa came home by bus, having forgotten where he had parked the car.

————————— 19. In those days anyone found guilty of even a minor crime was transported to a penal colony.

————————— 20. Having hiked to Lake Crescent in five hours, we took a much-needed rest.

EXERCISE 19
Infinitive Phrases

NAME _____ SCORE _____

DIRECTIONS: In the space at the left, write one of the following abbreviations to identify the use within the sentence of the italicized infinitive phrase:

    N. (noun—subject, delayed subject, direct   Adj. (adjective)
       object, subjective complement, object   Adv. (adverb)
       of preposition)

_____ 1. We raced from the stadium to the bus depot *to catch the last bus home.*

_____ 2. "I hope you'll try *to make the next payment on time,*" said the unpleasant cashier.

_____ 3. It might be a good idea *to postpone the game until the weather improves.*

_____ 4. No one in the office seemed willing *to help Marcia with her new duties.*

_____ 5. Show me the best way *to get from here to Bass Lake.*

_____ 6. *To help pay her college expenses,* Betty worked part-time in the library.

_____ 7. Do you want *to begin painting the garage today?*

_____ 8. The items *to be sold next week in the clearance sale* are marked with a red tag.

_____ 9. The officer ordered *Beth and me to wait in the hall.*

_____ 10. You and I should be able *to finish the chores by sundown.*

_____ 11. Wouldn't it be pleasant *to have more than two weeks for vacation?*

_____ 12. Yesterday the new student did little in class except *draw pictures in his notebook.*

_____ 13. Since high-school days his goal has been *to become lead singer in a rock group.*

_____ 14. The agent prepared a brochure picturing the properties *to be offered at auction next month.*

_____ 15. Ms. Hudson often lets *Jane and me clean the chalkboards.*

_____ 16. Fred turned down the invitation, saying that he was much too tired *to play another round of golf.*

_____ 17. After work Lee stopped at a market *to buy something for dessert.*

_____ 18. The scoutmaster showed the boys *how to start a campfire without the use of matches.*

_____ 19. Our manager could do nothing besides *make insulting remarks about the umpire.*

_____ 20. Sometimes it's difficult *to be civil to a person like Frisbee.*

83

Complements in Phrases

DIRECTIONS: In the first space at the left, write one of the following letters to identify the italicized phrase:

G. (gerund phrase)   I. (infinitive phrase)
P. (participial phrase)   A. (absolute phrase)

In the second space, write one of the following abbreviations to identify the use within the phrase of the complement printed in bold type:

D.O. (direct object)   I.O. (indirect object)
S.C. (subjective complement)   O.C. (objective complement)

_____ _____ 1. *Offering* **Tom** *a share of the prize* was generous of you.

_____ _____ 2. *Having played* **soccer** *as a youth in Germany*, Hank was able to explain the strategy to us.

_____ _____ 3. *My roommate having found a better* **job,** I now have extra space to rent.

_____ _____ 4. The county engineer advocates *leaving the road* **unpaved.**

_____ _____ 5. "This time your directors are able *to give you* **stockholders** *some good news*," she said.

_____ _____ 6. Shawn, *being a* **minor,** could not enter the cocktail lounge.

_____ _____ 7. One witness reported *having sent the accused* **man** *a check for two thousand dollars.*

_____ _____ 8. He maintains that he has perfected a method *to make electric power* **available** *to all at little cost.*

_____ _____ 9. Jasper had to find a new job, *his old firm having declared* **bankruptcy.**

_____ _____ 10. It was tactless of you *to call the referee an* **idiot.**

_____ _____ 11. The company recalled thousands of cars *declared* **unsafe** *because of faulty brakes.*

_____ _____ 12. Why don't you try *making the path* **wider?**

_____ _____ 13. According to the advertisement, reading the book will help *you become a* **leader** *in your community.*

_____ _____ 14. Fred surprised us by *keeping* **quiet** *during the debate.*

_____ _____ 15. *Placing one* **foot** *carefully in front of the other*, Janet slowly crossed the creek on the fallen log.

_____ _____ 16. No one wants *to be called a social* **outcast.**

_____ _____ 17. *All things being* **equal,** I'd vote for the incumbent.

_____ _____ 18. We often study at the library, *the fraternity house usually being too* **noisy.**

_____ _____ 19. *Declaring the ship* **ready** *for active duty*, the admiral's wife hurled the champagne bottle at the bow.

_____ _____ 20. The suspicious clerk called Art's bank before *giving* **him** *the money.*

12 Sentence Building: Misplaced Modifiers; Dangling Modifiers

PROPER arrangement of the parts of your sentence will help make your meaning clear. Ordinarily the main parts—the subjects, the verbs, the complements—cause no problems. Here we shall consider five possible trouble spots in the placing of modifiers.

1. Although usage sanctions a rather loose placing of some common adverbs, such as *only, nearly, almost,* and *hardly,* sentences of precise meaning result only when such adverbs are placed close to the words they modify:

> LOOSE: This will *only* take five minutes.
> I *nearly* earned a hundred dollars last week.
> BETTER: This will take *only* five minutes. [*Only* should modify *five,* not *take.*]
> I earned *nearly* a hundred dollars last week.

2. Words and phrases that attach themselves to the wrong word can confuse the reader:

> POOR: I wish every person in this class could know the man I'm going to talk about *personally.*
> I heard that Senator Jones had been shot *on the morning broadcast.*
> The Police Department will be notified of all reported obscene phone calls *by the telephone company.*
> BETTER: I wish every person in this class could know *personally* the man I'm going to talk about.
> *On the morning broadcast* I heard that Senator Jones had been shot.
> The Police Department will be notified *by the telephone company* of all reported obscene phone calls.

3. The squinting modifier is one that is placed between two units, either of which it could modify:

> POOR: Students who can already type *normally* are put into an advanced class.
> He said *after the dinner* some color slides would be shown.
> BETTER: Students who can already type are *normally* put into an advanced class.
> He said some color slides would be shown *after the dinner.*

4. The split infinitive results from the placing of an adverbial modifier between the *to* and the root verb of an infinitive. Although greatly overemphasized by some as an error, the split infinitive, particularly with a modifier consisting of more than one word, is usually avoided by careful writers:

> POOR: It was my custom to *at least once a month* visit my grandmother.
> BETTER: It was my custom to visit my grandmother *at least once a month.*

5. The correlatives *both . . . and, not only . . . but also, either . . . or,* and *neither . . . nor* are used in pairs and should be placed immediately before the parallel units that they connect:

> POOR: We sent invitations *both* to Webster *and* Jenkins.
> This man *not only* can get along with young people *but also* with their parents.

You must *either* promise me that you will come *or* send a substitute.

BETTER: We sent invitations to *both* Webster *and* Jenkins. [The parallel words are *Webster* and *Jenkins*.]

This man can get along *not only* with young people *but also* with their parents.

You must promise me that you will *either* come *or* send a substitute.

Dangling Modifiers

In a well-constructed sentence, any modifying phrase containing a participle, a gerund, or an infinitive (see Lesson 11) is attached to the word that it logically modifies. By this we mean that the noun or pronoun being modified could be a logical subject of the verb from which the verbal is derived:

Being a stubborn child, Ted usually gets his way. [Test: Ted is a stubborn child.]

After *leaving the dentist's office,* I bought my groceries. [Test: I left the dentist's office.]

To qualify for the job, an applicant must be able to type. [Test: An applicant qualifies for the job.]

If the modifying unit attaches itself to a noun or a pronoun that does not produce this logical subject–verb relationship, we say that the phrase dangles:

After *leaving the dentist's office,* my groceries had to be bought. [Test: My groceries left the dentist's office.]

Although danglers are occasionally detected in the writings of very good authors, a dangler is undesirable if it calls attention to itself, if it causes even momentary confusion, or if it gives a ludicrous meaning that the writer did not intend.

The easiest way to correct a dangler is to supply the word that the phrase should modify and to place the phrase next to that word. Another way is to change the dangling phrase to a subordinate clause with a subject and verb expressed.

1. The most common type of dangler is the participial phrase beginning a sentence:

DANGLER: *Stepping into the boat,* my camera dropped into the water. [Was the camera stepping into the boat? Of course not. The trouble here is that the word that the phrase should modify is not expressed in the sentence.]

Burned to a cinder, I could not eat the toast. [The sentence sounds as if *I* were burned to a cinder. The word that the dangler should modify is *toast,* but this word is too far from the phrase to be immediately associated with it.]

BETTER: Stepping into the boat, I dropped my camera into the water.

As I was stepping into the boat, my camera dropped into the water.

Burned to a cinder, the toast could not be eaten.

I could not eat the toast because it was burned to a cinder.

2. Another type of dangler is the gerund that follows a preposition. The phrase that contains the verbal must have a word to refer to, and that word must be close enough to the phrase so that the reader does not associate the phrase with the wrong word:

DANGLER: *After driving all day,* the motel was a welcome sight. [Was the motel doing the driving? That is not what is meant, and yet that is what the sentence states.]

> *On graduating from high school,* my father let me work in his office. [The sentence says that your father let you work in his office when *he,* not *you,* graduated from high school.]
> *Since breaking my leg,* my neighbors have helped with my farm chores. [A logical sentence only if the neighbors broke your leg.]
> BETTER: After driving all day, we welcomed the sight of the motel.
> After we had driven all day, the motel was a welcome sight.
> On graduating from high school, I was given a chance to work in my father's office.
> After I had graduated from high school, my father let me work in his office.
> Since breaking my leg, I have been helped with my farm chores by my neighbors.
> My neighbors have helped with my farm chores since I broke my leg.

3. One type of introductory elliptical clause (see Lesson 8) that must be used carefully is a "time" clause, usually introduced by *when* or *while.* The clause becomes a dangler if the understood subject of the adverb clause is different from the subject of the main clause. The reader wrongly assumes that both clauses have the same subject, and the result can be a ridiculous meaning that the writer never intended:

> DANGLER: *When ten years old,* my father sold the farm and moved to Dallas.
> *While weeding my vegetable garden,* a garter snake startled me.
> BETTER: When ten years old, I moved to Dallas after my father sold the farm.
> When I was ten years old, my father sold the farm and moved to Dallas.
> While weeding my vegetable garden, I was startled by a garter snake.
> While I was weeding my vegetable garden, a garter snake startled me.

4. You may occasionally have trouble with an introductory infinitive phrase. If the infinitive names a specific action, be sure that the word that the phrase attaches to names the logical doer of that action.

> DANGLER: *To enter the contest,* a box top must be sent with your slogan.
> BETTER: To enter the contest, you must send a box top with your slogan.
> If you want to enter the contest, a box top must be sent with your slogan.
> When you enter the contest, send a box top with your slogan.

Misplaced Modifiers

DIRECTIONS: From each of the following pairs of sentences, select the one that is clearer and write its letter in the space at the left. Be prepared to justify your choice.

_____ 1. A. Jill's first-year savings only paid for half of her school debts.

         B. Jill's first-year savings paid for only half of her school debts.

_____ 2. A. We urge you to as soon as possible return the survey.

         B. We urge you to return the survey as soon as possible.

_____ 3. A. In another month or so young Andy will be nearly as tall as his father.

         B. In another month or so young Andy will nearly be as tall as his father.

_____ 4. A. From our seats high in the stadium, we watched the parachutists float to earth.

         B. We watched the parachutists float to earth from our seats high in the stadium.

_____ 5. A. The book gave me neither enlightenment nor entertainment.

         B. The book neither gave me enlightenment nor entertainment.

_____ 6. A. The author lists what she considers the ten worst writing weaknesses in her preface.

         B. In her preface the author lists what she considers the ten worst writing weaknesses.

_____ 7. A. You ought to fertilize the vegetables every three weeks.

         B. You ought to every three weeks fertilize the vegetables.

_____ 8. A. Remember, not all students are interested in drama.

         B. Remember, all students are not interested in drama.

_____ 9. A. Eating junk food often is deplored by nutritionists.

         B. Eating junk food is often deplored by nutritionists.

_____ 10. A. I feel sure that you'll get the job after reading your flattering references.

         B. After reading your flattering references, I feel sure that you'll get the job.

DIRECTIONS: In the space at the left, write A or B to indicate the logical placing of the italicized modifier within the parentheses.

_____ 1. *(only)* Hurry, children; you A have B ten minutes left to finish your test.

_____ 2. *(either)* A You B pay the tax now or postpone payment and pay a penalty.

_____ 3. *(at least once a month)* A The Sunday-school teacher would give his standard lecture on obeying our parents B.

_____ 4. *(not only)* Ms. LaRue A is B a chemist but has an MBA from Stanford.

_____ 5. *(almost)* Hawkins A played in B every Tiger game for seven seasons.

_____ 6. *(every ten days)* Junior promised A to cut the lawn B.

_____ 7. *(once)* A neighbor of mine who had played lacrosse A tried B to explain the game to me.

_____ 8. *(either)* That broker of yours A is B very clever or unbelievably lucky.

_____ 9. *(neither)* The embattled prime minister vowed A to B resign nor even to apologize.

_____ 10. *(normally)* Applicants who can use word processors A are B given preference.

_____ 11. *(in spite of the rain)* We were determined to A finish our golf game B.

_____ 12. *(in his sermon)* A Dr. Thornton discussed the need for harmony B.

_____ 13. *(by the visiting nurse)* We were told A to raise our hands if we had already been vaccinated B.

_____ 14. *(not)* A All college professors are B vitally interested in conducting research.

_____ 15. *(only)* Jack decided to A invest B two hundred dollars in the project.

90

NAME _____ SCORE _____

DIRECTIONS: One sentence of each pair contains a dangling modifier. Underline the dangler. In the space at the left, write the letter that identifies the correct sentence.

_____ 1. A. Having misunderstood the assignment, I received a low grade on my paper.
         B. Having misunderstood the assignment, my paper got a low grade.

_____ 2. A. Exhausted after fourteen hours of driving, the exit to Denver was a welcome sight.
         B. Because we were exhausted after fourteen hours of driving, the exit to Denver was a welcome sight.

_____ 3. A. Having stood in the oily marinade for six hours, you are now ready to grill the meat.
         B. Having stood in the oily marinade for six hours, the meat is now ready to be grilled.

_____ 4. A. As the spider painstakingly repaired the damaged web, I marveled at its skill and patience.
         B. Painstakingly repairing the damaged web, I marveled at the spider's skill and patience.

_____ 5. A. Approaching the Continental Divide, there was a noticeable drop in temperature.
         B. Approaching the Continental Divide, we noticed a drop in temperature.

_____ 6. A. The archaeologists could not decipher the inscription covered with the grime of centuries.
         B. Covered with the grime of centuries, the archaeologists could not decipher the inscription.

_____ 7. A. To avoid overexposing the picture, use a light meter.
         B. To avoid overexposing the picture, a light meter should be used.

_____ 8. A. Meeting Lou after geology class, he suggested a handball game.
         B. Meeting Lou after geology class, I suggested a handball game.

_____ 9. A. If unable to attend, please call the reservation clerk.
         B. If unable to attend, a call to the reservation clerk would be appreciated.

_____ 10. A. Seen from miles away, the mountain looks like a cloud.
         B. Seen from miles away, one might think the mountain was a cloud.

_____ 11. A. Having only two days of holiday, it might be sensible just to stay home.
         B. Having only two days of holiday, we might just as well stay home.

_____ 12. A. This being payday, I am momentarily without financial worries.
         B. Being payday, I am momentarily without financial worries.

_____ 13. A. Having sprained my left shoulder badly, Dr. Johnson put it in a sling.
B. Having sprained my left shoulder badly, I asked Dr. Johnson to put it in a sling.

_____ 14. A. If you stay on the thruway to the Ninety-fifth Street exit, there should be no traffic problem.
B. Staying on the thruway to the Ninety-fifth Street exit, there should be no traffic problem.

_____ 15. A. My neighbor has done my shopping for me since breaking my toe.
B. My neighbor has done my shopping for me since I broke my toe.

_____ 16. A. Instead of folding the sheets of your theme, turn them in flat.
B. Instead of folding the sheets of your theme, they should be turned in flat.

_____ 17. A. While Jenny was still in junior high school, her grandfather set up a trust fund for her education.
B. While still in junior high school, Jenny's grandfather set up a trust fund for her education.

_____ 18. A. To be sure of getting a first printing, the book order must be received by March 15.
B. To be sure of getting a first printing, you should order the book by March 15.

_____ 19. A. Badly burned from too much cooking, Dad had to throw away the steaks.
B. Badly burned from too much cooking, the steaks had to be thrown away.

_____ 20. A. We found the kitten, frightened and crying piteously, on the garage roof.
B. Frightened and crying piteously, we found the kitten on the garage roof.

Dangling Modifiers

NAME _____ SCORE _____

DIRECTIONS: Rewrite each of the following sentences twice:
  a. Change the dangler to a complete clause with subject and verb.
  b. Retain the phrase but begin the main clause with a word that it can logically modify.

1. Working full time as a door-to-door salesperson, my car is indispensable.

   a.

   b.

2. While pruning some of her rose bushes, a hornet stung Mrs. Ross.

   a.

   b.

3. Upon hearing the damaging testimony, the prisoner's face turned pale.

   a.

   b.

4. To earn a B.A. degree, at least fifteen semester hours of a laboratory science must be taken.

   a.

   b.

5. Having picked up orders from seven of my old customers, the day can be called a success.

   a.

   b.

DIRECTIONS: Reduce the italicized material to a verbal phrase (a participial phrase or a gerund phrase) or an elliptical clause. Write the verbal phrase or the elliptical clause on the line provided. Then, in the space at the left, write A or B to designate the independent clause that the phrase or clause can logically modify.

> EXAMPLE:
>
> __B__   While *I was jogging this morning*, (A) A vicious dog chased me.
> (B) I was chased by a vicious dog.
> (While) jogging this morning, _____

_____   1. *I recalled our family picnics at Loon Lake.* (A) A feeling of sadness overcame me. (B) I felt sad.

_____   2. After *she had studied until 3 A.M.*, (A) Ginny had a headache. (B) Ginny's head ached.

_____   3. *We had already waited an hour.* (A) A further delay was unreasonable. (B) We thought a further delay was unreasonable.

_____   4. Before *you paint the metal*, (A) All surface dirt and grease should be removed. (B) You should remove all surface dirt and grease.

_____   5. *We are the parents of four teenagers.* (A) We really need a reliable washing machine. (B) A reliable washing machine is really needed.

_____   6. *I talked with Ted at the cafeteria.* (A) He told me he was leaving school. (B) I learned that he was leaving school.

_____   7. When *you are gathering notes for your report*, (A) Unlined 5 × 7 cards are best. (B) Use unlined 5 × 7 cards.

_____   8. *I labored through the knee-deep snow.* (A) I had visions of steaming hot coffee. (B) Visions of steaming hot coffee filled my mind.

_____   9. While *he was attempting a difficult move on the parallel bars*, (A) Ben's back was injured. (B) Ben injured his back.

_____   10. *I stepped onto the platform.* (A) My throat felt dry. (B) I became aware of my dry throat.

LESSON
13 Sentence Building: Completeness

A COMPLETE sentence contains a subject and a verb as its core. Without a subject and a verb, there is no complete sentence. A sentence, moreover, must be able to stand alone as an independent unit of communication. Therefore a clause introduced by a subordinating word cannot be a complete sentence even though it contains a subject and a verb, as all clauses must. The subordinating word makes it dependent instead of independent.

A group of words punctuated like a sentence but lacking subject, verb, or independence is an incomplete sentence, or **sentence fragment.** The mistake of punctuation that creates a sentence fragment is called a **period fault.** When they appear in writing, sentence fragments are usually considered serious errors.

The undesirable sentence fragments that inexperienced writers sometimes construct are almost always of the three following types:

1. A subordinate clause standing as a sentence. (But remember that *and, but, for, or,* and *nor* do not subordinate. A clause introduced by one of these words may stand as a sentence.)

> FRAGMENTS: I customarily mow my own lawn. *Although I cannot say that I enjoy the chore.*
> We saw a performance of *Tartuffe. Which is one of my favorite plays.*

2. A verbal phrase punctuated as a sentence:

> FRAGMENTS: The delegates agreed on a compromise wage scale. *Realizing that the strike could not go on indefinitely.*
> I hope to go on to New York City. *Especially to visit the UN Building.*

3. A noun followed by a phrase or a subordinate clause but lacking a verb to go with it:

> FRAGMENTS: The committee should include Ms. Tartar. *A tireless worker with many constructive ideas.*
> I hope you will let me have my old job back. *A chance to show you that I have learned my lesson.*
> You must play checkers with him. *A game of checkers being the old man's idea of the perfect way to spend an afternoon.*
> Junior will require a special kind of tutor. *Someone who will realize how sensitive the child really is.*

You can avoid sentence fragments if you have a working knowledge of the grammatical makeup of the sentence and if you practice reasonable care in your writing. If you have repeatedly had fragments called to your attention, try this technique: When you reread and revise what you have written, read the sentences in a paragraph in reverse order. Start with your last sentence and work back to your first. This process, by breaking the tie between a fragment and the sentence that it depends on, makes any grammatically incomplete sentence reveal itself prominently.

Then, when you have discovered a fragment in your writing, any one of the several possible corrections is easy to make. Sometimes you can attach the fragment to the preceding sentence by doing away with the fragment's capital letter and supplying the right punctuation. Or you can change the fragment to a subordinate clause and attach it to the appropriate main clause by means of the right connective. Or you can change the fragment to a separate sentence by supplying a subject or a verb or both.

CORRECTED: I customarily mow my own lawn, *although I cannot say that I enjoy the chore.*

We saw a performance of *Tartuffe, which is one of my favorite plays.*

The delegates agreed on a compromise wage scale *because they realized that the strike could not go on indefinitely.*

The committee should include Ms. Tartar, *a tireless worker with many constructive ideas.*

I hope you will let me have my old job back *and give me a chance to show you that I have learned my lesson.*

You must play checkers with him. *A game of checkers is the old man's idea of the perfect way to spend an afternoon.*

Junior will require a special kind of tutor. *He or she must be someone who will realize how sensitive the child really is.*

A few types of word groups, although lacking a complete subject–verb combination, are not objectionable fragments. They are accepted as legitimate language patterns. These are

1. Commands, in which the subject *you* is understood:

Please be seated. Put your name on a slip of paper. Pass the papers to the left aisle.

2. Exclamations:

What excitement! Only two minutes to go! Good Heavens, not a fumble? How terrible!

3. Bits of dialogue:

"New car?" she asked. "Had it long?"
"Picked it up last week," he replied.

4. Occasional transitions between units of thought:

On with the story.
And now to conclude.

You have very likely observed in your reading that experienced writers sometimes use sentence fragments, especially in narrative and descriptive writing. But they are skillful workers who know how to use fragments to achieve particular stylistic effects. You, as a beginning writer, must first master the fundamental forms of the sentence. Once you have learned to write clear, correct sentences without faltering, there will be plenty of time for experimenting.

EXERCISE 23
Completeness

NAME _____ SCORE _____

DIRECTIONS: Each numbered unit consists of a sentence followed by a fragment. Be prepared to discuss in class the structuring of the fragments. In the space provided, rewrite enough of the material to show how you would correct the error, by either attaching the fragment, properly punctuated, to the sentence or recasting the fragment so that it becomes a complete sentence.

1. From the field of archery have come many good old English family names. Such as Archer, Bowman, Arrowsmith, Stringer, and Fletcher.

2. The interest of scientists in the atom is far from being new. Going back, actually, as far as the fifth century before Christ.

3. According to the myth, Jason, to get the Golden Fleece, had to perform many daring deeds. The most terrifying being the yoking of two wild bulls to a plow.

4. Thoreau is best known for *Walden, or Life in the Woods.* An account of his hermitlike existence on the shores of Walden Pond.

5. Hank is, we all agreed, a capable fellow. But, unfortunately, one who never takes advantage of his opportunities.

6. Ellen remembered that she had left her keys in the trunk. Which by this time was well on its way to the airport.

7. Dad planted twelve bulbs of the regal lily. The hardiest and most beautiful of the whole *Lilium* genus.

8. Alice offered no explanation for her unusual conduct. Wanting, no doubt, to give the impression of being unconventional.

9. The newspaper gave an award to Ms. Agnes Elder. A woman who has risen to a position of leadership in civic affairs.

10. The pathetic old man's costume called attention to itself. His coat showing evidence of his having slept in it.

11. The teacher read "Richard Cory" to the class. The moral of which is that people we envy also have their troubles.

12. The outstanding alumnus award went to Dr. Eliot Lambert. A 1973 graduate who has distinguished herself in the field of medicine.

13. Ellen's grandfather has little interest in the rest of the country. Never having traveled, believe it or not, outside the state of Vermont.

14. With the decline in profits, nearly one third of the workers were laid off. Many with years of service to their credit.

15. It seems that Coach Lucas likes to do needlepoint. Which he has never admitted even to his closest friends.

16. This course has helped me improve my study habits. By planning my work so that I get all the studying, recreation, and sleep that I need.

17. The next ten years of my life will be divided into two parts. One period of four years and one of six.

18. The football season was a catastrophe. The first game being a dull affair showing the team's lack of training.

19. The novel impresses one with its surprising turns. Although, of course, many other writers have handled the same theme.

20. Winning the scholarship allowed Pete to quit his job. At the same time allowing him to work in a well-equipped laboratory.

LESSON
14 Sentence Building: Subordination

TWO COMMON faults among beginning writers are the habit of stringing short sentences together and the habit of tying clauses together by *and, but, so,* and *and so,* connectives that do not show that one idea is subordinate to another.

> POOR: My father's boss is Mr. Alterton. He can afford expensive meals. He eats only simple food. He has an ulcer.
>
> I tramped around town for three days but I couldn't find quarters and then I located this apartment and so I am comfortable.

If you determine the exact relationships between the parts of the sentences, your expression will be more mature, more economical, and more meaningful:

> IMPROVED: Although my father's boss, Mr. Alterton, can afford expensive meals, he eats only simple food because he has an ulcer.
>
> After tramping around town unsuccessfully for three days, I located this apartment, where I am comfortable.

Get in the habit of trying out the various methods of subordinating material. Notice in the following sentences how an idea can be expressed in diminishing degrees of emphasis:

> TWO SENTENCES: The small car was inexpensive to drive. It had only four cylinders.
>
> COMPOUND SENTENCE: The small car was inexpensive to drive, for it had only four cylinders.
>
> COMPOUND VERB: The small car had only four cylinders and was inexpensive to drive.
>
> ABSOLUTE PHRASE: The small car having only four cylinders, it was inexpensive to drive.
>
> ADVERBIAL CLAUSE: Because the small car had only four cylinders, it was inexpensive to drive.
>
> ADJECTIVE CLAUSE: The small car, which had only four cylinders, was inexpensive to drive.
>
> PARTICIPIAL PHRASE: The small car, having only four cylinders, was inexpensive to drive.
>
> Having only four cylinders, the small car was inexpensive to drive.
>
> The small car was inexpensive to drive, having only four cylinders.
>
> PREPOSITIONAL PHRASE: The small car with only four cylinders was inexpensive to drive.
>
> APPOSITIVE: The small car, a four-cylinder model, was inexpensive to drive.
>
> ADJECTIVE MODIFIER: The small, four-cylinder car was inexpensive to drive.

Note that the use of subordination produces more than a pleasing surface texture in writing. It also makes a crucial contribution to meaning by eliminating uncertainty about what is most important in a message.

> The management and union representatives announced an agreement. A strike had been threatened but was averted. The employees of Grantex Company reported for work today. They were relieved.

In this string of simple sentences there is no way of knowing which fact is most significant: The agreement? The avoidance of a strike? The workers' reporting for work? Their relief? Rewritten with proper subordination, the news reveals the writer's sense of significance:

> The relieved employees of Grantex Company reported for work today after the management and union representatives announced an agreement that averted a threatened strike.

The only independent clause in the sentence concerns the workers' return to work. That is the important message. A writer more interested in strikes and their effect on the general economy might report the event thus:

> The threatened strike was averted at Grantex Company when the management and union representatives announced an agreement, after which the relieved employees reported for work today.

A Note on Sentence Variety

Preceding lessons have demonstrated how subordinate clauses and phrases, by compressing material, help the writer avoid tiresome strings of independent clauses. You have also seen that certain subordinate units—adverbial clauses and participial phrases in particular—permit a variety of placements within the sentence and thus help prevent monotony of sentence structure.

Another unit useful for achieving compression and variety is the appositive. (See Lesson 10.) As noun renamers, appositives closely resemble—they might be called the final reduction of—Pattern 2 clause and phrase modifiers of nouns:

> Junior usually gets his way. Junior [or He] is a pampered only child. [Two independent clauses.]
> Junior, *who is a pampered only child*, usually gets his way. [Adjective clause.]
> Junior, *being a pampered only child*, usually gets his way. [Participial phrase.]
> Junior, *a pampered only child*, usually gets his way. [Appositive.]

Although the usual position of appositives is immediately following the nouns they rename, many of them, like many nonrestrictive participial phrases, can precede the main noun (in which case we call them *pre-positional appositives*); sometimes they are effectively placed at the end of the clause:

> Lawyer Somers, *a master of wit and guile*, cajoles and browbeats in the courtroom.
> *A master of wit and guile*, Lawyer Somers cajoles and browbeats in the courtroom.
> Lawyer Somers cajoles and browbeats in the courtroom, *a master of wit and guile*.

As a final example of language tools for renaming and modifying nouns, study this effective, compact sentence:

> One of the five largest towns in Roman England, home of King Arthur's legendary Round Table, seat of Alfred the Great, whose statue looks down its main street, early capital of England, and victim of Cromwell's destructive forces, Winchester is an enchanting cathedral city in which layer after layer of history is visibly present.
>
> Elisabeth Lambert Ortiz
> "Exploring Winchester," *Gourmet*,
> March 1978, p. 21

This sentence is made up of one independent clause, which includes an adjective clause, and five pre-positional appositives, the third of which contains an adjective clause. The statements underlying this sentence might be charted thus:

Winchester is an enchanting cathedral city.

In [this city] which layer after layer of history is visibly present.
Winchester was one of the five largest towns in Roman England.
Winchester was the home of King Arthur's legendary Round Table.
Winchester was the seat of Alfred the Great.

[Alfred the Great's] whose statue looks down its main street.
Winchester was the early capital of England.
Winchester was the victim of Cromwell's destructive forces.

We see here that eight statements—enough to make up a paragraph of clear but unrelieved simple sentences—have been shortened into one complex sentence, the layering of appositives and adjective clauses producing compression, sentence variety, and proper emphasis.

101

EXERCISE 24
Subordination

NAME _____   SCORE _____

DIRECTIONS: Reduce the italicized sentence to the grammatical structure indicated in the parentheses and rewrite each numbered unit as one sentence.

1. *Two of our star players were injured.* We lost the game.
   (adverbial clause of reason) _____
   _____

2. *Two of our star players were injured.* We won the game.
   (adverbial clause of concession) _____
   _____

3. *I saw no reason to continue the search.* I returned to camp.
   (participial phrase) _____
   _____

4. *The question of membership was settled.* The committee made plans for the dance.
   (adverbial clause of time) _____
   _____

5. *The question of membership was settled.* The committee made plans for the dance.
   (absolute phrase) _____
   _____

6. Put some rock salt on the driveway. *It will melt the ice.*
   (infinitive phrase) _____
   _____

7. *Put some rock salt on the driveway.* It will melt the ice.
   (gerund phrase) _____
   _____

8. *We finished our lunch.* We hiked to the beach.
   (preposition plus gerund phrase) _____
   _____

9. You might get help from Al Hughes. *He is a computer expert.*
   (adjective clause) _____
   _____

10. You might get help from Al Hughes. *He is a computer expert.*
    (appositive) _____
    _____

SUBORDINATION

DIRECTIONS: Rewrite each sentence by removing the coordinating conjunction *(and, but, or)* and changing the italicized material to the kind of unit indicated in the parentheses.

1. *I had taken good notes,* and I had no trouble with the test.
   (adverbial clause of reason) _____

2. *I had taken good notes,* and I had no trouble with the test.
   (participial phrase) _____

3. *I had taken good notes,* but I had trouble with the test.
   (adverbial clause of concession) _____

4. *Additional troops arrived,* and the rebels fled into the jungle.
   (adverbial clause of time) _____

5. *Additional troops arrived,* and the rebels fled into the jungle.
   (absolute phrase) _____

6. Mother sent Henry a new cookbook, and *it contained a recipe for tripe.*
   (adjective clause) _____

7. *Turn in your theme by Tuesday,* and you will receive full credit.
   (adverbial clause of condition) _____

8. *Turn in your theme by Tuesday,* or you will receive no credit.
   (adverbial clause of condition) _____

9. The job entails speech making, and *that's a skill in which I am deficient.*
   (appositive plus adjective clause) _____

10. *Today is payday,* and my worries are lessened somewhat.
    (absolute phrase) _____

Subordination

NAME _____ SCORE _____

DIRECTIONS: Preceding lessons have demonstrated for you various types of noun modification. When two sentences employ the same noun or pronoun, one sentence can be
incorporated into the other by being reduced to an adjective clause, a participial phrase,
or (in some cases) an appositive. In the following pairs of sentences, the word printed in
bold type in the first sentence is the noun or pronoun to be modified. Combine the
sentences by reducing the second sentence to the kind of unit indicated by the following
letters:

    A. Adjective clause
    B. Participial phrase following the noun
    C. Participial phrase preceding the noun
    D. Appositive

(You need not write the entire sentence; copy enough to show how the combining is
done.)

1. A *stranger* rang our doorbell. He was carrying our lost puppy.

    A. _____

    B. _____

2. To conduct the campaign, we hired a young *woman.* The national chairman
had recommended her strongly.

    A. _____

    B. _____

3. The amateur play was directed by *Ms. Arlene Staples.* She is a former ac-
tress.

    A. _____

    D. _____

4. *Mr. Bentley* hired a local guide. He wanted to see the Inca ruins.

    A. _____

    B. _____

    C. _____

5. *Freddy* wrote to his wealthy aunt. He desperately needed a loan.

    A. _____

    B. _____

    C. _____

6. *Johnson* should retire soon. He has worked here for thirty years.

    A. _____

    B. _____

    C. _____

7. *Grandmother* sat at the head of the table. She looked like an oldfashioned tintype.

    A. _____

    B. _____

    C. _____

8. The *Chow Hut* does a good business. It's the only restaurant near the campus.

    A. _____

    B. _____

    C. _____

    D. _____

9. *You* should make the presentation. You're the oldest employee.

    A. _____

    B. _____

    C. _____

    D. _____

10. *Jessie Loomis* knows this region well. She is an experienced hiker.

    A. _____

    B. _____

    C. _____

    D. _____

Subordination

DIRECTIONS: Rewrite each of the following numbered sections as one sentence. In each case use the italicized subject and verb for the main clause. Use a variety of the subordinating units listed for you in Lesson 14.

1. *Jake* is not ordinarily a good student. Last term he *earned* an A in biology. Biology was a subject that really interested him.

2. *Swift* hated the Irish but was forced to live in Ireland, and he *said* that being born in a stable did not make a man a horse.

3. I did not understand poetry, but many people whom I admire like it, and so *I registered* for a course in poetry.

4. At first Cedric did not like his teacher. She was strict and demanding. *He* soon *realized* that he was learning much from her.

5. *Dr. Johnson* disliked the Scots, and he *said* that oats are usually eaten by horses but in Scotland oats are eaten by people.

6. Many of the new students were often late for class. The *teacher* then *made* a new rule. It specified punishment for tardiness.

7. Last night we were all at the study table. Lois Shaw fell fast asleep. She was in charge of the study session. We *freshmen giggled.*

8. I have always enjoyed reading and I used to read three or four books a month, but now *I am* busy and read only a few magazines.

9. *Uncle Tim* usually says very little. He is a quiet man. He gave us a lecture on the proper respect for the flag. He *was* quite eloquent.

10. This *quilt* has been in our family for over sixty years. It *was made* by my grandmother. She was eighty years old when she made it.

11. I thought I was too old to take up golf. Gail insisted that I try the game. *I have enjoyed* it very much.

12. Jackson is a below-average student, but he is a good football player so *I suppose* he will be going to college.

13. The recipe calls for chopped pecans. *I used* chopped peanuts. Peanuts are more fitted to my limited budget.

14. *I* followed Lucy's advice and *went* to the Thrift Shop and found some secondhand patio furniture.

15. *Cranshaw* had served four years in the Army. He *had saved* some money. It was enough to see him through two years at Ohio State.

16. Bob had graduated with a degree in pharmacy. But now *he manages* a seed company. It's a large company. It's located in Oregon.

17. I knew Fred Haynes in college. He is now a successful commercial artist. *I was* surprised to learn this.

18. The truck *driver* was blinded by the reflections on the pavement. The pavement was wet. He *slammed* on the brakes. He wanted to avoid the dog.

19. *Susan* is my niece. She is six years old. She recently *startled* her parents. She said that she intended to marry her dentist.

20. Storch has been declared ineligible. He is our star quarterback. His grades are low. *We are* unhappy to learn this.

LESSON
15 Sentence Building: Parallel Structure; Comparisons

OUR EXAMINATION of the construction of effective sentences should deal with two other situations where underlying logic demands careful selection of sentence units.

Parallel Structure

When two or more parts of a sentence are similar in function, they should be expressed in the same grammatical construction; in other words, they should be made parallel. The principle of parallelism implies that, in a series, nouns should be balanced with nouns, adjectives with adjectives, prepositional phrases with prepositional phrases, clauses with clauses, and so forth. The following sentence owes much of its clarity and effectiveness to the careful parallel arrangement: Two adjective clauses are joined with *and*, two adverbs with *but*, and three noun direct objects with *and*.

Anyone ‖ who studies world affairs *and*
         ‖ who remembers our last three wars will realize, ‖ sadly *but*
                                                            ‖ inevitably,
   that another conflict will endanger ‖ the economic strength of our nation,
                                        ‖ the complacency of our political institutions,
                                        ‖ *and* the moral fiber of our people.

Here we shall deal with two types of errors, the false series and the *and who* construction, both of which use a coordinator to join unlike grammatical units.

1. The false or shifted series:

   WEAK: Most people play golf for exercise, pleasure, and so they can meet others. [The *and* ties an adverb clause to two nouns.]
   BETTER: Most people play golf for exercise, for pleasure, and for social contacts.
   WEAK: Our new teacher was young, tall, slender, and with red hair. [The *and* suggests that it will be followed by a fourth adjective, not a prepositional phrase.]
   BETTER: Our new teacher was young, tall, slender, and red-haired.
   WEAK: Mr. Little's speech was tiresome, inaccurate, and should have been omitted.
   BETTER: Mr. Little's speech was tiresome, inaccurate, and unnecessary.

2. The *and who* or *and which* construction:

   WEAK: She is a person with great talent *and who* should be encouraged.
   BETTER: She is a person who has great talent and who should be encouraged.
   She is a talented person who should be encouraged. [Here the series is avoided.]
   WEAK: I am taking Physics 388, a difficult course *and which* demands much time.
   BETTER: I am taking Physics 388, which is a difficult course and which demands much time.
   I am taking Physics 388, which is difficult and demands much time.

Skilled writers use parallel structure as a stylistic device to form patterns in their writing—patterns that are pleasing and appropriate. Note the following:

You are ‖ the rulers and the ruled,
　　　　‖ the lawgivers and the law-abiding,
　　　　‖ the beginning and the end.　　—Adlai Stevenson
For the individuals do not have ‖ the time,
　　　　　　　　　　　　　　　　‖ the opportunity, or
　　　　　　　　　　　　　　　　‖ the energy ‖ to make all the experiments and
　　　　　　　　　　　　　　　　　　　　　　‖ to discern all the significance
　that has gone into the making of the whole heritage of civilization.
　　　　　　　　　　　　　　　　　　　　　　　—Walter Lippmann

COMPARISONS

A common type of sentence is one in which a comparison or a contrast is made. This kind of sentence offers a few difficulties that you should be aware of.

1. Be sure that you compare only those things that are capable of being compared:

> FAULTY: The damage done by the fire was more severe than the earthquake. [What is wrong with this sentence is that two unlike things, *damage* and *earthquake*, are being compared.]
> The influence of the political leader is more ephemeral than the artist.
> IMPROVED: The damage done by the fire was more severe than *the damage done by* the earthquake.
> The damage done by the fire was more severe than *that done by* the earthquake.
> The influence of the political leader is more ephemeral than *the influence of* the artist.
> The influence of the political leader is more ephemeral than *that of* the artist.
> The political leader's influence is more ephemeral than *the artist's*.

2. When you are using the comparative form in a comparison, use *any other* when it is necessary to exclude the subject of the comparison from the group:

> The men's dormitory is larger than *any other* building on the campus. [If you were to say ". . . than any building on the campus," you would compare the men's dormitory to a group that *includes* the men's dormitory.]

3. When your sentence contains a double comparison, you should include all the words necessary to make the idiom complete.

> Glenn is as young *as*, if not younger *than*, you.
> Glenn is as young as you, if not younger.
> Jennie is one of the best *cooks*, if not the best *cook*, in town.
> Jennie is one of the best cooks in town, if not the best.

(See Supplement 1.)

Supplement 1

In addition to requiring the structural units already mentioned, comparison–contrast sentences place a few constraints on the *form* of the adjective or adverb.

When your comparison is limited to two things, use the comparative degree. Use the superlative for more than two things:

> Both Jane and Edwina sing well, but Jane has the *better* voice.
> Which takes *more* time, your studies or your job?
> January is the *worst* month of the year.

You learned in Lesson 2 that there are two ways of forming the comparative and superlative degrees. In general, *er* and *est* are used with short words, and *more* and *most* with longer words.

When I was *younger*, I was *more apprehensive* about thunder and lightning.
This encyclopedia is the *newest* and the *most comprehensive*.
Maria works *faster* than I and also *more accurately*.

Remember that in present-day standard English we don't combine *er* or *est* with *more* or *most* in the same word. We don't say, for example, *more pleasanter, most loveliest*, or *more faster*.

EXERCISE 27
Parallelism

NAME _____ SCORE _____

DIRECTIONS: In the space at the left of each pair of sentences, copy the letter identifying the sentence that is logically structured. Be prepared to point out in class the faulty parallelism in the sentences that you rejected.

_____ 1. A. Jake said what he did not only from spite but because he is jealous.
           B. Jake said what he did not only from spite but from jealousy.

_____ 2. A. This ground cover allows the water to seep in rather than to run off.
           B. This ground cover allows the water to seep in rather than running off.

_____ 3. A. The accountant was tall and quite thin, had a receding hairline, and was about forty.
           B. The accountant was tall and quite thin, receding hairline, and about forty.

_____ 4. A. Everyone admires people who have plenty of spirit and who will stand up for their rights.
           B. Everyone admires people with plenty of spirit and who will stand up for their rights.

_____ 5. A. Ted Powers is a man whose experience is wide and has good common sense.
           B. Ted Powers is a man who has wide experience and good common sense.

_____ 6. A. Having worked on a newspaper for years, she writes directly, forcefully, and with clearness.
           B. Having worked on a newspaper for years, she writes directly, forcefully, and clearly.

_____ 7. A. I look forward to turning over a new leaf next term and make an honest attempt to improve my grades.
           B. I look forward to turning over a new leaf next term and making an honest attempt to improve my grades.

_____ 8. A. Remember that a good study room should be comfortable and have plenty of fresh air and good light.
           B. Remember that a good study room should be comfortable, plenty of fresh air, and having good light.

_____ 9. A. And there was Uncle Lou, trying to finish the stack of hay before dark, and he sweated like a horse in that humid heat.
           B. And there was Uncle Lou, trying to finish the stack of hay before dark and sweating like a horse in that humid heat.

_____ 10. A. Some of us think that Judkins is more of a handicap than a help.
            B. Some of us think that Judkins is more of a handicap than helpful.

113

EXERCISE 27
Comparisons

DIRECTIONS: From each of the following pairs of sentences, select the one you prefer and write its letter in the space at the left. Be prepared to justify your choice.

_____ 1. A. You'll have to admit that working conditions here are different from Alaska.
   B. You'll have to admit that working conditions here are different from those in Alaska.

_____ 2. A. California has the most varied climate of any western state.
   B. California has the most varied climate of all western states.

_____ 3. A. Herb is one of the laziest boys, if not the laziest boy, in the class.
   B. Herb is one of the laziest, if not the laziest boy, in the class.

_____ 4. A. Who is the oldest, you or Betty?
   B. Who is the older, you or Betty?

_____ 5. A. He was short and heavy, with a bull neck and arms like a blacksmith's.
   B. He was short and heavy, with a bull neck and arms like a blacksmith.

_____ 6. A. Tom, who has little interest in science, found physics more difficult than his older sister Lucy.
   B. Tom, who has little interest in science, found physics more difficult than his older sister Lucy had.

_____ 7. A. Prices here are usually lower than our competitors.
   B. Prices here are usually lower than our competitors'.

_____ 8. A. Minnesota is reputed to have more lakes than any other state in the Union.
   B. Minnesota is reputed to have more lakes than any state in the Union.

_____ 9. A. His work is as dangerous, if not more dangerous, than a police officer.
   B. His work is as dangerous as that of a police officer, if not more dangerous.

_____ 10. A. Life here in Lakeview is really not much different from any other small town.
   B. Life here in Lakeview is really not much different from life in any other small town.

PART II PUNCTUATION
Lessons and Exercises

LESSON

16 Commas to Separate

COMMAS are used to separate certain parts of the sentence so that written communication will be clear and direct. Commas to separate are used in the following situations:

1. Before *and, but, for, or, nor,* and *yet* when they join the clauses of a compound sentence:

> I placed the typed sheet on his desk, and he picked it up and read it slowly. His face turned red, but he did not say a word. I knew he was angry, for he rose and stamped out of the room. [Note that no comma is used before the conjunction in a compound predicate.]

At this point you might reread Lesson 7. There you will find a detailed explanation, with examples, of this rule. Remember that a semicolon rather than a comma is usually required in a compound sentence when no coordinating conjunction is present.

2. Between the items of a series. A series is composed of three or more words, phrases, or clauses of equal grammatical rank. A series usually takes the form of *a, b, and c;* sometimes it may be *a, b, or c.* In journalistic writing the comma is omitted before *and* or *or;* in more formal writing it is generally not omitted. The beginning writer will do well to follow formal practice:

> The old house was empty, cold, dark, and uninviting. [Four adjectives.]
> The jury was made up of two preachers, six housewives, three laborers, and a farmer. [Four nouns.]
> She rushed into the house, up the stairs, and into her room. [Phrases.]
> I told him which way to go, what to carry, and how to dress. [Phrases.]
> Larry fetched the water, Mort built the fire, and I opened the cans. [Independent clauses.]

Notice the last example. Three or more short independent clauses arranged in the form of a series may be separated by commas. But long clauses—independent clauses especially, but sometimes dependent clauses, also—are better separated by semicolons, particularly if there is other punctuation within the clauses. The following sentences illustrate the punctuation between and within the long clauses. Although you would probably hesitate to attempt such sentences, you will encounter them in your reading:

> The first week of the tour called for long hops and little free time; the second week, with longer rest periods in Amsterdam and Antwerp, was less exhausting; but the third week, which took us to four countries in seven days, left us numb and bewildered. [Three lengthy independent clauses in series, with internal punctuation.]

These dark days will be worth all they have cost if they show us that happiness is not a matter of money; if they force upon us the joy of achievement, the thrill of creative effort; if they teach us that our true destiny is to serve, to the best of our ability, our fellows. [Three lengthy adverbial clauses in series, with internal punctuation.]

3. Between coordinate adjectives preceding a noun. A comma separating two adjectives signifies that the two adjectives are equal in their modifying force. A comma is not used when the modifier closer to the noun has more importance as an identifier of the noun. Thus we use a comma with "a difficult, unfair examination" but not with "a difficult midterm examination." Another explanation is that in the first example *difficult* and *unfair* modify *examination* with equal force, whereas in the second example *difficult* really modifies the unit *midterm examination*.

The problem here is to determine when adjectives are coordinate, that is, equal in modifying force. Two tests may prove helpful.

a. If the insertion of *and* between the modifiers produces a reading that still makes sense, the adjectives are equal and a comma should be used. "A difficult *and* unfair examination" would sound correct to most native speakers of English, but "a difficult *and* midterm examination" would not.

b. If the adjectives sound natural in reversed position, they are equal and should be separated by a comma. Thus we could say "an unfair, difficult examination" but not "a midterm difficult examination" without meaning something quite different from a difficult midterm examination.

When you use a noun preceded by more than two adjectives, you should test the adjectives by pairs, the first with the second, the second with the third, and so on. It may help you to know that we usually do not use commas before adjectives denoting size or age. And you must remember that we never use a comma between the last adjective and the noun.

Observe how use of the above-mentioned tests determines punctuation like the following:

a tall, dark, and handsome gentleman   a tall, dark, handsome gentleman
the dark, cold, drafty classroom   a neat, courteous little boy
a heavy, soiled leather ball   her funny little upturned nose
a mean old local gossip

4. After most introductory modifiers, especially if they are long and not obviously restrictive. In this situation modern usage varies considerably. You must depend on your own good sense and judgment. The following explanations will provide a general guide.

a. Put commas after introductory adverbial clauses except those that are short or in no need of special emphasis. No hard-and-fast rule governs this situation. The inexperienced writer would probably do well to use commas after all introductory adverbial clauses except very short clauses denoting time:

Although none of us really enjoyed the performance, we applauded politely.
If what you say is true, quick action is required.
Before undergraduates can participate in these sports, they must take a physical examination.
Whenever I see her I remember her youthful awkwardness.
When George sleeps the rest of us must be quiet.

b. Put commas after introductory verbal-phrase modifiers:

Having climbed the steep trail up Cougar Mountain, Bob decided to take some pictures. To get the best view of the valley, he walked to the edge of the cliff. After
opening his rucksack, he searched for his new telephoto lens.

c. Put a comma after an introductory absolute element, such as a phrase, a
sentence adverb, or a mild exclamation, and after *yes* and *no:*

In fact, there was no way to keep the front door closed.
Well, what are we to do now?
No, we are not in danger.
Certainly, I'll put a chair against it.

d. Ordinarily, do not put a comma after a prepositional phrase that precedes
a main clause unless the phrase is long or unless a comma is needed to add
special emphasis or to prevent a misreading.

After a heavy dinner we usually went for a short walk.
In early summer many birds nested there.
In spite of the very heavy wind and the pelting hailstones, the third race was com-
pleted.
In the name of justice, please help these people.
Shortly after two, forty-five marathon runners left the stadium.

5. Between any two words that might be mistakenly read together:

Before, he had been industrious and sober. [Not *before he had been.*]
Once inside, the dog scampered all over the furniture. [Not *inside the dog.*]
While we were eating, the table collapsed. [Not *eating the table.*]
After we had washed, Mother prepared breakfast. [Not *washed Mother.*]
Ever since, he has been afraid of deep water. [Not *ever since he has been.*]
Shortly after ten, thirty new recruits appeared. [Not *shortly after ten thirty.*]

EXERCISE 28

Commas to Separate

NAME _____ SCORE _____

DIRECTIONS: Each of the following sentences has two commas missing. Add the commas where they are necessary. Then, in the blanks at the left, write the numbers of the rules that apply to the commas you have added:

1. Before coordinate conjunction in a compound sentence
2. In a series
3. Between coordinate adjectives
4. After an introductory modifier
5. To prevent misreading

_____ 1. The plates, the cups and the saucers all fell to the floor with a loud
_____   crash and Mr. Blaze rushed into the kitchen.

_____ 2. Rising hurriedly from their seats the three men walked with quick
_____   nervous steps out of the auditorium.

_____ 3. The snake coiled swiftly, struck with blinding speed and grasped
_____   the terror-stricken immobilized lizard just behind the head.

_____ 4. Before we had gone five miles over the rocky dusty detour two of
_____   our tires had become dangerously soft.

_____ 5. My brother ordered an omelet, a Danish pastry and a cup of coffee
_____   but the rest of us did not order anything at all.

_____ 6. Instead of leaving the dog returned to the picnic table and ate the
_____   cake, the ice cream and all the cookies.

_____ 7. Led by several swift long-legged runners the vast crowd of mara-
_____   thon runners moved up the street and across the bridge.

_____ 8. Elaine had once been chased by a snarling vicious dog; ever since
_____   she has distrusted pets of all kinds.

_____ 9. Although the towns are far apart they nevertheless have similar
_____   schools, churches and public parks.

_____ 10. We don't usually spend that much money for dinner but perhaps
_____   we could make an exception this time in celebration of your exciting
           unexpected victory in the office bowling tournament.

COMMAS TO SEPARATE

DIRECTIONS: Under each rule, write two sentences of your own composition to illustrate the punctuation to be used. Bring your paper to class for discussion. The purpose of this exercise is to help you recognize punctuation situations in your own writing.

1. Comma used before a coordinate conjunction in a compound sentence.

    a.

    b.

2. Commas used in a series (one series of single words and one series of phrases).

    a.

    b.

3. Comma used after an introductory modifier (one adverb clause and one verbal phrase).

    a.

    b.

4. Comma used between coordinate adjectives.

    a.

    b.

5. Comma used to prevent misreading.

    a.

    b.

Commas and Semicolons to Separate

NAME _____ SCORE _____

DIRECTIONS: One sentence in each of the following pairs is correctly punctuated. Copy the identifying letter of the correct sentence in the space at the left. Be prepared to explain in class why the punctuation of the other sentence is faulty.

_____ 1. A. As the days passed my sister resisted calling the tall handsome boy in her class but she finally dialed his number.
        B. As the days passed, my sister resisted calling the tall, handsome boy in her class, but she finally dialed his number.

_____ 2. A. Thinking back to my childhood days, I remember starting a collection of snuffboxes; my first one was made of buffalo horn.
        B. Thinking back to my childhood days I remember starting a collection of snuffboxes, my first one was made of buffalo horn.

_____ 3. A. "I predict a long, bitterly fought campaign; the political writers are in the back rooms sharpening their pens," said the reporter.
        B. "I predict a long bitterly fought campaign, the political writers are in the back rooms, sharpening their pens," said the reporter.

_____ 4. A. The behavior of some delegates was rude and disruptive, for some of us the convention was a disappointment.
        B. The behavior of some delegates was rude and disruptive; for some of us the convention was a disappointment.

_____ 5. A. She has invested a small fortune in her car, a 40-watt stereo, special seats and a sophisticated alarm system were just a modest beginning of her effort.
        B. She has invested a small fortune in her car; a 40-watt stereo, special seats, and a sophisticated alarm system were just a modest beginning of her effort.

_____ 6. A. The dog eyed the meat hungrily but the small quick fox snatched it up, and ran into the thicket.
        B. The dog eyed the meat hungrily, but the small, quick fox snatched it up and ran into the thicket.

_____ 7. A. Noting a slight swirl in the water, Sue cast the lure into the center of it, and a huge trout struck just as the lure hit the water.
        B. Noting a slight swirl in the water Sue cast the lure into the center of it and a huge trout struck, just as the lure hit the water.

_____ 8. A. While she had been running the clock had stopped, it failed to record her best time ever in this long difficult race.
        B. While she had been running, the clock had stopped; it failed to record her best time ever in this long, difficult race.

_____ 9. A. Seeing the grouse rise out of the sage, the woman raised her gun, shot skillfully, and dropped the bird cleanly.
        B. Seeing the grouse rise out of the sage the woman raised her gun, shot skillfully and dropped the bird cleanly.

_____ 10. A. "When you walk, walk very carefully, but try not to look at the water two hundred feet below," advised the guide.
B. "When you walk walk very carefully but try not to look at the water, two hundred feet below," advised the guide.

_____ 11. A. Our teacher was a mild-mannered kindly old gentleman, he often went to obvious extremes to avoid embarrassing any of us.
B. Our teacher was a mild-mannered, kindly old gentleman; he often went to obvious extremes to avoid embarrassing any of us.

_____ 12. A. There is only one service station in our village, and the owner always goes home for lunch, sometimes not returning till the middle of the afternoon.
B. There is only one service station in our village and the owner always goes home for lunch; sometimes not returning till the middle of the afternoon.

_____ 13. A. The calm, friendly garage attendant assured us that the bridge had been repaired and was now safe to cross.
B. The calm, friendly, garage attendant assured us that the bridge had been repaired, and was now safe to cross.

_____ 14. A. Several kinds of exotic flowers grow in this warm humid climate, everywhere one sees hibiscus, oleander and orchids.
B. Several kinds of exotic flowers grow in this warm, humid climate; everywhere one sees hibiscus, oleander, and orchids.

_____ 15. A. Yesterday we awoke to find the ground covered with wet heavy snow, today's newspaper reports that not since 1937, have we had snow this late.
B. Yesterday we awoke to find the ground covered with wet, heavy snow; today's newspaper reports that not since 1937 have we had snow this late.

_____ 16. A. In the opinion of some, elementary-school teachers are more influential than parents in determining children's attitudes toward learning, and I agree with that opinion.
B. In the opinion of some elementary-school teachers are more influential than parents in determining children's attitudes toward learning and I agree with that opinion.

_____ 17. A. Many early automobiles were high, stately things; most of them were patterned after the horse-drawn carriage.
B. Many early automobiles were high stately things, most of them were patterned after the horse-drawn carriage.

_____ 18. A. Your lecture made a deep lasting impression on our class and we were still discussing it, several weeks later.
B. Your lecture made a deep, lasting impression on our class, and we were still discussing it several weeks later.

_____ 19. A. Forty years ago, I fished for bass, pike and muskellunge in Minnesota, in those days no one worried about polluted water.
B. Forty years ago I fished for bass, pike, and muskellunge in Minnesota; in those days no one worried about polluted water.

_____ 20. A. Wanting to buy postcards, candy bars, magazines and souvenirs; I checked my luggage, and searched the airport for a newsstand.
B. Wanting to buy postcards, candy bars, magazines, and souvenirs, I checked my luggage and searched the airport for a newsstand.

LESSON

17 Commas to Enclose

Commas are used to set off words, phrases, or clauses that break into the normal word order of a sentence. Notice that these interrupters are *set off* by commas. This means that although interrupters that begin or end a sentence have only one comma, any such unit that comes in the interior of the sentence has *two* commas, one before it and one after it.

The following are the most common types of interrupters:

1. Nonrestrictive adjective clauses and phrases. To understand this comma use, you should now reread pages 64–65 of Lesson 9 for an explanation of the difference between restrictive and nonrestrictive adjective clauses.

Other modifiers of nouns—participial phrases especially and, less frequently, prepositional phrases—must be set off by commas when they are nonrestrictive, that is, when they are not necessary for the *identification* of the noun modified. (The same distinction applies also to a few appositives, as noted in the next item of this lesson.)

Examine these additional examples contrasting restrictive and nonrestrictive modifiers of nouns. Notice in the last pair of sentences how the writer, by using or not using commas with the adjective clause, gives important information to the reader:

> One campus building *that needs immediate renovating* is Calhoun Hall. [Restrictive adjective clause.]
> Calhoun Hall, *which needs immediate renovating,* is the oldest building on the campus. [Nonrestrictive adjective clause.]
> Anyone *wishing more detailed information* should write to the secretary. [Restrictive participial phrase.]
> My father, *wishing more detailed information,* wrote to the secretary. [Nonrestrictive participial phrase.]
> A woman *at the far end of the head table* summoned a waiter. [Restrictive prepositional phrase.]
> Professor Angela Cheney, *at the far end of the head table,* summoned a waiter. [Nonrestrictive prepositional phrase.]
> My brother-in-law *who lives in Akron* is a chemist. [The writer has more than one brother-in-law. The restrictive clause is needed to distinguish this brother-in-law from other brothers-in-law.]
> My brother-in-law, *who lives in Akron,* is a chemist. [Identification is not explicit, so the writer is telling us that he has only one brother-in-law.]

2. Most appositives. An appositive is a noun unit that immediately follows a noun or a pronoun and stands for the same thing. (See pp. 70–71 of Lesson 10.)

> The new boy, *the one with red hair,* likes me.
> The colonel, *a friend of many years,* advised me to stay.
> Ms. McClure, *our science teacher,* told me about it.

Appositives like these are called *loose* or *nonrestrictive appositives* and are set off. But an appositive may sometimes function the same way that a restrictive

123

adjective clause functions; that is, it may identify a preceding noun that, without the appositive, could refer to any member of a class. An appositive of this sort is not set off:

my brother Jack, the poet Keats, the apostle Paul, the preposition *to*, Henry IV

3. **Absolute phrases.** An absolute phrase, which consists of a noun or a pronoun plus a verbal (see p. 79, Lesson 11), modifies the sentence as a whole, not any special part of it:

The cat being away, the mice will play.
My work having been finished, I went to see Alice.
He sat there in silence, *his left cheek twitching as usual*.
He stood in the doorway, *his wet cloak dripping water on the rug*, and waited for
   some sign of recognition.

4. **Parenthetical expressions.** These are words, phrases, or clauses that break into the sentence to explain, to emphasize, to qualify, or to point the direction of the thought:

The text, *moreover*, had not been carefully proofread.
You will find, *for example*, that the format is not attractive.
His appearance, *I must say*, was not prepossessing.

5. **Words used in direct address:**

I tell you, *Carol*, that we were all proud of you.
"You were justified, *Ms. Faire*," she said, "in refusing the gift."
"*Henry*, your theme must be rewritten," said his teacher.
And remember, *all good union members*, that every vote counts.

6. **Expressions designating the speaker in direct quotations:**

"With your permission," *he replied*, "there's nothing I'd rather do."
"That must do," *he said*, "until we think of something better."

Other marks may be used instead of the comma if the sentence justifies their use:

"How shall I tell him?" *asked Mary timidly*. [Question mark after question.]
"Silence!" *he shouted*. "Get to work at once!" [Exclamation point.]
"Two of the buildings are firetraps," *replied the comptroller*; "moreover, the library
   needs a new roof." [Semicolon required to avoid a comma fault between independent clauses.]

7. **Negative insertions used for emphasis, units out of their position, and short interrogative clauses combined with statements:**

Our plane was a DC-3, *not the jet we had expected*.
Tired and footsore, the hikers finally reached camp.
The hikers finally reached camp, *tired and footsore*.
[*But*] The tired and footsore hikers finally reached camp.
You had a good time, *didn't you?*
You recall, *don't you*, our first meeting?

8. **Degrees, titles, and the like when they follow names:**

Helen Lyle, *Ph.D.*, gave the opening address.
The new ambassador is Peter Jones, *Esq.*

9. In dates and addresses:

On July 14, *1904,* in a little cottage at 316 High Street, *Mayville, Illinois,* the wedding took place. [Journalistic practice usually omits the comma *after* the year and the state.]

When a year follows a month, rather than a day of the month, it is usually not set off. And a comma is not needed before a zip-code number:

As of March 1985 his mailing address was 1675 East Union Street, Seattle, Washington 98122.

EXERCISE 30
Commas to Enclose

NAME _____ SCORE _____

DIRECTIONS: Insert commas where they are necessary in the following sentences. Then, before each sentence, write one of the following numbers to indicate the rule that governs the punctuation of the sentence. Commas are used to enclose

1. a nonrestrictive clause or phrase.
2. an appositive.
3. a noun in direct address.
4. a parenthetical element.
5. the speaker in dialogue.
6. an absolute phrase.

_____ 1. My favorite flower the hyacinth is too odoriferous for some people.

_____ 2. I rode the bus this morning my car being in the shop.

_____ 3. "Once again" said the candidate "I must respond to the call of the people."

_____ 4. My reaction to his speech to be brutally frank was highly unfavorable.

_____ 5. My youngest sister who is still in high school hopes to become an astronaut.

_____ 6. "And now fellow citizens the time for action has arrived," said the mayor.

_____ 7. Cape Palmetto once a smugglers' haven has become a tourist center.

_____ 8. The once stately mansion it must be admitted is in a state of disrepair.

_____ 9. Let us remind you sir that your presence here is unwelcome.

_____ 10. The dress slightly faded from repeated washings was still attractive.

_____ 11. "I must ask you to repeat your question" said the chairwoman.

_____ 12. Its cash reserves running low the corporation applied for a loan.

_____ 13. The meal that Mrs. King served pleased Uncle Fred whose appetite is boundless.

_____ 14. At Cloverdale our next overnight stop we bought two new tires.

_____ 15. "From behind this post I can't see the stage" complained Ted.

_____ 16. The budget for next year I must emphasize will be severely cut.

_____ 17. And in conclusion good neighbors I urge you to cast an affirmative vote.

_____ 18. My landlord who formerly was a mechanic can repair anything.

_____ 19. Our little boat having a shallow draft maneuvered over the sandbar easily.

_____ 20. The rain having stopped we resumed our hike.

COMMAS TO ENCLOSE

DIRECTIONS: Each of the following sentences contains one adjective clause or one participial phrase. Underline the clause or phrase. Insert commas where they are needed. In the space at the left of each sentence write
    R. if the clause or phrase is restrictive.   N. if it is nonrestrictive.

_____   1. Can you recommend a course that will require little outside reading?

_____   2. I signed up for Philosophy 274 which requires much outside reading.

_____   3. We spent the winter in El Paso where the winters are mild.

_____   4. We want to move to some area where the winters are mild.

_____   5. Mr. Beech having hung up his hat and coat joined our group.

_____   6. A large man smoking an evil-smelling cigar sat down next to me.

_____   7. The first person who gives us the correct answer will win the prize.

_____   8. Lily Robbins who thought she knew the answer raised her hand.

_____   9. Our cruise ship stopped at Samoa where many of us went ashore.

_____   10. An island I'd like to visit is Samoa.

_____   11. Anyone knowing this man's whereabouts should notify the police.

_____   12. My eldest son having witnessed the accident called the police.

_____   13. Betty confided in her oldest friend whose opinion she valued highly.

_____   14. Betty's roommate is a girl whose parents live in Bermuda.

_____   15. This is Shirley Bascom of whom you have often heard me speak.

_____   16. Can't you think of someone from whom you could borrow the money?

_____   17. My unabridged dictionary badly scorched in the fire must be replaced.

_____   18. Books kept in the reserve library may be checked out after five o'clock.

_____   19. Our speaker today is a man who really needs no introduction.

_____   20. Our speaker today is Mayor Trueblood who really needs no introduction.

EXERCISE 31
Commas to Enclose; Commas: All Uses

DIRECTIONS: Recognizing typical punctuation situations in your own writing is a very important skill. In the spaces provided, write two sentences to illustrate each of the rules indicated. Punctuate your sentences correctly.

1. Two sentences with nonrestrictive adjective clauses.

    a.

    b.

2. Two sentences with nonrestrictive participial phrases.

    a.

    b.

3. Two sentences with appositives.

    a.

    b.

4. Two sentences with nouns used in direct address.

    a.

    b.

5. Two sentences with parenthetical elements.

    a.

    b.

6. Two sentences with absolute phrases.

    a.

    b.

DIRECTIONS: Insert commas where they are needed. Then, in the space at the left, write the number of commas you have used in each sentence.

_____ 1. Before you begin an exercise program you should buy new shoes get a thorough physical and find someone to exercise with you.

_____ 2. The next meeting which will be held in Joplin Missouri on May 1 1985 will concentrate on budgetary matters and ignore other questions.

_____ 3. "Once you have met Joan the new class president" said Mark "you should study the agenda most of which you will find very technical."

_____ 4. After we had talked to our coach we realized that we had a long hard season ahead of us.

_____ 5. Forgetting the plans we had so carefully prepared we decided to strike out cross-country walking as fast as we could.

_____ 6. His spirits boosted by the team's success the new owner who took over last week decided to repaint the ballpark hire new ushers and open a larger concession stand.

_____ 7. Shortly after they appointed three captains each one instructed to select four people who were willing to work on the project.

_____ 8. After she had found the dress selected shoes and chosen a purse she found that the total cost came to $351.06 an amount she could scarcely afford.

_____ 9. After the meeting started James Johnson one of the charter members of the club proposed a new project an idea that met with a less than enthusiastic reception we all thought.

_____ 10. Hungry tired but extremely happy the campers arrived at the train station on April 17 exactly six weeks after they had gathered for the session which was judged to be successful in every way.

EXERCISE 32
Commas and Semicolons: All Uses

NAME _____ SCORE _____

DIRECTIONS: The following sentences contain fifty numbered spots, some with punctuation and some with no punctuation. In the correspondingly numbered spaces at the left, write *C* if the punctuation is correct or *W* if the punctuation is incorrect.

1. _____
2. _____
(1) Inspired by the sight of the marathon runners, Marsh Jones dug her running shoes out of the back of the closet, and laced them onto her feet for another try at jogging.

3. _____
4. _____
(2) Many people still believe in the unicorn, a mythical animal with the body of a horse and a single horn in the middle of its head.

5. _____
6. _____
(3) Thank you, Mrs. Johnson, without your help we would have accomplished little or nothing this term.

7. _____
8. _____
(4) "You should find, friends," said the director, "that the first exercises are fairly easy, but the second session is a bit more strenuous."

9. _____
10. _____
(5) She said that the weather, although it is bitter cold, is perfect for skiing, and we ought to have a splendid weekend.

11. _____
12. _____
(6) Mary Ellen, everyone knows, is our best runner, she should anchor the relay team in tomorrow's track meet.

13. _____
14. _____
(7) As they began to spread out the crowd began to chant, "Encore! Encore!"

15. _____
16. _____
(8) My work in trigonometry is A minus or B plus, not the low C, that I thought I would earn.

17. _____
18. _____
(9) Instead of releasing employees when work is slow, which is common practice in our industry, we try to retrain them for work that is in demand.

19. _____
20. _____
(10) My friend has invented a low-calorie chocolate cake, he will soon be a rich, very famous, person.

21. _____
22. _____
(11) The Jones brothers have expanded their restaurant, their business having increased beyond the point where the dining room could handle the crowds.

23. _____ (12) When the salesperson smiled, and said, "This unit will cool
24. _____ your house far more cheaply than your present unit," I was
delighted.

25. _____ (13) My brother is taking care of Jim's Great Dane puppy this
26. _____ weekend, Jim is on a canoe trip in the nearby national park
where there is a whitewater river.

27. _____ (14) After the women left the gym, they went quickly to a restau-
28. _____ rant for cold drinks, dinner, and rich desserts.

29. _____ (15) In just a moment, you will see the first floats in the parade,
30. _____ however, the bands will not be along for about a half hour.

31. _____ (16) "And next friends," said the announcer, "we will select a new
32. _____ contestant and begin the preliminary questions."

33. _____ (17) The luscious, red strawberries are ripe, the corn has tasseled,
34. _____ and the peach trees are in full bloom.

35. _____ (18) Although John Maples is not extremely well known, experts say
36. _____ he has an excellent chance for victory in next year's primary
election.

37. _____ (19) The students in the new freshman class are extremely
38. _____ talented, in fact, some say that this may be the best group in
many years.

39. _____ (20) While the sun sank slowly in the west, the cowboy and the girl
40. _____ walked to the barn, and saddled the horses for their moonlight
ride.

41. _____ (21) So now, neighbors, the time has come, let's go quickly to the
42. _____ auditorium to watch the play.

43. _____ (22) Unless I've forgotten something or can't find my keys; I should
44. _____ be at your house within the hour.

45. _____ (23) The man stood and walked slowly to the ticket window; the
46. _____ ticket seller having finally returned from her lunch.

47. _____ (24) Alaska, you know, is the largest state, it has extraordinarily
48. _____ beautiful mountains and rivers.

49. _____ (25) The boss walked into my office, sat down slowly, and stared at
50. _____ the ceiling for a long time, then he told me that he'd been
transferred to New York City.

18 Apostrophes, Colons, Dashes, and Quotation Marks

1. The apostrophe (') has three uses: (a) to form the possessive case of nouns and indefinite pronouns; (b) to indicate contractions; and (c) to form the plurals of numbers, letters, and symbols.

a. Any noun, whether singular or plural, that does not end in *s* forms its possessive by adding an apostrophe and *s:*

a boy's hat, the horse's tail, Carol's car, men's shoes, children's toys

All plural nouns that end in *s* form the possessive by adding an apostrophe after the *s:*

boys' hats, horses' tails, the Smiths' home, ladies' dresses

In singular nouns ending in *s* or *z*, an apostrophe following the *s* or *z* is the usual way to form the possessive:

the countess' castle, Frances' reply, Archimedes' law, Mr. Gomez' report

However, for short words ending in *s*, usage is divided. If the possessive form can be easily pronounced with an extra syllable, an added *s* may be used following the apostrophe:

the boss' [or boss's] answer, Mr. Jones' [or Jones's] house, Keats' [or Keats's] poetry

The indefinite pronouns, but not the personal pronouns, form the possessive with the aid of the apostrophe:

somebody's sweater, anyone's opinion, anybody's game [But note the possessive forms of these pronouns: his, hers, its, theirs, ours, yours, whose.]

b. The apostrophe is used to stand for the omitted material in contractions:

doesn't [does not], won't [will not], she's [she is, she has], o'clock [of the clock]

You must learn to distinguish carefully between the following pairs of contractions and possessives:

it's [it is, it has]	its	who's [who is, who has]	whose
there's [there is, there has]	theirs	you're [you are]	your
they're [they are]	their		

c. Plurals of letters, numbers, symbols, words used as words, and abbreviations are formed with the apostrophe. (Do not use an apostrophe to form the plural of either a common noun or a proper noun.)

Your *T*'s and *7*'s look alike. So do your *3*'s and *8*'s. Your *n*'s, *m*'s, and *u*'s all look like a wavy line. Don't use so many *and*'s in your writing, and never use *&*'s as substitutes for them.

2. The colon (:) is a formal mark announcing a list, an explanation, or a quotation to follow. (Notice, for example, its use in the first rule on this page.)

My fellow Americans: My speech tonight will examine . . .
All hikers must bring the following: a flashlight, a small ax, and a waterproof tarpaulin.

Do not use a colon to separate a verb from its complement or a preposition from its object:

FAULTY: All hikers must bring: a flashlight, a small ax, and a waterproof tarpaulin.
FAULTY: The things a hiker must bring are: a flashlight, a small ax, and a waterproof tarpaulin.
FAULTY: The hiker's equipment should consist of: a flashlight, a small ax, and a waterproof tarpaulin.

3. The dash (—) is used to show an abrupt change in thought in the sentence. It must be used sparingly and never as a substitute for other marks:

Superior students—notice that I said *superior*—will not have to take the test.
New surroundings, new friends, a challenging new job—all these helped Eugene overcome his grief.

4. Quotation marks (" ") are used to enclose quoted material and words used in some special way.
a. Use double quotation marks (" ") to enclose the exact words of a quoted speech.

Quotation marks always come in pairs. The marks show the beginning and the end of a speech, whether it is part of a sentence, one sentence, or several sentences. If a speech is interrupted by material showing who said it, quotation marks set off the quoted material from the explanatory material. Use quotation marks where the directly quoted material begins and where it ends or is interrupted.

Indirect quotations are *not* set off by quotation marks:

"I am sure," said Tom, "that your answer is right." [Note that the explanatory material is set off from the direct quotation.]
Peggy answered, "I worked hard on this. I checked all my data." [More than one sentence.]
Peggy answered that she had worked hard and checked all her data. [This is an indirect quotation. Words not directly quoted do not need quotation marks.]

b. Use double quotation marks to set off subdivisions of books, names of songs, and titles of units of less than book length, such as short stories, short poems, essays, and articles:

The second chapter of *Moby Dick* is entitled "The Carpet-Bag."
Nanki-Poo sings "A Wandering Minstrel I" early in Act I of *The Mikado*.
Our anthology includes "Threes," a poem from Sandburg's *Smoke and Steel*.
The first article I read for my research paper was John Lear's "How Hurricanes Are Born" in the *Saturday Review*.

NOTE: In printed copy, titles of books, magazines, and newspapers are usually set in italic type. In handwritten or typewritten papers, underlining (typescript like this) is the equivalent of italics in printed material (*type like this*).
c. Use double quotation marks to set off slang words used in serious writing. Quotation marks are also sometimes used to set off words when they are referred to as words:

The witness had only recently been released from the "slammer."
Words like "seize" and "siege" are often misspelled.

Usage is divided on these uses of quotation marks. In printed material the two words in the second example would almost certainly appear in italics. Student writers of handwritten or typed material should underline such words or set them off by quotation marks, the first method being the more common practice.

d. Follow this usage in the placing of quotation marks in relation to other marks: (1) commas and periods always inside quotes; (2) semicolons and colons always outside quotes; (3) question marks and exclamation points inside if they belong to the quoted part, outside if they do not:

"Come in," said my uncle, "and take off your coats." [Comma and period.]

Mr. Lowe said, "I heartily endorse this candidate"; unfortunately most of the audience thought he said *hardly* instead of *heartily*. [Semicolon outside.]

"Heavens!" he exclaimed. "Is this the best you can do?" [Exclamation point and question mark.]

Mother asked, "Where were you last night?" [No double punctuation.]

Did she say, "I came home early"? [Question mark belongs to the whole sentence, not to the quoted part.]

Did Mother ask, "Where were you last night?" [Note that there is only one question mark after a double question like this.]

e. Use single quotation marks to enclose a speech within a speech:

"I wonder what he meant," said Betty, "when he said, 'There are wheels within wheels.'" [You may not write many sentences like this one, but just the same, you should note that when you have quotes within quotes, the period comes inside both single and double quotes.]

Apostrophes, Colons, Dashes, and Quotation Marks

NAME _____ SCORE _____

DIRECTIONS: In the spaces at the left, write *C* if the punctuation is correct or *W* if it is incorrect. Within the incorrect sentences, correct the faulty punctuation by adding, removing, or changing marks.

_____ 1. It's true, isn't it, that another person's name appeared on the list where your's belongs?

_____ 2. We've announced the names of all the winner's, haven't we?

_____ 3. "Whats going on here?" asked the reporter. "I'm not able to find anybodys notes on that story."

_____ 4. She finished the paper with a final, stirring exhortation: "Lets carry on now, even in the face of all thats happened to our hopes."

_____ 5. This morning's paper carried ads for: womens shoes, men's suits, and childrens books.

_____ 6. "Today's test," said the teacher, "will cover all the material from— but I already told you that information yesterday, didn't I?"

_____ 7. The glove compartment of the suspects car contained the following: a handgun, a stocking mask, and a pair of gloves.

_____ 8. "These books don't belong to me," said Jane. "Perhaps they're Ms. Jones; she's always leaving her's lying around the room."

_____ 9. We'll be there about nine o'clock with: our uniforms, our shoes, and our drum's and bugle's.

_____ 10. My grandmother used an old saying that ought to hang in every garage: if it isn't broken, don't fix it.

_____ 11. "Everyone's got a chance to make the team," said the coach. "However, you can't make the team if you don't try out."

_____ 12. My brothers only response to my request was that he'd do the best he could to make A's and B's this next term.

_____ 13. When the tired hiker opened her pack, she found: a two weeks supply of vitamin pills and two of her brother's stale ham sandwiches.

_____ 14. James' presence at this meeting is explained by the fact that his club postponed it's regularly scheduled meeting until nine oclock tomorrow night.

_____ 15. Up until a few year's ago—maybe you can remember the year—it was illegal to sell automobiles on Sunday in my hometown.

DIRECTIONS: Sentences 1–5 are indirect quotations. In the space provided, rewrite each sentence as a direct quotation. Sentences 6–10 are direct quotations. Rewrite each as an indirect quotation. You will have to alter some verb forms and some pronoun forms as well as the punctuation.

1. Ms. Johnson said that she had forgotten the date of our next meeting.

2. The woman replied that she would help us as soon as she had finished her report.

3. Joan explained that her sister has always been extremely shy.

4. The manager asked if we had brought the receipt for the glasses with us.

5. Did the teacher announce that the test is tomorrow in this room?

6. The driver said to me, "You must have correct change in order to ride this bus."

7. The president looked around the table and said, "Perhaps you are wondering why I called you here today."

8. The unhappy customer complained, "Every time I started this electric saw, it blew a fuse."

9. The reporter walked up to me and asked, "Would you mind answering a few questions for our viewing audience?"

10. Didn't you see the sign that said, "Hard hats required beyond this point"?

19 End Marks; Summary of Punctuation Rules

T HE PERIOD is used after a complete declarative sentence and after ordinary abbreviations. Its use as end punctuation after sentences needs no examples. Its use after abbreviations is a little more complicated.

A few abbreviations are proper in the ordinary sort of writing, such as *Mr.*, *Mrs.*, *Ms.*, *Messrs.*, and *Dr.*, before names; *Jr.*, *Sr.*, *Esq.*, *D.D.*, *Ph.D.*, and so forth, after names. No period is used with *Miss. Ms.*, used instead of *Miss* or *Mrs.* when marital state is not indicated, is usually considered an abbreviation and uses a period, although some modern dictionaries have entries for it either with or without a period.

The following, correct in footnotes, bibliographies, and tabulations, should be written out in ordinary writing: *e.g. (for example), etc. (and so forth), i.e. (that is), p., pp. (page, pages),* and *vol. (volume).*

A.D., B.C., A.M., and *P.M.* (usually set in small caps in printed matter) are used only with figures and where necessary for clearness.

The following are acceptable in addresses but should be spelled out in ordinary writing: *St. (Street), Ave. (Avenue), Blvd. (Boulevard), Dr. (Drive), Rd. (Road), Co. (Company),* and *Inc. (Incorporated).* Conventionally, periods have been used with abbreviations of the states *(Mass., Minn., Tex., W. Va.).* However, the two-letter capitalized symbols authorized by the U.S. Postal Service *(MA, MN, TX, WV)* do not require periods.

> POOR: Last Mon. P.M. I met my two older bros., who live in N.Y: Chas. works for a mfg. co. there. Thos. attends NYU, preparing himself for a gov't. job. He's coming home for Xmas.
>
> RIGHT: Last Monday afternoon I met my two older brothers, who live in New York. Charles works for a manufacturing company there. Thomas attends New York University, preparing himself for a government job. He's coming home for Christmas.

In modern usage, the "alphabet" name forms, or acronyms, of various governmental or intergovernmental agencies, social or professional organizations, and units of measurement used in scientific contexts are usually not followed by periods: *CARE, CBS, CIA, FBI, GNP, HEW, ICBM, NASA, NATO, SEC, TVA, UNESCO, mpg, mph, rpm.* When in doubt, consult your dictionary; be prepared to find apparent inconsistencies and much divided usage.

The **question mark** is used after a direct question, which is an utterance that calls for an answer. (See Lesson 6.) But we do not use a question mark after an indirect question, which is a *statement* giving the substance of a question but not the words that would be used in a direct question.

> DIRECT: Who goes there? Is that you? When do we eat? How much do I owe you? "Who goes there?" he demanded. [In dialogue.]
> Did he ask, "Where does this road lead?" [Note single question mark.]
>
> INDIRECT: She asked me how old I was. I wondered why she would ask such a question. [Note that periods are used. These are statements, not direct questions.]

The **exclamation point** is used sparingly in modern writing and should be reserved for statements of strong feeling. Mild exclamations, such as *oh, goodness, well, yes,* and *no,* are followed by commas, not exclamation points. Be sure to place the exclamation mark after the exclamation itself.

"Help! I'm slipping!" he shouted. [Note period after *shouted.*]
"Stop that!" she screamed. [Do not put the exclamation point after *screamed.*]
Well, it was exciting, wasn't it? Oh, I had a pleasant time.

Summary of Punctuation Rules

Punctuation is not complex, nor are the rules many and involved; they can be learned quickly. In this review we shall simplify them still more by listing only the important ones that you use constantly in your everyday writing. You can see how few of them there actually are. Colons, dashes, parentheses, brackets, and even question marks and exclamation points do have other uses for special occasions or effects; but these occasional applications rarely cause problems for most writers.

The important thing for you to do now is to study these really indispensable rules until you are perfectly at home with them. And then, of course, if all of this is to do you any good, you must use your knowledge in everything you write, whether it is "for English," or in a letter to a friend, or in a notebook for a course in biology.

Commas to Separate: Five rules

1. Coordinate clauses
2. Items in a series
3. Coordinate adjectives
4. Introductory modifiers
5. Words that may be misread together

Commas to Enclose: Eight rules

1. Nonrestrictive clauses and phrases
2. Appositives
3. Absolute phrases
4. Parenthetical expressions
5. Words in direct address
6. The speaker in dialogue
7. Negative insertions
8. Dates, addresses, degrees, and titles

Semicolon: One rule

1. In compound sentences without conjunction

Apostrophe: Two rules

1. With possessives
2. With contractions

Quotation Marks: Three rules

1. About direct quotations
2. About titles
3. About words used in some special way

Period: Two rules

1. After declarative sentences
2. After most abbreviations

Question Mark: One rule

1. After direct questions

End Marks

NAME _____ SCORE _____

DIRECTIONS: Draw a circle around each error in punctuation. If the punctuation is wrong, write *W* in the space before the sentence. If the punctuation is correct, write *C* in the space.

_____ 1. Is your address at school 743 N.W. 3rd Ave., Baltimore, MD 10512?

_____ 2. Next summer Ms. Johnson will be working in Washington, D C. for DOT.

_____ 3. SEC can stand for *Securities and Exchange Commission* or *Southeastern Conference.*

_____ 4. Joanne Robinson, DDS, has developed a new method for repairing damaged teeth.

_____ 5. We cannot allow the operation of radios, cameras, computers, etc while the plane is in flight.

_____ 6. The first marathon was run in 490 B.C, wasn't it?

_____ 7. "Hurry," she cried! "The train is pulling out."

_____ 8. "Do you intend to work for a Ph.D. or an Ed.D." my father asked?

_____ 9. Every morning at 9 A.M. Mr Adams, Mrs. Williams, and Ms. Walker begin the day by drinking coffee together.

_____ 10. The correct reference for that article reads: Vol 2, No. 10, p. 121.

_____ 11. "Will you be able to find that restaurant," asked Mrs. Morton?

_____ 12. "My stars and body!" exclaimed the old man. "I thought you'd never get here!"

_____ 13. Ms. Wilson asked how to order another pack of paper?

_____ 14. "Help! Help! I'm trapped in my office by a flood of paperwork!" shouted the bureaucrat.

_____ 15. We could leave, couldn't we, about 10 A.M. tomorrow?

_____ 16. John asked me whether that date is A.D. 323 or 323 B.C.?

_____ 17. "I'll be leaving for work about 7:15 A.M.," said the boss.

_____ 18. Do you know whether she works for NASA or NOAA?

_____ 19. Many early Americans, e.g., John Paul Jones, were truly heroic figures.

_____ 20. "Just a minute, please," said the receptionist. "Mr. Shorter is not ready to see you yet."

EXERCISE **34**

Review of Punctuation

DIRECTIONS: In the following sentences correct every error in punctuation. Then, in the column of figures at the left, circle every number that represents an error in that sentence. Use these numbers:

1. Comma omitted
2. Apostrophe omitted or misused
3. Comma misused for semicolon
4. Semicolon misused for comma

1 2 3 4   (1) For anyone who would like to know our location; we are 95 nautical miles due south of Corpus Christi, Texas heading home as fast as we can go.

1 2 3 4   (2) I believe we should begin to diversify, there are many opportunities, you know in developing innovative programs for business applications.

1 2 3 4   (3) Joan, remembering my aversion to mathematics said, "This course of study does require knowledge of math and it's applications to engineering."

1 2 3 4   (4) My new friends, the Anderson's, live near a steel mill; a situation that prevents them from getting a good night's sleep unless the mill is closed.

1 2 3 4   (5) "Not one of my friends," said Alice, "is as interesting as your's but they call regularly and come to visit on special occasions."

1 2 3 4   (6) Lets try not to be late for our nine oclock appointment, we need to get our class schedules as early as possible.

1 2 3 4   (7) If you will call me early in the morning after you get up; I'd like to have you look at my garden which needs a great deal of work.

1 2 3 4   (8) The manager walked up to Jim and me, chuckled a little, and said, "We seem to have a slight problem here, we did not, unfortunately, expect you two until tomorrow night."

1 2 3 4   (9) Jane Collins our lawyer for the past five years, cant understand why we don't want to deal with a young associate in her firm.

1 2 3 4   (10) Looming large and threatening over the valley is a tall snow-capped mountain Mount Baldy; its icy winds seeming to chill the entire area below it.

EXERCISE 35
Review of Punctuation

NAME _____ SCORE _____

DIRECTIONS: The following sentences contain fifty numbered spots between words or beneath words. (The number is beneath the word when the punctuation problem involves the use of an apostrophe in that word.) In the correspondingly numbered spots at the left, write *C* if the punctuation is correct or *W* if it is incorrect.

1. _____
2. _____

(1) The sportscaster on the local television station has resigned,[1] in his final broadcast he said he'd found a place where people are[2] better sports than they are here.

3. _____
4. _____

(2) After I had read the new womens'[3] magazine, I gave the copy to Janie Schultz, who is a free-lance[4] writer of some note.

5. _____
6. _____

(3) My eccentric uncle left me some unusual items in his will:[5] an antique sewing machine, three advertising posters, and a small[6] leather satchel.

7. _____
8. _____

(4) Someone—I don't really want to know who—[7]has left a long[8] jagged scratch on the side of my new car.

9. _____
10. _____

(5) Looking up from behind the book and smiling shyly[9] Melissa said, "It must be time for the party to start;[10] I hear the band tuning up."

11. _____
12. _____

(6) The weather being, as far as I was concerned, far too cold for gardening;[11] I picked up a book that I'd[12] been trying to read for some time.

13. _____
14. _____

(7) You need the following items to make a good omelette:[13] eggs, milk, butter, cheese, bacon, and a good omelette pan.[14]

15. _____
16. _____

(8) "I checked the list before I[15] went into the store, but I couldn't find it when I got in the store," said Grandma,[16] who is a trifle absent-minded.

17. _____
18. _____

(9) At last the girls have arrived,[17] their luggage has been here for day's[18] cluttering up the front hallway.

19. _____
20. _____

(10) As there is no other way out of the valley;[19] we cleared the logging road using:[20] axes, shovels, pickaxes, and good old muscle power.

21. _____   (11) I think I'll try to buy a new car, my old one is very dirty on

21
22. _____   the inside, and it's trunk has a big dent in it.

22

23. _____   (12) Many industries in this country are beginning to follow the pat-
24. _____   tern of Japanese management; with company songs,

23
      calisthenics, and quality circles.

24

25. _____   (13) I'm delighted to say that I'm finally going to fulfill one of my

25
26. _____   dreams, I'm going to take a trip to the Grand Canyon.

26

27. _____   (14) Gathering his belongings up the stairs he walked and left the

27
28. _____   meeting; those left at the table were completely surprised.

28

29. _____   (15) "Thats going to be a great boon to this small town," said Joan

29
30. _____   Shields, "not many towns have their own telephone company."

30

31. _____   (16) After all our club is very small, we can not expect to compete

31   32
32. _____   with a large club from a major city.

33. _____   (17) My boss called me and said, "Jones, my boy, youre going to

33
34. _____   love your next assignment; and that's an order."

34

35. _____   (18) "Somebody else's car would be better than mine, yours, Joan,

35   36
36. _____   is especially well suited to carrying trash," laughed Harry.

37. _____   (19) Mr. Wells smiled and asked, "Can I interest anyone in a free
38. _____   dinner at a dark, expensive, French restaurant?"

37   38
39. _____   (20) A new worker entered the room and asked, "What time is

39
40. _____   lunch around here and how far is the cafeteria from here?"

40

41. _____   (21) All the members had arrived by nine oclock, but the president

41   42
42. _____   and the secretary were very late that day.

43. _____   (22) When our friends the Williams's moved to a new house, they

43
44. _____   took their menagerie of five cats and seven dogs with them, the

44
      neighborhood is much quieter now.

45. _____   (23) "I wonder why none of my friends is willing to go on a trip to
46. _____   wild wonderful Alaska with me?" said Charlie.

45   46
47. _____   (24) Our leader Amy Johnson, will lead us this Saturday on a hike

47
48. _____   through River Park, in which there is a small canyon.

48

49. _____   (25) "Everyone must be at my house before nine o'clock," said
50. _____   Michele, "its going to take a few minutes to get started."

49   50

144

NAME _____ SCORE _____

DIRECTIONS: One sentence in each of the following pairs is correctly punctuated. Copy the identifying letter of the correct sentence in the space at the left. Be prepared to explain in class why the punctuation of the other sentence is faulty.

_____ 1. A. According to the latest surveys, which were completed, I under-stand, about a month ago, there are many jobs available in Aus-tin, Texas; Seattle, Washington; and Santa Fe, New Mexico.

B. According to the latest surveys, which were completed, I under-stand about a month ago; there are many jobs available in Aus-tin, Texas, Seattle, Washington, and Santa Fe, New Mexico.

_____ 2. A. The coach stood up in the meeting and said, "Several of our starting players are in a slump and are batting only in the upper 300's and lower 400's."

B. The coach stood up in the meeting, and said, "Several of our starting player's are in a slump, and are batting only in the up-per 300's and lower 400's.

_____ 3. A. "The characters, the plot, the setting—everything works to-gether to perfection," cried Jim Robinson, the local drama critic.

B. "The characters, the plot, the setting; everything works together to perfection," cried Jim Robinson the local drama critic.

_____ 4. A. R. L. Morgan and Tommy Johnson wrote the script for our se-nior class play, "One More Time"; its story was only mildly in-teresting, and the play was not very well received by the audi-ence.

B. R. L. Morgan and Tommy Johnson wrote the script for our se-nior class play "One More Time," it's story was only mildly in-teresting and the play was not very well received by the audi-ence.

_____ 5. A. Jim announced "that he had tried to make hotel reservations' for the game on July 4, 1985 but his efforts were to no avail, be-cause the hotel was booked solid."

B. Jim announced that he had tried to make hotel reservations for the game on July 4, 1985, but his efforts were to no avail be-cause the hotel was booked solid.

_____ 6. A. "If you will review the last four assignments I'm sure you will find all you need to know for Mondays test," said the instructor.

B. "If you will review the last four assignments, I'm sure you will find all you need to know for Monday's test," said the instructor.

_____ 7. A. If your brothers new car is as fast as he says it is why doesn't he enter it in the next showroom stock sports-car race.

B. If your brother's new car is as fast as he says it is, why doesn't he enter it in the next showroom stock sports-car race?

_____ 8. A. A man at the back of the room stood quietly and asked, "If we elect the same board of directors again, we will get essentially the same performance from the company as we got last year, won't we?"

B. A man at the back of the room stood quietly, and asked, "If we elect the same board of directors again we will get essentially the same performance from the company as we got last year won't we.

_____ 9. A. "Hot humid days like this one," said Dr Thorpe, "remind me of Noel Coward's famous line, 'Mad dogs and Englishmen go out in the midday sun."

B. "Hot, humid days like this one," said Dr. Thorpe, "remind me of Noel Coward's famous line, 'Mad dogs and Englishmen go out in the midday sun.'"

_____ 10. A. When we built our cabin in that remote mountain valley, we purposely left out most of the modern conveniences that people seem to expect.

B. When we built our cabin in that remote, mountain valley we purposely left out most of the modern conveniences, that people seem to expect.

_____ 11. A. "We've given you the best possible education, now its your turn to make use of that education in building your career," said Dr. Caldwell the luncheon speaker.

B. "We've given you the best possible education; now it's your turn to make use of that education in building your career," said Dr. Caldwell, the luncheon speaker.

_____ 12. A. It is great fun to talk baseball with my grandmother who is a dyed-in-the-wool Yankee fan, the talk always ends, however when we bring up their losing seasons.

B. It is great fun to talk baseball with my grandmother, who is a dyed-in-the-wool Yankee fan; the talk always ends, however, when we bring up their losing seasons.

_____ 13. A. "Coach," asked the reporter, "how can you hope to go to a bowl game? Your record is worse than anyone else's in the whole conference."

B. "Coach," asked the reporter, "how can you hope to go to a bowl game. Your record is worse than anyone elses in the whole conference?"

_____ 14. A. After polling 1,276 adults, the Alton Liebler Company, a firm that does opinion polling, has concluded that 73 percent of all adult Americans prefer ice cream to cookies for dessert.

B. After polling 1,276 adults the Alton Liebler Company a firm that does opinion polling, has concluded that 73 percent of all adult Americans prefer ice cream to cookies for dessert.

_____ 15. A. Our town recently saw the opening of three new businesses: a store selling computer software, a beauty parlor for dogs, and a restaurant whose specialty is Japanese food.

B. Our town recently saw the opening of three new businesses, a store selling computer software, a beauty parlor for dogs, and a restaurant who's specialty is Japanese food.

146

PART **III** USAGE
Lessons and Exercises

LESSON

20 Using Verbs Correctly: Principal Parts

IN LESSON 2 you learned that verbs are either regular or irregular and that the principal parts of the two classes are formed in different ways. We shall now examine certain trouble spots where incorrect forms sometimes appear because of confusion in the use of the principal parts. (See Supplement 1.)

To gain assurance in your use of verbs, you must remember how the past tense and the past participle are used:

The **past tense** is always a single-word verb; it is never used with an auxiliary:

I *ate* my lunch. [*Not* I *have ate* my lunch.]

The **past participle** is never a single-word verb; it is used with the auxiliary *have* (to form the perfect tenses) or the auxiliary *be* (to form the passive voice):

I *have done* the work. The work *was done*. [*Not* I *done* the work.]

(The past participle is, of course, used as a single word when it is a modifier of a noun: the *broken* toy, the *worried* parents, some *known* criminals.)

Four groups of verbs that often cause confusion are illustrated in this lesson, each group containing verbs that have similar trouble spots. The basic solution for the problem in each group is to master the principal parts of the verbs; they are the ones that account for most of the verb form errors found in writing. The principal parts are listed in the customary order: base form, past tense, and past participle.

1. The error in the form of the verb results from a confusion of the past tense and the past participle:

Later, their actions *became* [not *become*] offensive.	become	became	become
They *began* [not *begun*] to laugh at us.	begin	began	begun
Someone had *broken* [not *broke*] the window.	break	broke	broken
She should not have *chosen* [not *chose*] that hat.	choose	chose	chosen
Yesterday the child *came* [not *come*] home.	come	came	come
I *did* [not *done*] what she told me to do.	do	did	done
He *drank* [not *drunk*] some water.	drink	drank	drunk
I had *driven* [not *drove*] all day.	drive	drove	driven
The lamp had *fallen* [not *fell*] over.	fall	fell	fallen
The bird has *flown* [not *flew*] away.	fly	flew	flown
The rope had *frozen* [not *froze*] stiff.	freeze	froze	frozen
Dad has *given* [not *gave*] me a car.	give	gave	given
Theresa has *gone* [not *went*] to school.	go	went	gone
I've never *ridden* [not *rode*] a horse.	ride	rode	ridden
We ran out when the fire alarm *rang* [not *rung*].	ring	rang	rung

147

Swensen had never *run* [not *ran*] the mile.	run	ran	run
I *saw* [not *seen*] her staring at me.	see	saw	seen
It must have *sunk* [not *sank*] in deep water.	sink	sank	sunk
She should have *spoken* [not *spoke*] louder.	speak	spoke	spoken
The car had been *stolen* [not *stole*].	steal	stole	stolen
The witness was *sworn* [not *swore*] in.	swear	swore	sworn
John has *swum* [not *swam*] across the lake.	swim	swam	swum
The letter had been *torn* [not *tore*] in two.	tear	tore	torn
You should have *worn* [not *wore*] a hat.	wear	wore	worn
I have already *written* [not *wrote*] my essay.	write	wrote	written

2. The error results from a confusion of regular and irregular verb forms:

He *blew* [not *blowed*] smoke into my face.	blow	blew	blown
John *brought* [not *bringed*] Mary some flowers.	bring	brought	brought
The children *built* [not *builded*] a fort.	build	built	built
Barbara *caught* [not *catched*] two trout.	catch	caught	caught
Slowly they *crept* [not *creeped*] up the stairs.	creep	crept	crept
He *dealt* [not *dealed*] me a good hand.	deal	dealt	dealt
The men quickly *dug* [not *digged*] a pit.	dig	dug	dug
She *drew* [not *drawed*] a circle on the sand.	draw	drew	drawn
All the men *grew* [not *growed*] long beards.	grow	grew	grown
Larry *hung* [not *hanged*] the mistletoe on the door.	hang	hung	hung
I *knew* [not *knowed*] him at college.	know	knew	known
A friend *lent* [not *lended*] me a dime.	lend	lent	lent
The sun *shone* [not *shined*] all day yesterday.	shine	shone	shone
I soon *spent* [not *spended*] the money.	spend	spent	spent
She *threw* [not *throwed*] a stone at me.	throw	threw	thrown

3. The error results from the use of an obsolete or dialectal form of the verb, a form not considered standard now:

I *am* [not *be*] working regularly.	be*	was, were	been
I *have been* [not *I been*] working regularly.			
The child *burst* [not *busted*] out crying.	burst	burst	burst
I've *bought* [not *boughten*] a car.	buy	bought	bought
I *climbed* [not *clumb*] a tree for a better view.	climb	climbed	climbed
The men *clung* [not *clang*] to the raft.	cling	clung	clung
You could not have *dragged* [not *drug*] me there.	drag	dragged	dragged
The boy was nearly *drowned* [not *drownded*].	drown	drowned	drowned
At the picnic I *ate* [not *et*] too many hot dogs.	eat	ate	eaten
I forgot that I had already *paid* [not *payed*] her.	pay	paid	paid
It had been *shaken* [not *shooken*] to pieces.	shake	shook	shaken
He had never *skinned* [not *skun*] a cat.	skin	skinned	skinned
A bee *stung* [not *stang*] me as I stood there.	sting	stung	stung
The girl *swung* [not *swang*] at the ball.	swing	swung	swung
I wonder who could have *taken* [not *tooken*] it.	take	took	taken

4. The error results from a confusion of forms of certain verbs that look or sound almost alike but are actually quite different in meaning, such as *lie, lay; sit, set;* and *rise, raise.* Note that three of these troublesome verbs—*lay, set,*

---

* As you learned in Lesson 2, the irregular verb *be* has three forms *(am, are, is)* in the present tense and two forms *(was, were)* in the past tense.

148

and *raise*—in their ordinary uses take an object. The other three—*lie, sit, rise*—do not take an object.

Please *lay* your books on the table. Mary *laid* several logs on the fire. The men have *laid* some boards over the puddle.	lay	laid	laid
The old dog *lies* [not *lays*] on the grass. Yesterday he *lay* [not *laid*] on the floor. Your dress must have *lain* [not *laid*] on the floor all night.	lie	lay	lain
She *sets* the plate in front of me. Tom *set* out some food for the birds. I had *set* the camera at a full second.	set	set	set
I usually *sit* in that chair. Yesterday he *sat* in my chair. I have *sat* at my desk all morning.	sit	sat	sat
At her command they *raise* the flag. The boy quickly *raised* his hand. He had *raised* the price of his old car.	raise	raised	raised
He *rises* when we enter the room. Everyone *rose* as the speaker entered the room. The water has *risen* a foot since midnight.	rise	rose	risen

The rules and illustrations given here will serve as a guide in most situations. They show the importance of knowing the principal parts of these verbs. Note, however, that there are a few exceptions, such as the intransitive uses of *set:*

A *setting* [not *sitting*] hen *sets* [that is, *broods;* of course, a hen, like a rooster or any other appropriate entity, may be said to *sit* when that is what is meant.]
The sun *sets* in the west.
Cement or a dye *sets*.
A jacket *sets (fits)* well.

With a few verbs special meanings demand different principal parts. For example, the past tense and the past participle of *shine,* when the verb is used as a transitive verb, are *shined:*

This morning I *shined* [not *shone*] my shoes.

The verb *hang* with the meaning "to execute by suspending by the neck until dead" uses *hanged,* not *hung,* for the past tense and the past participle. When in doubt, always refer to your dictionary.

Supplement 1

Mention should be made here of another slight change in verb form that is possible. In Lesson 2 you saw a partial conjugation of three verbs. That conjugation showed only the indicative mood (or mode), those forms that are used to make nearly all statements or to ask questions. A second mood, the imperative, causes no complications: It is merely the base form of the verb when used to give a command or a request, with the subject *you* generally not expressed:

Be here by noon.
Please *come* to my office.

A third mood, the subjunctive, is sometimes shown by a change in the form of the verb. In this change *be* is used instead of *am, is,* or *are; were* is used instead of *was;* and, rarely, a third-person singular verb is used without the *s,* for instance, "he *leave*" instead of "he *leaves.*"

There is really only one situation in modern English in which the subjunctive form *were* is regularly used instead of *was,* and that is in an *if* clause making a statement that is clearly and unmistakably contrary to fact. The most obvious example is the everyday expression "If I *were* you, I'd . . . ." Remember the "If-I-were-you" set pattern to remind you of other "contrary-to-fact" clauses in which the subjunctive *were* would be expected in serious writing and speaking:

If I *were* able to fly . . . *Were* I president of this country . . . If she *were* thirty
years younger . . .

Divided usage prevails in a few other remnants of earlier subjunctive uses, especially in formal writing, for example in "wish" clauses (reflecting also a contrary-to-fact situation):

On frigid days like this, I wish I *were* in Tahiti.

The subjunctive is also found in certain set patterns of resolutions and demands:

I move that Mr. Shaw *be* appointed.
The chairman demanded that the reporter *leave* the room.
It is imperative that you *be* here by 10 o'clock.

In many of these and similar sentence situations in which older English insisted on subjunctive forms, modern speakers and writers often choose either an indicative form or one of the modal auxiliaries, such as *should, may,* or *might.*

Using Verbs Correctly: Principal Parts

NAME _____ SCORE _____

DIRECTIONS: In the space at the left, write the correct form of the verb shown within the parentheses. Do not use any *ing* forms.

1. If you had (bring) a note from a parent, the school would have (give) you permission to go on the field trip.
2. A month or so ago, the school principal (become) aware that several items from the library had been (steal).
3. After dinner we (sit) on the porch and watched the sun as it (sink) behind the mountain.
4. By dinner time Jane and Dad had (drag) away the alder tree that the storm had (blow) across the road.
5. Before lunch yesterday we (swim) across the bay and then (lie) on the beach for an hour.
6. "I had (wear) this dress only twice when I (tear) a rip in the sleeve," complained Emily.
7. My uncle has often (speak) of the time he fell off this dock and nearly (drown).
8. Mother never let us leave the table until we had (eat) our vegetables and had (drink) all our milk.
9. Before long Jake (begin) to realize that he had (pay) too much for the broken-down motorcycle.
10. When the guide screamed and (swing) the ax over his head, the bobcat turned and (run) into the underbrush.
11. I (see) Dr. Roberts nearly a month ago, but I have not (see) her since.
12. After he retired, Professor Duncan (choose) to live at Seaport among people he had (know) since childhood.
13. The landlord took the witness stand and (swear) that he had not (write) the notice.
14. The bottle of milk had (sit) on the porch overnight, and the milk was (freeze) solid.
15. The children put the puppy in the hole they had (dig) on the beach, but the puppy soon (climb) out.
16. Yesterday I (take) back three useless items that I had (buy) at the department store.
17. "My old truck has (shake) itself nearly to pieces in the ten years I've (drive) it on these roads," he complained.
18. "This is the third time that I've (lend) you money, and I've (grow) tired of supporting you," he answered.
19. The architect who has (draw) these plans is the one who (build) the warehouse on South Elm Street.
20. By January 5 I had (break) my resolution; I (spend) most of my allowance on a silly video game.

DIRECTIONS: Each sentence contains two italicized verb forms. If the verb is in the form proper in serious writing, write *C* in the corresponding space at the left. If the verb is incorrect, write the correct form at the left.

1. That was a brave thing you *done* when you rushed into the heavy traffic to help the woman who had *fallen.*

2. The clever spy decided to *lay* low for a while; she had learned that the enemy had *laid* a trap for her.

3. We couldn't have *chose* a worse day for our hike; by the time we finished I was nearly *froze.*

4. You must *rise* early tomorrow; any good fisherman is on the lake by the time the sun has *rose.*

5. For some reason or other, not all of the pickled eels that Mr. Haslic *brought* to the picnic were *ate.*

6. Although he had never *rode* a horse in his life, Jerry bravely *swung* himself into the saddle.

7. The sun has *shone* brightly ever since it *burst* out from behind the early morning clouds.

8. "I *been* around the world twice and have *seen* just about everything worth seeing," he replied.

9. "Why don't you *lay* down your books and then *lay* down for a short rest?" asked Dotty.

10. After breakfast one of the young girls *come* running to the camp nurse and reported that a bee had *stung* her.

11. The stranger got out of the car, *crept* slowly to the porch, and *lay* the mysterious package on the top step.

12. Mother had just *laid* down for a nap when someone *rang* the doorbell.

13. Yesterday some of the islanders *begun* to salvage cargo from the ship that *sank* in the bay.

14. As soon as the visitors had *gone* through the gate, we *set* on the porch and laughed.

15. Crawford rushed to the control room and *threw* the emergency switch, and warning bells *rung* out in the factory.

16. That huge jet *setting* on the runway has just *flown* in from Tokyo.

17. The parachute was *caught* in a tall tree, and the pilot *hanged* there about thirty feet from the ground.

18. "Your skis have been *laying* on the garage floor ever since you *laid* them there two days ago," complained Dad.

19. The official photographer has *taken* several pictures of the distinguished guests *setting* at the head table.

20. After the rescued swimmer had *drank* some hot tea, he *begun* to feel better.

LESSON
21 Using Verbs Correctly: Subject–Verb Agreement

I earn	We earn
You earn	You earn
He, She, It earns	They earn

EXAMINE this conjugation and observe that in the present tense the third-person singular form (*He, She, It earns*) differs from the third-person plural (*They earn*). This change we call a change in number: **Singular number** means that only one thing is talked about; **plural number** means that more than one thing is talked about. Notice how verbs and nouns differ in this respect: The *s* ending on nouns is a plural marker, but on verbs it designates the singular form.

The following examples show how the number of the subject (one or more than one) affects the form of the verb. The verbs *have, do,* and *be* are important because they have auxiliary uses as well as main-verb uses. *Be* is an exceptional verb; it changes form in the past tense as well as in the present tense.

SINGULAR	PLURAL
She *walks* slowly.	They *walk* slowly.
Mother *seems* pleased.	My parents *seem* pleased.
Mary *has* a new dress.	All of the girls *have* new dresses.
He *has traveled* widely.	They *have traveled* widely.
She *does* her work easily.	They *do* their work easily.
Does he *have* enough time?	*Do* they *have* enough time?
He *is* a friend of mine.	They *are* friends of mine.
My brother *is coming* home.	My brothers *are coming* home.
His camera *was taken* from him.	Their cameras *were taken* from them.

The relation of verb form to subject follows an important principle of usage: **The verb always agrees in number with its subject.** Although the principle is simple, some of the situations in which it applies are not. You will avoid some common writing errors if you keep in mind the following seven extensions of the principle. The first is probably the most necessary.

1. The number of the verb is not affected by material that comes between it and the subject. Determine the *real* subject of the verb; watch out for intervening words that might mislead you. Remember that the number of the verb is not altered when other nouns are attached to the subject by means of prepositions such as *in addition to, together with, as well as, with, along with.* Remember also that indefinite pronoun subjects like *either, neither, each, one, everyone, no one, somebody* take singular verbs:

Immediate *settlement* of these problems *is* [not *are*] vital. [The subject is *settlement*. *Problems*, being here the object of the preposition *of*, cannot also be a subject.]

The *cost* of replacing the asbestos shingles with cedar shakes *was* [not *were*] considerable.

Tact, as well as patience, *is* [not *are*] required.

Mr. Sheldon, together with several other division heads, *has* [not *have*] left.

Each of the plans *has* [not *have*] its good points.
Is [not *Are*] *either* of the contestants ready?

None may take either a singular or a plural verb, depending on whether the writer wishes to emphasize "not one" or "no members" of the group:

None of us *is* [or *are*] perfect.

2. A verb agrees with its subject even when the subject follows the verb. Be especially careful to find the real subject in sentences starting with *there:*

Behind these gates *stands* one *guard*. [*Guard stands.*]
Behind these gates *stand* three *guards*. [*Guards stand.*]
He handed us a piece of paper on which *was* scribbled a *warning*. [*Warning was* scribbled.]
There *was* barely enough *time* remaining.
There *were* only ten *minutes* remaining.
There *seems* to be an extra *player* on the field.
There *seem* to be some extra *players* on the field.

3. Compound subjects joined by *and* take a plural verb:

A little *boy* and his *dog were* playing in the yard.
On the platform *were* a *table* and four *chairs*.

But the verb should be singular if the subjects joined by *and* are thought of as a single thing, or if the subjects are considered separately, as when they are modified by *every* or *each:*

Plain *vinegar* and *oil is* all the dressing my salad needs. [One thing.]
Every *man* and every *woman is* asked to help. [Considered separately.]

4. Singular subjects joined by *or* or *nor* take singular verbs:

Either a *raincoat* or an *umbrella is* advisable.
Neither *he* nor his *assistant is* ever on time.
Was either *China* or *India* represented at the conference?

In some sentences of this pattern, especially in questions like the last example, a plural verb is sometimes used, both in casual conversation and in writing. In serious and formal writing, the singular verb is considered appropriate.

If the subjects joined by *or* or *nor* differ in number, the verb agrees with the subject nearer to it:

Neither the *mother* nor the two *boys were* able to identify him.
Either the *players* or the *coach is* responsible for the defeat.

5. Plural nouns of amount, distance, and so on, when they are used as singular units of measurement, take singular verbs:

A hundred *dollars was* once paid for a single tulip bulb.
Thirty *miles seems* like a long walk to me.
Seven *years* in prison *was* the penalty that he had to pay.

6. A collective noun is considered singular when the group is regarded as a unit; it is plural when the individuals of the group are referred to. Similarly words like *number, all, rest, part, some, more, most, half* are singular or plural, depending on the meaning intended. A word of this type is often accompanied by a modifier or referred to by a pronoun, either of which gives a clue to the number intended. When the word *number* is a subject, it is considered singular if it is preceded by *the* and plural if it is preceded by *a:*

The *audience is* very enthusiastic tonight.
The *audience are* returning to their seats.[Notice pronoun *their.*]
The *band is* playing a rousing march.
Now the *band are* putting away their instruments. [Again note *their.*]
Most of the book *is* blatant propaganda.
Most of my friends *are* happy about the election.
The *rest* of the lecture *was* dull.
The *rest* of the cars *are* on sale.
The *number* of accidents *is* increasing.
A *number* of the officers *are* resigning.

7. When the subject is a relative pronoun, the antecedent of the pronoun determines the number (and person) of the verb:

He told a joke *that was* pointless. [*Joke was.*]
He told several jokes *that were* pointless. [*Jokes were.*]
I paid the expenses of the trip, *which were* minimal. [*Expenses were.*]
Jack is one of those boys *who enjoy* fierce competition.

The last example, sometimes called the "one of those . . . who" sentence, is particularly troublesome. Generally we find a plural verb used. If we recast the sentence to read "Of those boys who enjoy fierce competition, Jack is one," it becomes clear that the logical antecedent of *who* is the plural noun *boys.* However, usage is divided. And notice that a singular verb must be used when the pattern is altered slightly:

Jack is the only *one* of my friends *who enjoys* fierce competition.

Because a relative pronoun subject nearly always has an antecedent that is third-person singular or third-person plural, we are accustomed to pronoun–verb combinations like these:

A boy *who is* . . .
Boys *who are* . . .
A man *who knows* . . .
Men *who know* . . .

But in those occasional sentences in which a relative pronoun subject has an antecedent that is in the first or second person, meticulously correct usage calls for subject–verb combinations like the following:

I, *who am* in charge here, should pay the bill. [*I . . . am.*]
They should ask me, *who know* all the answers. [*I . . . know.*]

You, *who are* in charge here, should pay the bill. [*You . . . are.*]
They should ask you, *who know* all the answers. [*You . . . know.*]

Using Verbs Correctly: Subject–Verb Agreement

NAME _____ SCORE _____

DIRECTIONS: These sentences are examples of structures that often lead to errors of subject–verb agreement. In the space at the left, copy the correct verb from within the parentheses. In each sentence the subject of the verb is printed in bold type.

_____ 1. The **decision** to suspend operations at four money-losing mills (is, are) affecting hundreds of families.

_____ 2. The study shows that the **percentage** of our graduates who earn college degrees (has, have) increased steadily.

_____ 3. There (is, are) many **indications** that the new legislature will be a conservative one.

_____ 4. High on the list of building priorities (is, are) the **construction** of playing fields and swimming pools for the inner city.

_____ 5. Neither the summer **heat** nor his advanced **years** (seems, seem) to slow down Mr. Watson.

_____ 6. Neither his advanced **years** nor the summer **heat** (seems, seem) to slow down Mr. Watson.

_____ 7. (Has, Have) **either** of your two supervisors mentioned anything about early retirement?

_____ 8. Not **one** of the stocks your broker recommended to my wife and me (has, have) increased in value.

_____ 9. A total **disregard** for the rights of other students (gives, give) your reform group a bad name.

_____ 10. A long **record** of reforms and social changes (makes, make) Thompson the favorite for reelection.

_____ 11. **Ms. Sherwood,** along with most of the other division heads, (has, have) decided to boycott the meeting.

_____ 12. **One** of the rarely mentioned causes of air pollution in this area (is, are) the dust particles carried by wind from the desert.

_____ 13. Either **Ms. Seely** or **one** of her associates (stays, stay) in the office during the lunch hour.

_____ 14. Not one **penny** from the last two state budgets (has, have) been spent on special-education classes.

_____ 15. The officer told the reporters that there (seems, seem) to be some **evidence** of foul play.

DIRECTIONS: If you find an error in subject–verb agreement, underline the incorrect verb and write the correct form in the space at the left. Circle the subject of every verb you correct. Some of the sentences may be correct.

1. The speaker emphasized the fact that electricity and natural gas, the cleanest of the modern fuels available, has no sulfur problems.

2. She showed us a scroll on which was recorded the awards and honors that she had won in her long career of public service.

3. The judge ruled that neither Hal nor his brother have any legitimate claim on the reward money.

4. Our records show that the bill of sale, together with a receipt for the final payment, were mailed to you on July 10.

5. Not far from our new condominium is a well-stocked supermarket, a garage, and a branch library.

6. Among my problems during the first few weeks of boot camp was my inability to make new friends easily.

7. Either the treasurer or someone else authorized to pay the club's bills have to be insured and bonded.

8. It's true, isn't it, that the sale of tickets for this season's basketball games have declined?

9. With a flourish the magician produced the two playing cards, on both of which were the mark I had made with red ink.

10. Does either the back door or the window in the reception room show signs of having been tampered with?

11. The additional cost of transporting several assistants on these foreign junkets has been criticized by some commentators.

12. Our team claimed the victory, but in our hearts there were neither pride in our methods nor any real sense of accomplishment.

13. But haven't you and the claims adjuster agreed that ninety dollars is the amount needed for repairs?

14. There was, according to several informants, good reasons for the outbreak of protests and riots.

15. In these reports the danger of sending back into rivers the superheated water from nuclear plants has been minimized.

EXERCISE **39**

Using Verbs Correctly: Subject–Verb Agreement

NAME _____ SCORE _____

DIRECTIONS: These sentences are examples of structures that often lead to errors of subject–verb agreement. In the space at the left, copy the correct form from within the parentheses. In each sentence the subject of the verb is printed in bold type.

_____ 1. **No one** except members of Congress and U.S. Supreme Court justices (is, are) invited to attend the ceremony.

_____ 2. Jerry has two home computers, **neither** of which (has, have) yet been paid for.

_____ 3. The **number** of arrests for driving without a license (has, have) increased lately.

_____ 4. A **number** of my close friends (has, have) offered to lend me the money.

_____ 5. Ninety **dollars** (is, are) more than I usually pay for a pair of running shoes.

_____ 6. On the platform (was, were) a **lectern** and a dozen **chairs** for the honored guests.

_____ 7. Ms. Jensen's **account** of her narrow escape from the rebellious natives of the island always (fascinates, fascinate) youthful audiences.

_____ 8. The **complexity** of the economic and social problems facing these developing countries (demands, demand) strong leadership.

_____ 9. To be included in the plans for the new annex (is, are) a **gymnasium** for girl students, in addition to a dozen staff offices.

_____ 10. Seated across the aisle from us (was, were) a talkative **woman** and two equally noisy **children.**

_____ 11. We have been told that there (is, are) only a few **tickets** available for the big game.

_____ 12. (Has, Have) **anyone** in this room seen Dr. Long's briefcase?

_____ 13. Slightly injured in the collision (was, were) the truck **driver** and two **passengers** in the other car.

_____ 14. At the new center the **variety** of activities for senior citizens (is, are) impressive.

_____ 15. Because a heavy snowstorm is predicted, (doesn't, don't) **it** seem sensible to postpone our trip?

DIRECTIONS: If you find an error in subject–verb agreement, underline the incorrect verb and write the correct form in the space at the left. Circle the subject of every verb you correct. Some of the sentences may be correct.

_____ 1. Nine weeks does seem to me to be a long enough period for you to complete your term paper.

_____ 2. The identity of the injured people and of the other passengers have not yet been made public.

_____ 3. Only one of my last six term papers have received a decent grade.

_____ 4. Is there any other matters you'd like to bring up before I adjourn the meeting?

_____ 5. Transferring student fees from cultural activities to athletics has brought about vigorous protests.

_____ 6. Neither my older sister nor I play a musical instrument.

_____ 7. Neither my older sister nor my brother plays a musical instrument.

_____ 8. One thing Lewis neglected to mention in his application letter were his five arrests for reckless driving.

_____ 9. The suggestion to increase the sales tax to provide funds for the greater number of retirees are being opposed by many.

_____ 10. The number of home video units our store has sold this month has increased greatly.

_____ 11. The annual influx of transient workers seeking jobs picking fruit in the local orchards always place added burdens on our schools.

_____ 12. The pilot, together with three of his passengers, were injured.

_____ 13. One or the other of the two proposals you submitted are certain to be accepted.

_____ 14. Fortunately, strengthening the engine supports on the older planes seems to have solved the problem.

_____ 15. Not one of the dozens of cars stolen from our streets this month have yet been recovered.

LESSON

22 Using Pronouns Correctly: Reference and Agreement

A PRONOUN is a word that substitutes for a noun or another pronoun. The word for which a pronoun stands is called its **antecedent:**

I invited *Joan,* but *she* could not attend. [*She* substitutes for *Joan. Joan* is the antecedent of *she.*]

Because *Joan and Mary* were on vacation, I did not see *them.* [The antecedent of *them* is the plural unit *Joan and Mary.*]

I have lost *my* wristwatch.

One of the boys lost *his* wristwatch.

Two of the boys lost *their* wristwatches.

In order to use pronouns effectively and without confusing your reader, you must follow two basic principles:

1. You must establish a clear, easily identified relationship between a pronoun and its antecedent.

2. You must make the pronoun and its antecedent agree in person, number, and gender.

Let us examine these requirements more fully.

1. Personal pronouns should have definite antecedents and should be placed as near their antecedents as possible. Your readers should know exactly what a pronoun stands for. They should not be made to look through several sentences for its antecedent, nor should they be asked to manufacture an antecedent for it. When you discover in your writing a pronoun with no clear and unmistakable antecedent, your revision, as many of the following examples demonstrate, will often require rewriting to remove the faulty pronoun from your sentence:

FAULTY: A strange car followed us closely, and *he* kept blinking his lights at us.

IMPROVED: A strange car followed us closely, and the driver kept blinking his lights at us.

FAULTY: Although Jenny was a real sports fan, her brother never became interested in *them.*

IMPROVED: Although Jenny really liked sports, her brother never became interested in them.

FAULTY: Jack is a good piano player, although he has had no formal training in *it.*

IMPROVED: Jack is a good piano player, although he has had no formal training in music.

The indefinite *you* or *they* is quite common in speech and in chatty, informal writing, but one should avoid using either in serious writing:

FAULTY: In Alaska *they* catch huge king crabs.

IMPROVED: In Alaska huge king crabs are caught. [Often the best way to correct an indefinite *they* or *you* sentence is to use a passive verb.]

FAULTY: Before the reform measures were passed, *you* had few rights.

IMPROVED: Before the reform measures were passed, people had few rights.

Before the reform measures were passed, one had few rights.

FAULTY: At the placement office *they* told me to get three recommendations.

IMPROVED: A clerk at the placement office told me to get three recommendations.
At the placement office I was told to get three recommendations.

A pronoun should not appear to refer equally well to either of two antecedents:

FAULTY: Bob told Jim that *he* was getting bald. [Which one was getting bald?]
IMPROVED: "You are getting bald," said Bob to Jim. [In sentences of this type, the direct quotation is sometimes the only possible correction.]

The "it says" introduction to statements, although common in informal language, is objectionable in serious writing:

FAULTY: *It* says on the bottle that the chemical will kill weeds but not grass.
IMPROVED: The directions on the bottle say that the chemical will kill weeds but not grass.
FAULTY: *It* said on the morning news program that a bad storm is coming.
IMPROVED: According to the morning news program, a bad storm is coming.

(See Supplement 1.)
Avoid vague or ambiguous reference of relative and demonstrative pronouns:

FAULTY: Only twenty people attended the lecture, *which* was due to poor publicity.
IMPROVED: Because of poor publicity, only twenty people attended the lecture.
FAULTY: Good writers usually have large vocabularies, and *this* is why I get poor grades on my themes.
IMPROVED: I get poor grades on my themes because my vocabulary is inadequate; good writers usually have large vocabularies.

A special situation relates to the antecedent of the pronouns *which, this,* and *that.* In a sentence such as "The children giggled, *which* annoyed the teacher" or "The children giggled, and *this* annoyed the teacher," the thing that annoyed the teacher is not the *children* but "the giggling of the children" or "the fact that the children giggled." This kind of reference to a preceding idea rather than to an expressed noun is unobjectionable provided that the meaning is instantly and unmistakably clear. But you should avoid sentences like the following. In the first one readers would be hard pressed to discover exactly what the *which* means, and in the second they must decide whether the antecedent is the preceding idea or the noun immediately preceding the *which:*

FAULTY: Hathaway's application was rejected because he spells poorly, *which* is very important in an application letter.
IMPROVED: Hathaway's application was rejected because he spells poorly; correct spelling is very important in an application letter.
FAULTY: The defense attorney did not object to the judge's concluding remark, *which* surprised me.
IMPROVED: I was surprised that the defense attorney did not object to the judge's concluding remark.

2. Pronouns should agree with their antecedents in person, number, and gender. The following chart classifies for you the three forms of each personal pronoun on the basis of person, number, and gender:

	SINGULAR	PLURAL
1st person	[the person speaking] *I, my, me*	[the persons speaking] *we, our, us*
2nd person	[the person spoken to] *you, your, you*	[the persons spoken to] *you, your, you*

| 3rd person | [the person or thing spoken of]
he, his, him
she, her, her
it, its, it | [the persons or things spoken of]

they, their, them |

A singular antecedent is referred to by a singular pronoun; a plural antecedent is referred to by a plural pronoun.

> Jack says that *he* is sure that *his* new investment will pay *him* well.
> Jack and Joan say that *they* are sure that *their* new investment will pay *them* well.

This principle of logical pronoun agreement is not as simple as these two examples might suggest. Recent language practices have given rise to two situations for which "rules" that apply in every instance cannot possibly be made. Student writers must, first of all, be aware of certain changing ideas about pronoun usage; then they must prepare themselves to make decisions among the choices available.

The first of these two troublesome situations relates to some of the indefinite pronouns: *one, everyone, someone, no one, anyone, anybody, everybody, somebody, nobody, each, either,* and *neither.* These words have generally been felt to be singular; hence pronouns referring to them have customarily been singular and, unless the antecedent specifies otherwise, masculine. Singular pronouns have also been used in formal writing and speaking to refer to noun antecedents modified by singular qualifiers such as *each* and *every.* The four following examples illustrate the traditional, formal practice:

> Everybody has *his* faults and *his* virtues.
> Each of the sons is doing what *he* thinks is best.
> England expects every man to do *his* duty.
> No one succeeds in this firm if Dobbins doesn't like *him.*

The principal difficulty with this usage is that these indefinites, although regarded by strict grammarians as singular in form, carry with them a group or plural sense, with the result that people are often unsure whether pronouns referring to them should be singular or plural. Despite traditional pronouncements, every day we hear sentences of the "Everyone-will-do-*their*-best" type. Beginning writers, however, would do well to follow the established practice until they feel relatively secure about recognizing the occasional sentence in which a singular pronoun referring to an indefinite produces a strained or unnatural effect even though it does agree in form with its antecedent.

Closely related to this troublesome matter of pronoun agreement is a second problem, this one dealing with gender. The problem is this: What reference words should be used to refer to such a word as *student?* Obviously there are female students and there are male students. With plural nouns there is no problem: *they, their,* and *them* refer to both masculine and feminine. But for singular nouns the language provides *she, her, her* and *he, his, him* but not a pronoun to refer to third-person singular words that contain both male and female members.

Here again, as with the reference to third-person singular indefinites, the traditional practice has been to use masculine singular pronouns. Eighty or so years ago Henry James wrote the following sentence: "We must grant the artist his subject, his idea, his *donné:* our criticism is applied only to what he makes of it." In James's day that sentence was undoubtedly looked upon as unexceptionable; the pronouns followed what was then standard practice. But attitudes have changed. In the 1980's, if that sentence got past the eyes of an editor and appeared on the printed page, its implication that artists are exclusively male would make the sentence unacceptably discriminatory to many readers.

Reliance on the *he-or-she* pronoun forms is an increasingly popular solution to some of these worrisome problems of pronoun reference. The *he-or-she* forms agree in number with the third-person singular indefinites. And the use of these forms obviates any possible charge of gender preference. However, a piling up of *he-or-she's*, *his-or-her's*, and *him-or-her's* is undesirable. (Notice the cumbersome result, for instance, if a *he-or-she* form is substituted for all four of the third-person singular masculine pronouns in the Henry James sentence.)

Here is a very important point for you to remember: When you are worried about a third-person singular masculine pronoun you have written, either because its reference to an indefinite antecedent sounds not quite right to you or because it shows an undesirable gender preference, you can remove the awkwardness, in nearly every instance that arises, by changing the antecedent to a plural noun, to which you then refer by using *they*, *their*, and *them*.

By way of summary, study these four versions of a sentence as they relate to the two problems just discussed:

> Every member of the graduating class, if *he* wishes, may have *his* diploma mailed to *him* after August 15. [This usage reflects traditional practice that is still quite widely followed. The objection to it is that the reference words are exclusively masculine.]
>
> Every member of the graduating class, if *he or she* wishes, may have *his or her* diploma mailed to *him or her* after August 15. [The singular reference is satisfactory, but the avoidance of masculine reference has resulted in clumsy wordiness.]
>
> Every member of the graduating class, if *they* wish, may have *their* diplomas mailed to *them* after August 15. [This version, particularly if used in spoken English, would probably not offend many people, but the lack of proper number agreement between the pronouns and the antecedent would rule out its appearance in edited material.]
>
> Members of the graduating class, if *they* wish, may have *their* diplomas mailed to *them* after August 15. [In this version the pronouns are logical and correct in both number and gender.]

A few other matters of pronoun reference, mercifully quite uncomplicated, should be called to your attention. If a pronoun refers to a compound unit or to a collective noun, the pronoun is singular or plural depending on the number of the antecedent. (See Lesson 21.)

> Both she and her daughter have changed the color of *their* hair.
> Either Tom or Floyd will bring *his* camera.
> The rest of the lecture had somehow lost *its* point.
> The rest of the women will receive *their* paychecks when new funds arrive.

An antecedent in the third person should not be referred to by *you*. This misuse develops when writers, forgetting that they have established the third person in the sentence, shift the structure and begin to talk directly to the reader:

> FAULTY: In a large university a *freshman* can feel lost if *you* have grown up in a small town.
> If a *person* really wants to become an expert golfer, *you* must practice every day.
>
> IMPROVED: In a large university a freshman can feel lost if *he or she* has grown up in a small town.
> If a person really wants to become an expert golfer, *she or he* must practice every day.

Supplement 1

At this point you should be reminded that *it* without an antecedent has some uses that are completely acceptable in both formal and informal English. One of these is in the delayed subject or object pattern. (See Lesson 10.) Another is its use as a kind of filler word in expressions having to do with weather, time, distance, and so forth.

It is fortunate that you had a spare tire.
I find *it* difficult to believe Ted's story.
It is cold today; *it* snowed last night.
It is twelve o'clock; *it* is almost time for lunch.
How far is *it* to Phoenix?

EXERCISE 40
Using Pronouns Correctly: Reference and Agreement

DIRECTIONS: In the space at the left, copy the correct pronoun, or pronoun–verb combination, from within the parentheses. Circle in the sentence the antecedent of the pronoun.

_____   1. We all agreed that nobody in (his or her, their) right mind would try to smuggle uncut diamonds into the country.

_____   2. The newly formed Lakeside Improvement Club will hold (its, it's, their) first meeting next Thursday.

_____   3. It's quite rare to find a father over fifty who freely admits that (he was, they were) once young and rebellious.

_____   4. Sheldon's Upholstery Shop has lost (its, it's, their) lease and must move to new quarters.

_____   5. "Viewing the Grand Canyon from the air certainly makes a person realize how insignificant (you are, he is)," said Mrs. Dow to her husband.

_____   6. A student who wants to drop a course must have the permission of (his or her, your, their) adviser.

_____   7. Cy never admits his mistakes; he usually finds some way to blame someone else for (it, them).

_____   8. Not one of the dozens of people reached by the survey admitted that (he or she, they) had sat through to the end of the telecast.

_____   9. "At this camp we teach a boy how to survive and how to take care of (himself, themself, themselves) in the forest," said Chuck.

_____   10. No one likes to admit that (she or he has, you have, they have) been cheated in a business deal.

_____   11. The local retail clerks' union has an emergency educational fund, to be drawn on by children of (its, it's, their) members.

_____   12. "The first thing I teach one of my boys," said the boxing coach, "is how to protect (himself, theirself, themself)."

_____   13. "Whoever did the overhaul job on your car surely knew what (he was, they were) doing," said the owner of the garage.

_____   14. "In my day," said Grandfather, "we were taught that, if one wanted to sing and dance, (he, you, they) had to pay the piper."

_____   15. Every one of these young men seems to believe that (he, you, they) will never grow old.

DIRECTIONS: Each sentence contains at least one reference word that is poorly used. In the space at the left, copy the pronoun or pronouns that have vague or incorrect reference. In the space below each sentence, rewrite enough of the sentence to make the meaning clear.

_____ 1. Dean Lee always tells anyone showing an interest in a career in journalism that they have to be really tough to become a good one.

_____ 2. It says in this brochure that whoever wants a copy of the annual report can get one if you send a self-addressed envelope.

_____ 3. On the early morning broadcast they reported that yesterday they had an earthquake in Chile.

_____ 4. All through school Al indicated that he wanted to be a teacher, despite his father's reminders that you can't earn much money from it.

_____ 5. If anyone is dissatisfied with the magazine, you can send back your first copy and get a refund.

_____ 6. Motorists going through Elmhurst should be reminded that they give you a ticket if you go over thirty miles an hour.

_____ 7. The company has had a few lean years, I admit, but right now their prospects are favorable.

_____ 8. One good thing about Upland Acres: any skier, regardless of their proficiency, can find a slope that fits their needs.

_____ 9. Fred told his younger brother that he has few close friends because he is too critical of others.

_____ 10. If a stranger to these parts leaves their car parked on the street overnight, in the morning they often find that they have hauled it away.

EXERCISE 41
Using Pronouns Correctly: Reference and Agreement

NAME _____   SCORE _____

DIRECTIONS: One sentence in each of the following pairs is correct, and the other contains at least one reference word that is poorly used. In the space at the left, write the letter that identifies the correct sentence. In the other sentence, circle the pronoun or pronouns that have vague or incorrect reference.

_____   1. A. For the second time in four months, the Holcombs' summer home was broken into, and this time they took most of her jewelry.
              B. For the second time in four months, the Holcombs' summer home was broken into, and this time most of Mrs. Holcomb's jewelry was taken.

_____   2. A. As my father is a doctor, I have always admired doctors and intend to make medicine my life work.
              B. As my father is a doctor, I have always admired them and intend to make it my life work.

_____   3. A. All outgoing flights were canceled because, according to the weather report, there were bad storms west of Chicago.
              B. All outgoing flights were canceled because it said in the weather report that they were having bad storms west of Chicago.

_____   4. A. Anyone who has been a heavy smoker should be given love and understanding when they give it up.
              B. Anyone who has been a heavy smoker should be given love and understanding when he or she gives up smoking.

_____   5. A. In this unhappy country, they often throw you into jail and then they forget all about you.
              B. In this unhappy country, people are often thrown into jail and then forgotten.

_____   6. A. It was a tough test; apparently they expected you to have memorized the entire textbook.
              B. It was a tough test; apparently one was expected to have memorized the entire textbook.

_____   7. A. If someone calls while I am gone, have her or him leave a number and I'll return the call later.
              B. If someone calls while I am gone, have them leave their number and I'll return it later.

_____   8. A. How should a girl respond when she greets a long-lost boyfriend who then calls her by the wrong name?
              B. How should a girl respond when she greets a long-lost boyfriend and then they call you by the wrong name?

_____   9. A. The oncoming truck sent glaring, blinding light into our eyes, and he didn't dim them as we passed.
              B. The oncoming truck sent glaring, blinding light into our eyes, and the driver didn't dim the headlights as we passed.

_____ 10. A. The soft drink machine on the fourth floor of the dormitory is broken; a student now has to go down to the lobby if he or she wants a soft drink.

   B. The soft drink machine on the fourth floor of the dormitory is broken; a student now has to go down to the lobby if they want one.

_____ 11. A. According to the notice on the bulletin board this morning, all students must pay their fees by next Friday.

   B. On the bulletin board this morning, it said that every student must pay their fees by next Friday.

_____ 12. A. We inquired about accommodations, and they told us that every unit at the motel was taken.

   B. We inquired about accommodations and were told that every unit at the motel was taken.

_____ 13. A. The supervisor told Larry that he had a good chance of being promoted.

   B. The supervisor said to Larry, "You have a good chance of being promoted."

_____ 14. A. Can you blame me for complaining when, after standing in this line for three hours, I am told that there are no more tickets?

   B. Can you blame me for complaining when, after standing in this line for three hours, they tell me that they have no more tickets?

_____ 15. A. Senator Bliss has introduced two tax bills, neither of which has much to recommend them.

   B. Senator Bliss has introduced two tax bills, neither of which has much to recommend it.

LESSON

23   Using Pronouns Correctly: Case

IN LESSON 22 a chart classified the forms of the personal pronouns on the basis of person, number, and gender. For each pronoun the three forms that were listed—first-person singular, *I, my, me;* third-person plural, *they, their, them;* and so on—illustrate the three case forms. *I* and *they* are nominative, *my* and *their* are possessive, and *me* and *them* are objective, for example.

The way you use these pronouns in everyday language, in sentences such as "Two of *my* books have disappeared; *they* cost *me* twenty dollars, and *I* must find *them*," shows you that the case form you choose depends on how the word is used within the sentence. In this lesson we shall examine some spots where the wrong choice of pronoun form is possible.

The only words in modern English that retain distinctions between nominative and objective case forms are a few pronouns. These two forms are identical in nouns, and the correct use of the distinctive form, the possessive, requires essentially only a knowledge of how the apostrophe is used. (See Lesson 18.)

Here are the pronouns arranged according to their case forms. The first eight are the personal pronouns; notice that the only distinctive form of *you* and *it* is the possessive. The last two pronouns, which we shall examine separately from the personal pronouns, are used only in questions and in subordinate clauses.

Nominative	*Possessive*	*Objective*
I	my, mine	me
you	your, yours	you
he	his, his	him
she	her, hers	her
it	its, its	it
we	our, ours	us
you	your, yours	you
they	their, theirs	them
who	whose	whom
whoever	whosever	whomever

The **possessive case** is used to show possession. Three possible trouble spots should be noted.

1. The preceding chart shows two possessive forms for the personal pronouns. The first form for each pronoun is used as a *modifier* of a noun. The second form is used as a nominal; in other words, it fills a noun slot, such as the subject, the complement, or the object of a preposition:

> This is *your* umbrella; *mine* has a white handle.
> Mary found *my* books, but one of *hers* is still missing.
> *Their* team was faster, but the final victory was *ours.*

2. The indefinite pronouns use an apostrophe to form the possessive case: *everybody's* duty, *one's* lifetime, *everyone's* hopes, someone *else's* car. But the personal pronouns do not:

> These seats are *ours* [not *our's*]. *Yours* [not *Your's*] are in the next row.

Learn to distinguish carefully between the following possessives and contractions that are pronounced alike: *its* (possessive), *it's* (it is, it has); *theirs* (possessive), *there's* (there is, there has); *their* (possessive), *they're* (they are); *whose* (possessive), *who's* (who is, who has); *your* (possessive), *you're* (you are):

> *It's* obvious that the car has outworn *its* usefulness.
> *There's* new evidence that *they're* changing *their* tactics.

3. Formal usage prefers the possessive form of pronouns (occasionally of nouns also) preceding gerunds in constructions like the following:

> The teacher objected to *my* [not *me*] addressing the student body.
> Al's injury certainly contributed to *our* [not *us*] losing the game.

The rules governing the uses of the other two cases are very simple.
A pronoun is in the **nominative case** when it is used:

1. As a subject: *I* know that *he* is honest.
2. As a subjective complement: This is *she* speaking.
3. As an appositive of a nominative noun: *We* children ate the ice cream.

A pronoun is in the **objective case** when it is used:

1. As an object of a verb or verbal: John gave·*me* the key. I enjoyed meeting *them*.
2. As an object of a preposition: No one except *me* knew the answer.
3. As the subject of an infinitive: The policeman ordered *me* to halt.
4. As an appositive of an objective noun: Two of *us* children ate the ice cream.

We need not examine in detail every one of these applications. As one grows up using the English language, he or she learns that such usages as "*Them* arrived late" and "I spoke to *she*" do not conform to the system of the language. Instead, we should examine the trouble spots where confusion may arise. When we use the personal pronouns, we must exercise care in the following situations:

1. When the pronoun follows *and* (sometimes *or*) as part of a compound unit, determine its use in the sentence and choose the appropriate case form. The temptation here is usually to use the nominative, although the last example in the following list shows a trouble spot where the objective case is sometimes misused. Test these troublesome constructions by using the pronoun by itself, and you will probably discover which form is the correct one:

> The man gave Sue and *me* some candy. [Not Sue and *I*. Both words are indirect objects. Apply the test. Notice how strange "The man gave . . . *I* some candy" sounds.]
> Send your check to either my lawyer or *me*. [Not "to . . . *I*."]
> Have you seen Bob or *her* lately? [Direct objects require the objective case.]
> Just between you and *me*, the lecture was a bore. [Never say "between you and *I*." Both pronouns are objects of the preposition *between*. If this set phrase is a problem for you, find the correct form by reversing the pronouns: You would never say "between I and you."]
> Mrs. Estes took *him* and *me* to school. [Not *he* and *I* or *him* and *I*. Both pronouns are direct objects.]
> Will my sister and *I* be invited? [Not *me*. The subject is *sister* and *I*.]

2. In comparisons after *as* and *than*, when the pronoun is the subject of an understood verb, use the nominative form:

> He is taller than *I* [*am*]. I am older than *he* [*is*].
> Can you talk as fast as *she* [*can talk*]? No one knew more about art than *he* [*did*].

Sentences like these nearly always call for nominative case subjects. Occasionally the meaning of a sentence may demand an objective pronoun. Both of the following sentences are correct; notice the difference in meaning:

> You apparently trust Mr. Alton more than *I*. [The meaning is ". . . more than I (trust Mr. Alton").]
> You apparently trust Mr. Alton more than *me*. [The meaning here is ". . . more than (you trust) me."]

3. Ordinarily use the nominative form for the subjective complement. The specific problem here concerns such expressions as *It's me* or *It is I*, *It was they* or *It was them*. Many people say *It's me*, but they would hesitate to say *It was her*, *It was him*, or *It was them*, instead of *It was she*, *It was he*, or *It was they*. However, this is a problem that does not arise often in the writing of students. The following are examples of correct formal usage:

> It is *I*.
> It could have been *he*.
> Was it *she?*
> Was it *they* who called?

4. See that the appositive is in the same case as the word that it refers to. Notice particularly the first three examples that follow. This usage employing *we* and *us* as an appositive modifier preceding a noun is a real trouble spot:

> *We* boys were hired. [The unit *We boys* is the subject and requires the nominative.]
> Two of *us* boys were hired. [The object of a preposition requires the objective case.]
> Mr. Elder hired *us* boys. [Not *we boys* for a direct object.]
> Two boys—you and *I*—will be hired. [In apposition with the subject.]
> Mr. Elder will hire two boys—you and *me*. [In apposition with the object.]

The only other pronouns in standard modern English that have distinctive nominative and objective forms are *who/whom* and *whoever/whomever*. The rules that apply to the personal pronouns apply to these words as well: In the subject position *who/whoever* should be used; in the direct object position *whom/whomever* should be used; and so forth. (These pronouns, it should be noted, are never used as appositives.)

The special problem in the application of the case rules to these words comes from their special use as interrogatives and as subordinating words. As you learned in Lessons 6, 9, and 10, these words, because they serve as signal words, always stand at the beginning of their clauses. To locate the grammatical function of the pronoun within its clause, you must examine the clause to determine the normal subject–verb–complement positioning.

1. In formal usage, *whom* is required when it is a direct object or the object of a preposition, even though it stands ahead of its subject and verb:

> *Whom* did Mr. Long hire? [If you are troubled by this sort of construction, try substituting a personal pronoun and placing it after the verb, where it normally comes: "Did Mr. Long hire *him?*" You would never say "Did Mr. Long hire *he?*" The transitive verb *hire* requires a direct object pronoun in the objective case.]
> He is a boy *whom* everyone can like. [*Whom* is the object of *can like.*]
> Wilson was the man *whom* everybody trusted. [Everybody trusted *whom.*]
> She is the girl *whom* Mother wants me to marry. [Object of the verbal *to marry.*]
> *Whom* are you going with? [With *whom* are you going?]
> *Whom* was she speaking to just then? [To *whom* was she speaking?]

2. When *who(m)* or *who(m)ever* begins a subordinate clause that follows a verb or a preposition, the use of the pronoun *within its own clause* determines its case form:

> Do you know *who* sent Jane the flowers? [*Who* is the subject of *sent*, not the direct object of *do know*.]
>
> No one knows *who* the intruder was. [*Who* is the subjective complement in the noun clause.]
>
> No one knows *whom* the mayor will appoint. [The objective form *whom* is used because it is the direct object of *will appoint*. The direct object of *knows* is the whole noun clause.]
>
> I will sell the car to *whoever* offers the best price. [The whole clause, *whoever offers the best price*, is the object of the preposition *to*. A subject of a verb must be in the nominative case.]

3. When the pronoun subject is followed by a parenthetical insertion like *do you think, I suspect, everyone believes*, or *we know*, the nominative case form must be used:

> *Who* do you think *is* their strongest candidate? [*Who* is the subject of *is*. The *do you think* is merely parenthetical.]
>
> Jenkins is the one *who* I suspect *will make* the best impression. [Determine the verb that goes with the pronoun. If you are puzzled by this type of sentence, try reading it this way: "Jenkins is the one *who will make* the best impression—I suspect."]

But if the pronoun is not the subject of the verb, the objective form should be used:

> Mr. Bass is the suitor *whom* we hope Portia will accept. [*Whom* is the direct object of *will accept*.]

EXERCISE 42
Using Pronouns Correctly: Case

NAME _____ SCORE _____

DIRECTIONS: Each italicized pronoun in these sentences is correctly used. In the space at the left, write one of the following numbers to identify the use of the pronoun:

1. Subject
2. Subjective complement
3. Appositive modifier of a nominative noun
4. Direct or indirect object
5. Object of a preposition
6. Appositive modifier of an objective noun

_____ 1. As usual, the kitchen chores were left to my sister and *me*.

_____ 2. The old hermit would throw stones at *whoever* walked on his property.

_____ 3. Some of us wonder *who* Betty's new boyfriend is.

_____ 4. Some of us wonder *whom* Betty will take to the prom.

_____ 5. Some of us wonder *who* sent Betty the flowers.

_____ 6. The drill sergeant led *us* recruits into the mess hall.

_____ 7. Several club members have told me that the committee should have included you and *me*.

_____ 8. Mary Lou is too timid; it couldn't have been *she* who sent you the ribald valentine.

_____ 9. The officer gave Fred and *me* a speeding ticket but spared us the usual lecture.

_____ 10. The ones who will suffer most from this drastic budget cut will be *we* students.

_____ 11. *Who* did you say will deliver the commencement address?

_____ 12. Mr. Thiel always votes for *whomever* his wife recommends.

_____ 13. Mr. Thiel always votes for *whoever* promises to lower taxes.

_____ 14. The reward should have been divided between the watchman and *me*.

_____ 15. I could not recall *who* Lincoln's secretary of war was at the beginning of the conflict.

_____ 16. Butch rarely encounters anyone who is as tall as *he*.

_____ 17. The free tax advice is a great service to *us* pensioners.

_____ 18. Ms. Denny deserves most of the credit; no one else worked harder at the rummage sale than *she*.

_____ 19. *We* seniors did not have to attend the lecture.

_____ 20. Some of *us* seniors wanted to hear the lecture.

DIRECTIONS: Each numbered unit contains one incorrectly used pronoun. Underline the pronoun and write the correct form in the space at the left.

_____ 1. The dean would not tell us committee members whom it was that started the petition.

_____ 2. Helen, who is slightly older than me, often gives advice to us beginning skaters.

_____ 3. Is this notebook your's? It doesn't belong to Leo or me.

_____ 4. The mansion was built by Jeb Witherspoon, whom business associates said once borrowed a king's ransom.

_____ 5. Jenny maintains that the responsibility should be someone else's, not just her's.

_____ 6. The news had been leaked to only three of us in the office: Louise, Alice, and I.

_____ 7. Who do you think Mrs. Baxter will invite to her anniversary party?

_____ 8. Jepson has never liked you or me; it was probably him who kept us out of the club.

_____ 9. I hope you don't object to me lowering the light; it's shining right into my eyes.

_____ 10. Regardless of who made the original error, all of we salespersons must share the blame.

_____ 11. You say this umbrella is not yours, and it's not mine. I wonder who's it is.

_____ 12. Everyones favorite, young Pete Osgood, won his match and now has only eighteen holes between him and the club championship.

_____ 13. Certainly you agree with my wife and me that the accident was the truck driver's fault, not our's.

_____ 14. "Whom do you suppose could have sent copies of this vicious editorial to my board of directors and me?" asked Ms. Calhoun.

_____ 15. My lawnmower is broken, but my new neighbors, whom I met only a week ago, are letting me use their's.

_____ 16. When Wilkins threw the bat toward the mound, some of us rookies ran out onto the field to get between he and the opposing pitcher.

_____ 17. Most of us reporters believe the appointment will go to some liberal whom the governor thinks will share her political philosophy.

_____ 18. Whom can you recommend to teach my wife and I how to play bridge?

_____ 19. Jerry, who is, I admit, more patient than me, suggested that we sit down and talk things over.

_____ 20. Isn't that suitcase yours, the one with the green name tag attached to it's handle?

EXERCISE 43
Using Pronouns Correctly: Reference and Case

NAME _____ SCORE _____

DIRECTIONS: Whenever you find an incorrectly used pronoun, circle it and write the correct form in the proper space at the left. Leave the spaces blank when no revision is needed.

_____ 1. This car would be an excellent buy for you; it's original owner always drove as carefully as you or me.

_____ 2. We committee members have already decided whom the next social chairperson will be.

_____ 3. Don Ewings, whom some people thought would win the tournament easily, now has two yawning sand traps between he and the eighteenth green.

_____ 4. The sneak thief, whomever he was, must have known the daily routine followed by my wife and I.

_____ 5. Anyone who's birthday falls on February 29 can play jokes on people when asked their age.

_____ 6. No one else in the family has had fewer accidents than me, and yet Dad usually objects to me driving after dark.

_____ 7. A guest in our restaurant can ask for any special dish even if you don't see them on the printed menu.

_____ 8. Every fellow in my office except Morrison, Levy, and I has already received their income tax refund.

_____ 9. Someone at the meeting—I've forgotten whom it was— suggested that any member whose dues are in arrears should be required to turn in their card.

_____ 10. The police have not yet announced who the informer is, and I'm afraid some people might think it was I who provided the evidence.

_____ 11. The boss gave the new job to Ms. Bishop, not I, in spite of the fact that my sales record is better than her's.

_____
_____ 12. In five games the young quarterback, whom most of us fans believe will become a great NFL player, has unimpressive stats.

_____
_____ 13. The counselor suggested that a private tutor could help you and I with our problem, but I really can't afford that.

_____
_____ 14. If a person is licensed to drive, you ought to carry it always as an excellent means of identification.

_____
_____ 15. I've always worried about snake bite; I'm sure that I'd faint dead away if I ever accidentally stepped on one.

_____
_____ 16. The young woman who I was giving the test to complained that the instructional pamphlet contained too many facts and figures for you to memorize.

_____
_____ 17. Most of the legislators whom I've interviewed think that the Senate should finish it's business by next Friday.

_____
_____ 18. Does a personnel officer have the right to ask an applicant personal questions, such as whom their closest friends are?

_____
_____ 19. Can you figure out why everyone in our division except Virgil and I has already been given their Christmas bonus?

_____
_____ 20. This duffle bag must be someone else's; it's larger than your's and smaller than mine.

LESSON
24 Using Modifiers and Prepositions Correctly

IN LESSON 2 you learned that an adjective is a word that describes or limits a noun or a pronoun. An adverb modifies a verb, an adjective, or another adverb. Many adverbs end in *ly*, such as *happily, beautifully*, and *extremely*. (But some adjectives—*lovely, likely, deadly, neighborly*, and *homely*, for instance—also end in *ly*.) Some adverbs do not end in *ly*, and these happen to be among the most frequently used words in speech and writing: *after, always, before, far, forever, here, not, now, often, quite, rather, soon, then, there, too*.

Some words can be used either as adjectives or as adverbs, as the following examples show:

ADVERBS	ADJECTIVES
She came *close*.	That was a *close* call.
She talks too *fast*.	She's a *fast* thinker.
Hit it *hard*.	That was a *hard* blow.
She usually arrives *late*.	She arrived at a *late* hour.
He went *straight* to bed.	I can't draw a *straight* line.

Some adverbs have two forms, one without and one with the *ly: cheap, cheaply; close, closely; deep, deeply; hard, hardly; high, highly; late, lately; loud, loudly; quick, quickly; right, rightly; slow, slowly*. In some of these pairs the words are interchangeable; in most they are not. The idiomatic use of adverbs is a rather complex matter; no rules can be made that govern every situation. We can, however, make a few generalizations that reflect present-day practice:

1. The shorter form of a few of these—*late, hard*, and *near*, for example—fill most adverbial functions because the corresponding *ly* forms have acquired special meanings:

We must not stay *late*.	I have not seen him *lately* [recently].
I studied *hard* last night.	I *hardly* [scarcely] know him.
Winter is drawing *near*.	I *nearly* [almost] missed the last flight.

2. The *ly* form tends toward the formal, with the short form lending itself to more casual, informal speech and writing:

It fell *close* to the target.	You must watch him *closely*.
They ate *high* off the hog.	She was *highly* respected.
Drive *slow*!	Please drive more *slowly*.
	He *slowly* removed his glasses.
Must you sing so *loud*?	He *loudly* denied the charges.
We searched far and *wide*.	She is *widely* known as an artist.

3. Because the short form seems more direct and forceful, it is often used in imperative sentences:

Hold *firm* to this railing.
"Come *quick*," yelled the officer.

4. The short form is often the one used when combined with an adjective to make a compound modifier preceding a noun:

a *wide*-ranging species	The species ranges *widely*.
a *slow*-moving truck	The truck approached *slowly*.

For the sake of simplifying the problem of the right use of adverbs and adjectives, we may say that there are three main trouble spots:

1. Misusing an adjective for an adverb. A word is an adverb if it modifies a verb, an adjective, or another adverb. The words that usually cause trouble here are *good, bad, well; sure, surely; real, really; most, almost; awful, awfully;* and *some, somewhat:*

I did *well* [not *good*] in my test. [Modifies the verb *did.*]
This paint adheres *well* [not *good*] to concrete. [Modifies the verb *adheres.*]
Almost [not *Most*] every student owns a car. [Modifies the adjective *every.*]
Today my shoulder is *really* [or *very*—not *real*] sore. [Modifies the adjective *sore.*]
We left the room *really* [or *very*—not *real*] fast. [Modifies the adverb *fast.*]
This rain has been falling *steadily* [not *steady*] for a week.
The champion should win his first match *easily* [not *easy*].
You'll improve if you practice *regularly* [not *regular*].
She wants that prize very *badly* [not *bad*].

2. Misusing an adverb for an adjective in the subjective complement. The most common verb to take the subjective complement is *be;* fortunately mistakes with this verb are nearly impossible. A few other verbs—like *seem, become, appear, prove, grow, go, turn, stay,* and *remain,* when they are used in a sense very close to that of *be*—take subjective complements. This complement must be an adjective, not an adverb.

The house *seems empty.* [House *is* empty.]
Their plans *became apparent.* [Plans *were* apparent.]
The work *proved* very *hard.* [Work *was* hard.]

The adjective subjective complement is also used with another group of verbs, the so-called verbs of the senses. These are *feel, look, smell, sound,* and *taste:*

You shouldn't feel *bad* about this. [Not *badly.*]
His cough sounds *bad* this morning. [Not *badly.*]
The street noises sound *loud* tonight. [Not *loudly.*]
Doesn't the air smell *sweet* today? [Not *sweetly.*]

The verb *feel* is involved in two special problems. In the first place, it is often used with both *good* and *well.* These two words have different meanings; one is not a substitute for the other. When used with the verb *feel, well* is an adjective meaning "in good health." The adjective *good,* when used with *feel,* means "filled with a sense of vigor and excitement." Of course, both *well* and *good* have other meanings when used with other verbs. In the second place, the expression "I feel badly" has been used so widely, especially in spoken English, that it should not be considered an error in usage. Many careful writers, however, prefer the adjective here, with the result that "feel bad" is usually found in formal written English.

3. Misusing a comparative or a superlative form of a modifier. (For a discussion of the comparison of adjectives, see Lesson 2.) Most adverbs are compared in the same way as adjectives. Some common adverbs cannot be compared, such as *here, now, then, when,* and *before.* As you learned in Lesson 15, we use the comparative degree *(taller, better, more intelligent, more rapidly)* in a comparison limited to two things. We use the superlative degree *(tallest, best, most intelligent, most rapidly)* for more than two things. Two other problems, both of minor importance, are involved in comparisons. First, we do not combine the two forms *(more + er, most + est)* in forming the comparative and superlative degrees:

After Al worked on my motorcycle,it sounded *quieter* [not *more quieter*].
Please drive *slower* [not *more slower*].
Please drive *more slowly* [not *more slower*].

Second, some purists object to the comparison of the so-called absolute qualities, such as *unique* ("being the only one"), *perfect, round, exact,* and so forth. They argue that, instead of such uses as *most perfect, straighter, more unique,* the intended meaning is *most nearly perfect, more nearly straight, more nearly unique.* General usage, however, has pretty well established both forms.

Three reminders should be made about the use of prepositions. One problem is the selection of the exact preposition for the meaning intended:

1. Many words, especially verbs and adjectives, give their full meaning only when modified by a prepositional phrase. In most cases the meaning of the preposition dictates a logical idiom: to sit *on* a couch, to walk *with* a friend, to lean *against* a fence, and so on. For some more abstract concepts, however, the acceptable preposition may seem to have been selected arbitrarily. Here are a few examples of different meanings of different prepositions:

agree *to* a proposal, *with* a person, *on* a price, *in* principle
argue *about* a matter, *with* a person, *for* or *against* a proposition
compare *to* to show likenesses, *with* to show differences [sometimes similarities]
correspond *to* a thing, *with* a person
differ *from* an unlike thing, *with* a person
live *at* an address, *in* a house or city, *on* a street, *with* other people

NOTE: Any good modern dictionary will provide information about and examples of the correct usage of prepositions.

2. Although at colloquial levels of language we sometimes find unnecessary prepositions used, examples like the following are improved in serious contexts if written without the words in brackets:

I met [up with] your uncle yesterday.
We keep our dog inside [of] the house.
Our cat, however, sleeps outside [of] the house.
The package fell off [of] the speeding truck.
The garage is [in] back of the cottage.

Avoid especially the needless preposition at the end of a sentence or the repeated preposition in adjective clauses and in direct or indirect questions:

Where is your older brother *at*?
He is one of the few people *to* whom I usually feel superior *to*. [Use one or the other, but not both.]
To what do you attribute your luck at poker *to*?

3. When two words of a compound unit require the same preposition to be idiomatically correct, the preposition need not be stated with the first unit:

CORRECT: We were both *repelled* and *fascinated by* the snake charmer's act.
But when the two units require different prepositions, both must be expressed.

INCOMPLETE: The child shows an *interest* and a *talent for* music. [interest . . . *for* (?)]

CORRECT: The child shows an *interest in* and a *talent for* music.

INCOMPLETE: I am sure that Ms. Lewis would both *contribute* and *gain from* a summer workshop.

CORRECT: I am sure that Ms. Lewis would both *contribute to* and *gain from* a summer workshop.

Instructor's Free

Examination Copy.

Incomplete and Not

for Sale.

DIRECTIONS: In the space at the left, copy the correct form from within the parentheses.

_____ 1. Did you notice that one word in that TV commercial was spelled (incorrect, incorrectly)?

_____ 2. April and May were miserably cold, but the weather has now warmed up (some, somewhat).

_____ 3. Marybeth did quite (good, well) in the field events.

_____ 4. When we opened the cottage this spring, we discovered that the roof had leaked (bad, badly).

_____ 5. The storm developed so (sudden, suddenly) that most residents were not prepared for it.

_____ 6. In which class, chemistry or political science, do you get the (better, best) grades?

_____ 7. Landers deserves a promotion; she's worked (good, well) for us all year.

_____ 8. (Most, Almost) everyone in town has fought with cranky old Mr. Weeks.

_____ 9. Which of your two daughters is the (better, best) driver?

_____ 10. Bob certainly looks (different, differently) now that he has shaved off his beard.

_____ 11. Bob certainly swings his golf club (different, differently) now that he has taken some lessons.

_____ 12. Sports fans are (awful, very) pleased with the team's performance this season.

_____ 13. The child looked (sad, sadly) at the departing ambulance.

_____ 14. The child looked (sad, sadly) as the ambulance departed.

_____ 15. Creston is the (likeliest, most likeliest) site for the proposed factory.

_____ 16. This cleanser works (good, well) on other surfaces besides glass.

_____ 17. Do you think this picture would look (good, well) hanging behind my desk in the office?

_____ 18. Jimmy is not a very good tennis player; you should be able to beat him (easy, easily).

_____ 19. Last night we saw a (real, really) exciting hockey game.

_____ 20. The tutoring you have given our daughter has helped her (considerable, considerably).

_____ 18. Ms. Carver dresses well and always looks neat; she is, in fact, a perfectionist with whom I never feel completely comfortable with.

_____ 19. We hurriedly threw together a quick lunch, one that all of us freely admitted tasted terrible.

_____ 20. You'll feel good knowing that you've done your job today really well.

_____ 21. "I'm sorry to have to tell you this, Ms. Jacobs," said Glenn, "but your poodle behaved real bad at obedience school today."

_____ 22. Although we rowed as hard as we could, our progress was slow because the water was awful choppy.

_____ 23. The guide drove the car so fast and so reckless that two of her passengers felt mildly ill.

_____ 24. Although Rodrigez was the heavier of the two boxers, Sanchez fought more cleverly and won the match easy.

_____ 25. The town, although considerable smaller than Walt remembered it, still seemed friendly and comfortable.

_____ 26. The developing of the film will proceed more faster if you use slightly warmer developer.

_____ 27. Like most young fellows, Jake is awful excited about getting started with his driving lessons.

_____ 28. Have you noticed how differently the engine's horn blast sounds in this clear, subzero weather?

_____ 29. Most everyone who has seen the play says that the acting of the amateur group is surprisingly good.

_____ 30. Driving in Centerville on a busy Saturday is not necessarily more easier than driving in a big city.

_____ 31. "Where in the world have you kids been at?" asked Aunt Louise crankily.

_____ 32. Jennifer, the younger of Mrs. Allen's two daughters, happily reported that her mother's condition had improved noticeably.

_____ 33. "The teachers I had in the early grades lacked, unfortunately, any curiosity or knowledge of good literature," she replied.

_____ 34. If you can fine-tune with these two knobs careful enough, your radio reception will be really good.

_____ 35. Almost all the girls I know did real good on the final examination.

in "Galileo was among the most talented people of his age," or "The estate was divided among his three sons." *Between* usually refers to two things, as in "between you and me," "between two points," "between dawn and sunset."

Amount, number. Use *number*, not *amount*, in reference to units that can actually be counted:

> the *amount* of indebtedness, the *number* of debts.

And etc. Because *etc. (et cetera)* means "and so forth," *and etc.* would mean "and and so forth." You should not use *etc.* to replace some exact, specific word, but if you do use it, be sure not to spell it *ect.* And remember that *etc.* requires a period after it.

Anyplace, anywheres. Colloquial and dialectal forms for *anywhere*. Similar colloquial forms are *anyways* for *anyhow*, *everyplace* for *everywhere*, *no place* or *nowheres* for *nowhere*, *someplace* or *somewheres* for *somewhere*.

> I looked for my books everywhere. They must be hidden somewhere.

As, like. See *Like*.

As to whether. *Whether* is usually enough.

Awful, awfully. Like *aggravate*, these words have two distinct uses. In formal contexts, they mean "awe-inspiring" or "terrifying." Often in conversation and sometimes in writing of a serious nature, *awful* and *awfully* are mild intensifiers, meaning "very."

Because. See *Reason is because*.

Because of. See *Due to*.

Being that, being as how. Substandard for *because*, *as*, or *since*.

Beside, besides. These two prepositions are clearly distinguished by their meanings. *Beside* means "at the side of" and *besides* means "in addition to."

Lucy sits beside me in class.
Did anyone besides you see the accident?

Between. See *Among*.

But what, but that. Colloquial for *that*.

> Both sides had no doubt that [not *but what*] their cause was just.

Can, may. *Can* suggests ability to do something. *May* is the preferred form when permission is involved.

> Little Junior can already count to ten.
> May [not *Can*] I borrow your pencil?

Can't hardly, couldn't hardly, can't scarcely, couldn't scarcely. Substandard for *can hardly, could hardly, can scarcely, could scarcely*. These are sometimes referred to as double negatives.

> They could hardly [not *couldn't hardly*] hear his shout for help.
> He could scarcely [not *couldn't scarcely*] walk when they found him.

Caused by. See *Due to*.

Complected. Dialectal or colloquial for *complexioned*.

> Being light-complexioned [not *light-complected*], Sue must avoid prolonged exposure to sunlight.

Contact. Used as a verb meaning "to get in touch with," this word, probably because of its association with sales-promotion writing, annoys enough people to warrant caution in its use in serious writing.

Continual, continuous. A fine distinction in meaning can be made if you remember that *continual* means "repeated regularly and frequently" and that *continuous* means "occurring without interruption," "unbroken."

Could(n't) care less. This worn-out set phrase indicating total indifference is a colloquialism. A continuing marvel of language behavior is the large

Fewer [not *Less*] students are taking courses in literature this year.

Food costs less, but we have less money to spend.

Figure. Colloquial for *consider, think, believe, suppose.*

He must have thought [not *figured*] that nobody would see him enter the bank.

Fine. Colloquial, very widely used, for *well, very well.*

The boys played well [not *just fine*].

Had(n't) ought. *Ought* does not take an auxiliary.

You ought [not *had ought*] to apply for a scholarship.

You ought not [not *hadn't ought*] to miss the lecture.

Hardly. See *Can't hardly.*

Healthy, healthful. *Healthy* means "having health," and *healthful* means "giving health." Thus a person or an animal is healthy; a climate, a food, or an activity is healthful.

Immigrate. See *Emigrate.*

Imply, infer. Despite the increasing tendency to use these words more-or-less interchangeably, it is good to preserve the distinction: *Imply* means "to say something indirectly," "to hint or suggest," and *infer* means "to draw a conclusion," "to deduce." Thus you *imply* something in what you say and *infer* something from what you hear.

Incredible, incredulous. An unbelievable *thing* is incredible; a disbelieving *person* is incredulous.

In regards to. The correct forms are *in regard to* or *as regards.*

Inside of. *Inside* or *within* is preferred in formal writing.

We stayed inside [not *inside of*] the barn during the storm.

Invite. Slang for *invitation.*

They will be sent an invitation [not *invite*] to join us in a peace conference.

Irregardless. Substandard or humorous for *regardless.*

The planes bombed the area regardless [not *irregardless*] of consequences.

Is when, is where. The *is-when, is-where* pattern in definitions is clumsy and should be avoided. Write, for example, "An embolism is an obstruction, such as a blood clot, in the bloodstream," instead of "An embolism is where an obstruction forms in the bloodstream."

Kind, sort. These words are singular and therefore should be modified by singular modifiers. Do not write *these kind, these sort, those kind, those sort.*

I cannot wear this kind [not *these kind*] of shoes.

Who could believe that sort [not *those sort*] of arguments?

Kinda, sorta, kind of a, sort of a. Undesirable forms.

Kind of, sort of. Colloquial for *somewhat, in some degree, almost, rather.*

They felt somewhat [not *sort of*] depressed.

Learn, teach. *Learn* means "to acquire knowledge"; *teach* means "to give or impart knowledge."

Ms. Brown taught [not *learned*] me Spanish.

Leave. Not to be used for *let.*

Let [not *Leave*] me carry your books for you.

Less. See *Fewer.*

Let. See *Leave.*

Let's us. The *us* is superfluous, because *let's* means "let us."

Like, as, as if. The use of *like* as a conjunction (in other words, to introduce a clause) is colloquial. It should be avoided in serious writing.

190

an adjective, to modify another adjective or an adverb is colloquial. In formal contexts *really* or *very* should be used.

> We had a really [not *real*] enjoyable visit.
> The motorcycle rounded the corner very [not *real*] fast.

Reason is because, reason is due to, reason is on account of. In serious writing, a *reason is* clause is usually completed with *that*, not with *because*, *due to*, or *on account of*.

> The reason they surrendered is that [not *because*] they were starving.
> The reason for my low grades is that I have poor eyesight [not *is on account of my poor eyesight*].

Same. The use of *same* as a pronoun, often found in legal or business writing, is inappropriate in most other types of writing.

> I received your report and look forward to reading it [not *the same*].

Scarcely. See *Can't hardly.*

So, such. These words, when used as exclamatory intensifiers, are not appropriate in a formal context. Sentences like the following belong in informal talk: "I am *so* tired," "She is *so* pretty," or "They are having *such* a good time."

Some. Colloquial for *somewhat, a little.*

> The ailing senator was reported as being somewhat [not *some*] better this morning.

Somewheres, someplace. See *Anyplace.*

Sort. See *Kind.*

Such. See *So.*

Suppose to. See *use to.*

Sure. *Sure* is correctly used as an adjective:

> We are not sure about her plans.
> He made several sure investments.

Sure is colloquial when used as an adverbial substitute for *surely, extremely, certainly, indeed, very, very much.*

> The examination was surely [not *sure*] difficult.
> Certainly [not *Sure*], your objections will be considered by the court.

Sure and. See *Try and.*

Suspicion. *Suspicion* is a noun; it is not to be used as a verb in place of *suspect.*

> No one suspected [not *suspicioned*] the victim's widow.

Swell. Not to be used as a general term of approval meaning *good, excellent, attractive, desirable,* and so on.

Teach. See *Learn.*

That there, this here, those there, these here. Substandard for *that, this, those, these.*

Them. Substandard when used as an adjective.

> How can you eat those [not *them*] parsnips?

Try and, sure and. *Try to, sure to* are the preferred forms in serious writing.

> We shall try to [not *try and*] make your visit a pleasant one.
> Be sure to [not *sure and*] arrive on time.

Type. Colloquial when used as a modifier of a noun. Use *type of* or *kind of.*

> I usually don't enjoy that type of [not *type*] movie.

Uninterested. See *Disinterested.*

Use to, suppose to. Although these incorrect forms are difficult to detect in spoken English, remember that the correct written forms are *used to, supposed to.*

Want in, want off, want out. Colloquial and dialectal forms for

DIRECTIONS: Each sentence contains two italicized words or expressions. If you think that a word or expression is inappropriate in serious writing, write an acceptable form in the space at the left. If an expression is correct, write *C* in the space.

1. I had the bad fortune of being seated *besides* a man who was *awful* talkative.

2. We were not allowed to get *off of* the ship until the next morning *due to* a strike by dock workers.

3. You'll like this *type* raincoat; it's *so* attractive and yet protects you well.

4. My *prof* read my report and said that it was *alright*.

5. The reason Bob ate his lunch in his office is *because* he is expecting some *real* important calls.

6. Our profit margin is *somewhat* better this year, and we hope for *further* improvement in sales.

7. Ben wasn't aware that the "RSVP" on the *invite* meant that he was *suppose to* respond before the event.

8. You *should of* gone to the party, *irregardless* of the fact that you hate to play bridge.

9. *Most* all business people agree that the decline in the rate of inflation is having a *most* beneficial effect.

10. *Let's us* all *try and* be on time for the next meeting.

11. The judge acted *like* the witness's flippant remarks were beginning to *aggravate* her.

12. *Because of* the bad weather, *less* than a dozen people heard the lecture.

13. Be *sure and* tell the driver that you *want off* at the courthouse.

14. Jeff's first tryout for the lacrosse team *learned* him that the game requires *lots of* endurance.

15. You won't find *anywheres* in this town a better bargain than *that there* Mustang I showed you yesterday.

16. You *sure* can't hold our company reponsible for shipment delays *due to* the bus drivers' strike, can you?

17. "I always thought that a referee is *suppose to* be completely *disinterested*," complained the coach.

18. From your reply, I *infer* that you think I *ought to of* notified the police earlier.

19. Jackson apparently *figured* that college basketball wouldn't be much *different than* the high-school kind.

20. "People seem *enthused* about my new book *everywhere* I go," said Ms. Stern.

The common exceptions to this rule may be easily remembered if you memorize the following sentence: Neither financier seized either species of weird leisure.

Rule 3: In words of one syllable and words accented on the last syllable, ending in a single consonant preceded by a single vowel, double the final consonant before a suffix beginning with a vowel.

WORDS OF ONE SYLLABLE—SUFFIX BEGINS WITH A VOWEL

ban —banned	hit —hitting	rid —riddance
bid —biddable	hop —hopping	Scot —Scottish
dig —digger	quit —quitter	stop —stoppage
drag —dragged	["qu" —consonant]	wet —wettest

ACCENTED ON LAST SYLLABLE—SUFFIX BEGINS WITH A VOWEL

abhor —abhorrence	equip —equipping
acquit —acquitted	occur —occurrence
allot —allotted	omit —omitted
begin —beginner	prefer —preferring
commit —committing	regret —regrettable
control —controlled	repel —repellent

NOT ACCENTED ON LAST SYLLABLE—SUFFIX BEGINS WITH A VOWEL

differ —different	open —opener
happen —happening	prefer —preference
hasten —hastened	sharpen —sharpened

SUFFIX BEGINS WITH A CONSONANT

allot —allotment	mother —motherhood
color —colorless	sad —sadness
equip —equipment	sin —sinful

(See Supplement 1.)

An apparent exception to this rule affects a few words formed by the addition of *ing, ed,* or *y* to a word ending in *c*. To preserve the hard sound of the *c*, a *k* is added before the vowel of the suffix, resulting in such spellings as *frolicking, mimicked, panicked, panicky, picnicked,* and *trafficking.*

Another irregularity applies to such spellings as *quitting* and *equipped*. One might think that the consonant should not be doubled, reasoning that the final consonant is preceded by two vowels, not by a single vowel. But because *qu* is phonetically the equivalent of *kw,* the *u* is a consonant when it follows *q*. Therefore, because the final consonant is actually preceded by a single vowel, the consonant is doubled before the suffix.

Rule 4: Words ending in *y* preceded by a vowel retain the *y* before a suffix; most words ending in *y* preceded by a consonant change the *y* to *i* before a suffix.

ENDING IN Y PRECEDED BY A VOWEL

boy —boyish	coy —coyness	enjoy —enjoying
buy —buys	donkey —donkeys	stay —staying

ENDING IN Y PRECEDED BY A CONSONANT

ally —allies	easy —easiest	pity —pitiable
busy —busily	icy —icier	study —studies
cloudy —cloudiness	mercy —merciless	try —tried

DIRECTIONS: A sentence may have no misspelled words, one misspelled word, or two misspelled words. Underline the misspelled words and write them, correctly spelled, in the spaces at the left.

_____
_____
1. Earlier in the trial the famous and conceited writer had admitted receiving copies of a contract for printing nineteen short stories.

_____
_____
2. Seizing the properties of these companies was extremly regrettable and entirely illegal.

_____
_____
3. The chief casheir is quitting; he chose early retirment although he is only in his mid-sixties.

_____
_____
4. After a conferrence, the attorneys representing labor and management submitted plans for a peaceable settlement.

_____
_____
5. "I am hopeful that you will paint the ceiling of my dinning room in your leisure time," said my niece.

_____
_____
6. The authorities now believe that the thief's successes lately have made him careless.

_____
_____
7. The chimneys on a few factories were severly damaged during the feirce storm.

_____
_____
8. Unfortunately many local people remember the outrageous and shameful happennings of John's youth.

_____
_____
9. In all liklihood the opposing armys in the coastal territories have made preparations for a long siege.

_____
_____
10. The visiting expert referred briefly to the desireable opportunities offered in the field of writing biographies.

Fourth. We planned a picnic for the Fourth of July.

Incidence. Better sanitation lowered the incidence of communicable diseases.

Incidents. Smugglers were involved in several incidents along the border.

Instance. For instance, she was always late to class.

Instants. As the car turned, those brief instants seemed like hours.

Its. Your plan has much in its favor. [Possessive of *it*.]

It's. It's too late now for excuses. [Contraction of *it is, it has*.]

Later. It is later than you think.

Latter. Of the two novels, I prefer the latter.

Lead. Can you lead [lēd—verb] us out of this jungle? Lead [lĕd—noun] is a heavy, soft, malleable metallic element.

Led. A local guide led us to the salmon fishing hole.

Loose. He has a loose tongue. The dog is loose again.

Lose. You must not lose your purse.

Passed. She smiled as she passed me. She passed the test.

Past. It is futile to try to relive the past.

Personal. Write him a personal letter.

Personnel. The morale of our company's personnel is high.

Pore. For hours they pored over the mysterious note.

Pour. Mrs. Cook poured hot water into the teapot.

Precedence. Tax reform takes precedence over all other legislative matters.

Precedents. The judge quoted three precedents to justify his ruling.

Presence. We are honored by your presence.

Presents. The child demanded expensive presents.

Principal. The principal of a school; the principal [chief] industry; the principal and the interest.

Principle. He is a man of high principles.

Quiet. You must keep quiet.

Quite. You have been quite good all day.

Rain. A soaking rain would help our crops greatly.

Reign. Samuel Pepys was briefly imprisoned during the reign of William III.

Rein. Keep a tight rein when you ride this spirited horse.

Shone. The cat's eyes shone in the dark.

Shown. He hasn't shown us his best work.

Stationary. The benches were stationary and could not be moved.

Stationery. She wrote a letter on hotel stationery.

Statue. It was a statue of a pioneer.

Stature. Athos was a man of gigantic stature.

Statute. The law may be found in the 1917 book of statutes.

Than. She sings better than I.

Then. He screamed; then he fainted.

Their. It wasn't their fault. [Possessive pronoun.]

There. You won't find any gold there. [Adverb of place.]

They're. They're sure to be disappointed. [Contraction of *they are*.]

Thorough. We must first give the old cabin a thorough [adjective] cleaning.

Through. The thief had entered through [preposition] a hole in the roof.

To. Be sure to speak to her. [Preposition.]

Too. He is far too old for you. [Adverb.]

Two. The membership fee is only two dollars. [Adjective.]

DIRECTIONS: If a sentence contains a misspelled word, underline the word and write it, correctly spelled, in the space at the left. No sentence contains more than one misspelled word; some sentences may contain none.

_____ 1. The parole officer should counsel the boy to altar his behavior before it's too late.

_____ 2. A few instants later the elderly lady replied, "The pain has left; I'm quite all right, thank you."

_____ 3. The fixture should be stationary because if it is loose the water pressure might be affected.

_____ 4. Don't lose sight of the fact that our lawyers have found precedents on which to base our case.

_____ 5. Marilyn is the kind of teacher who's intellectual stature and high principles impress the students.

_____ 6. Later that afternoon the visitors were driven passed the site of the new infirmary.

_____ 7. Of course, it's not going to be easy to raise enough capitol for our venture.

_____ 8. Before leaving the dining room, the French consul sent his complements to the cook.

_____ 9. "In this heavy rain they're in danger of losing there way," said the guide.

_____ 10. "The desserts here are altogether to high in calories," Everett complained.

_____ 11. A few quite radical reforms were effected during the reign of King Leopold.

_____ 12. I advise you not to use motel stationery for a personal letter.

_____ 13. The new personnel directer is much younger then the man whose place she is taking.

_____ 14. The principal of the school finished his speech and then lead the graduates off the stage.

_____ 15. These incidents have shone us the need for a thorough review of the tax structure.

_____ 16. Serious students expect to find the library quiet when they're pouring over class notes for an exam.

_____ 17. I wish to compliment you, Ms. Lewis; you're the only class member whose paper was not too messy to read.

_____ 18. The members of the city council were not altogether pleased with the advise I gave them.

_____ 19. The young lawyer cited three statutes on which she had based her principal argument.

_____ 20. I'm quite sure you're going to enjoy this play; it's plot is really intriguing.

208

curriculum, curriculums, curricula   fungus, funguses, fungi
memorandum, memorandums, memoranda   index, indexes, indices
tableau, tableaus, tableaux

WARNING: Do *not* use an apostrophe to form the plural of either a common or a proper noun.

WRONG: Our neighbor's, the Allen's and the Murray's, recently bought new Honda's.
RIGHT: Our neighbors, the Allens and the Murrays, recently bought new Hondas.

Capitals

A capital letter is used for the first letter of the first word of any sentence, for the first letter of a proper noun, and often for the first letter of an adjective derived from a proper noun. Following are some reminders about situations that cause confusion for some writers.

1. Capitalize the first word of every sentence, every quoted sentence or fragment, and every transitional fragment. (See Lesson 13.)

The building needs repairs. How much will it cost? Please answer me. Mr. James said, "We'll expect your answer soon." She replied, "Of course." And now to conclude.

Traditionally, a capital letter begins every line of poetry. This convention, however, is not always followed by modern poets; when you quote poetry, be sure to copy exactly the capitalization used by the author.

2. Capitalize proper nouns and most adjectives derived from them. A proper noun designates by name an individual person, place, or thing that is a member of a group or class. Do not capitalize common nouns, which are words naming a group or class:

Doris Powers, woman; France, country; Tuesday, day; January, month; Christmas Eve, holiday; Shorewood High School, high school; Carleton College, college; *Mauretania,* ship; Fifth Avenue, boulevard; White House, residence

Elizabethan drama, Restoration poetry, Chinese peasants, Indian reservation, Red Cross assistance

3. Do not capitalize nouns and derived forms that, although originally proper nouns, have acquired special meanings. When in doubt, consult your dictionary:

a set of china; a bohemian existence; plaster of paris; pasteurized milk; a mecca for golfers; set in roman type, not italics

4. Capitalize names of religions, references to deities, and most words having religious significance:

Bible, Baptist, Old Testament, Holy Writ, Jewish, Catholic, Sermon on the Mount, Koran, Talmud

5. Capitalize titles of persons when used with the person's name. When the title is used alone, capitalize it only when it stands for a specific person of high rank:

I spoke briefly to Professor Jones. He is a professor of history.
We visited the late President Johnson's ranch in Texas.
Jerry is president of our art club.
Tonight the President will appear on national television.

Capitals

NAME _____ SCORE _____

DIRECTIONS: The following selection contains fifty numbered words. If you think the word is correctly capitalized, write *C* in the space at the left with the corresponding number. If you think the word should not be capitalized, write *W* in the space.

1	2	3
4	5	6
7	8	9
10	11	12
13	14	15
16	17	18
19	20	21
22	23	24
25	26	27
28	29	30
31	32	33
34	35	36
37	38	39
40	41	42
43	44	45
46	47	48
49	50	

Dear Uncle Fred: This is final examination week here [1] at Beloit College. I have tests in three of my courses [2] [3] this Semester, one in Sociology, one in Modern [4] [5] [6] French History, and one in the English Novel. It's a [7] [8] [9] [10] busy week; I must also finish a term paper on George Eliot's *The Mill On The Floss*. [11] [12] [13] [14] [15]

I am finishing my Sophomore year. I live in [16] Belnap Hall, the largest dormitory on the Campus. [17] [18] [19] My roommate, Terry Jackson, took his first-year work at a Junior College in the East. His Father works for [20] [21] [22] [23] the Federal Bureau Of Investigation. After finishing [24] [25] [26] [27] High School, Terry spent two years in the U.S. [28] [29] Navy. He tells me tales about the South Seas and the [30] [31] [32] Middle East. He once sailed around the Cape Of [33] [34] [35] [36] Good Hope. Last semester he took Geology 272. As [37] [38] [39] a result of this course and of talks he had with Dr. [40] Sanders, his favorite Professor, he plans to become a [41] Mineralogist. He plans to work next Summer in the [42] [43] Black Hills of South Dakota. [44] [45]

In a recent letter, Mother reported that you will [46] soon be heading North for Lake Goodwin. Have a [47] [48] pleasant vacation. Give my regards to Aunt Letty and [49] to my three Cousins. [50]

LESSON
29 Spelling List

T HIS LIST includes words frequently misspelled by high school and college students. Each word is repeated to show its syllabic division. Whether this list is used for individual study and review or in some kind of organized class activity, your method of studying should be the following: (1) Learn to pronounce the word syllable by syllable. Some of your trouble in spelling may come from incorrect pronunciation. (2) Copy the word carefully, forming each letter as plainly as you can. Some of your trouble may come from bad handwriting. (3) Pronounce the word carefully again. (4) On a separate sheet of paper, write the word from memory, check your spelling with the correct spelling before you, and, if you have misspelled the word, repeat the learning process.

abbreviate	ab-bre-vi-ate	barbarous	bar-ba-rous
absence	ab-sence	basically	ba-si-cal-ly
accidentally	ac-ci-den-tal-ly	beneficial	ben-e-fi-cial
accommodate	ac-com-mo-date	boundaries	bound-a-ries
accompanying	ac-com-pa-ny-ing	Britain	Brit-ain
accomplish	ac-com-plish	bureaucracy	bu-reau-cra-cy
accumulate	ac-cu-mu-late	business	busi-ness
acknowledge	ac-knowl-edge	calendar	cal-en-dar
acquaintance	ac-quaint-ance	candidate	can-di-date
acquire	ac-quire	category	cat-e-go-ry
across	a-cross	cemetery	cem-e-ter-y
additive	ad-di-tive	certain	cer-tain
admissible	ad-mis-si-ble	characteristic	char-ac-ter-is-tic
aggravate	ag-gra-vate	chosen	cho-sen
always	al-ways	commission	com-mis-sion
amateur	am-a-teur	committee	com-mit-tee
among	a-mong	communicate	com-mu-ni-cate
analysis	a-nal-y-sis	communism	com-mu-nism
analytical	an-a-lyt-i-cal	comparative	com-par-a-tive
apparatus	ap-pa-ra-tus	competent	com-pe-tent
apparently	ap-par-ent-ly	competition	com-pe-ti-tion
appearance	ap-pear-ance	completely	com-plete-ly
appreciate	ap-pre-ci-ate	compulsory	com-pul-so-ry
appropriate	ap-pro-pri-ate	computer	com-put-er
approximately	ap-prox-i-mate-ly	concede	con-cede
arctic	arc-tic	conference	con-fer-ence
argument	ar-gu-ment	confidentially	con-fi-den-tial-ly
arithmetic	a-rith-me-tic	conscience	con-science
association	as-so-ci-a-tion	conscientious	con-sci-en-tious
astronaut	as-tro-naut	conscious	con-scious
athletics	ath-let-ics	consistent	con-sist-ent
attendance	at-tend-ance	continuous	con-tin-u-ous
audience	au-di-ence	controversial	con-tro-ver-sial
auxiliary	aux-il-ia-ry	convenient	con-ven-ient
awkward	awk-ward	counterfeit	coun-ter-feit

criticism	crit-i-cism	government	gov-ern-ment
criticize	crit-i-cize	grammar	gram-mar
curiosity	cu-ri-os-i-ty	grievous	griev-ous
curriculum	cur-ric-u-lum	guarantee	guar-an-tee
decision	de-ci-sion	guerrilla	guer-ril-la
definitely	def-i-nite-ly	harass	ha-rass
describe	de-scribe	height	height
description	de-scrip-tion	hindrance	hin-drance
desperate	des-per-ate	humorous	hu-mor-ous
détente	dé-tente	hurriedly	hur-ried-ly
dictionary	dic-tion-ar-y	hypocrisy	hy-poc-ri-sy
difference	dif-fer-ence	imagination	im-ag-i-na-tion
dilapidated	di-lap-i-dat-ed	immediately	im-me-di-ate-ly
disappear	dis-ap-pear	impromptu	im-promp-tu
disappoint	dis-ap-point	incidentally	in-ci-den-tal-ly
disastrous	dis-as-trous	incredible	in-cred-i-ble
discipline	dis-ci-pline	independence	in-de-pend-ence
dissatisfied	dis-sat-is-fied	indispensable	in-dis-pen-sa-ble
dissident	dis-si-dent	inevitable	in-ev-i-ta-ble
dissipate	dis-si-pate	influential	in-flu-en-tial
doesn't	does-n't	initiative	in-i-ti-a-tive
dormitory	dor-mi-to-ry	intelligence	in-tel-li-gence
during	dur-ing	intentionally	in-ten-tion-al-ly
efficient	ef-fi-cient	intercede	in-ter-cede
eligible	el-i-gi-ble	interesting	in-ter-est-ing
eliminate	e-lim-i-nate	interpretation	in-ter-pre-ta-tion
embarrass	em-bar-rass	interrupt	in-ter-rupt
eminent	em-i-nent	irrelevant	ir-rel-e-vant
emphasize	em-pha-size	irresistible	ir-re-sist-i-ble
enthusiastic	en-thu-si-as-tic	irritation	ir-ri-ta-tion
entrepreneur	en-tre-pre-neur	knowledge	knowl-edge
environment	en-vi-ron-ment	laboratory	lab-o-ra-to-ry
equipment	e-quip-ment	laser	la-ser
equivalent	e-quiv-a-lent	legitimate	le-git-i-mate
especially	es-pe-cial-ly	liable	li-a-ble
exaggerated	ex-ag-ger-at-ed	library	li-brar-y
exceed	ex-ceed	lightning	light-ning
excellent	ex-cel-lent	literature	lit-er-a-ture
exceptionally	ex-cep-tion-al-ly	livelihood	live-li-hood
exhaust	ex-haust	loneliness	lone-li-ness
existence	ex-ist-ence	maintenance	main-te-nance
exorbitant	ex-or-bi-tant	marriage	mar-riage
experience	ex-pe-ri-ence	mathematics	math-e-mat-ics
explanation	ex-pla-na-tion	memento	me-men-to
extraordinary	ex-traor-di-nar-y	miniature	min-i-a-ture
extremely	ex-treme-ly	miscellaneous	mis-cel-la-ne-ous
familiar	fa-mil-iar	mischievous	mis-chie-vous
fascinate	fas-ci-nate	misspelled	mis-spelled
February	Feb-ru-ar-y	murmuring	mur-mur-ing
finally	fi-nal-ly	mysterious	mys-te-ri-ous
foreign	for-eign	naturally	nat-u-ral-ly
forty	for-ty	necessary	nec-es-sar-y
frantically	fran-ti-cal-ly	ninety	nine-ty
fundamentally	fun-da-men-tal-ly	ninth	ninth
genealogy	ge-ne-al-o-gy	nowadays	now-a-days
generally	gen-er-al-ly	nuclear	nu-cle-ar

216

obedience	o-be-di-ence	representative	rep-re-sent-a-tive
oblige	o-blige	respectfully	re-spect-ful-ly
obstacle	ob-sta-cle	respectively	re-spec-tive-ly
occasionally	oc-ca-sion-al-ly	restaurant	res-tau-rant
occurrence	oc-cur-rence	rhetoric	rhet-o-ric
omission	o-mis-sion	rhythm	rhythm
opportunity	op-por-tu-ni-ty	ridiculous	ri-dic-u-lous
optimistic	op-ti-mis-tic	sacrilegious	sac-ri-le-gious
original	o-rig-i-nal	sandwich	sand-wich
pamphlet	pam-phlet	satellite	sat-el-lite
parallel	par-al-lel	satisfactorily	sat-is-fac-to-ri-ly
parliament	par-lia-ment	schedule	sched-ule
particularly	par-tic-u-lar-ly	scientific	sci-en-tif-ic
partner	part-ner	secretary	sec-re-tar-y
pastime	pas-time	separately	sep-a-rate-ly
performance	per-form-ance	sergeant	ser-geant
permissible	per-mis-si-ble	significant	sig-nif-i-cant
perseverance	per-se-ver-ance	similar	sim-i-lar
perspiration	per-spi-ra-tion	sophomore	soph-o-more
persuade	per-suade	specifically	spe-cif-i-cal-ly
physically	phys-i-cal-ly	specimen	spec-i-men
politics	pol-i-tics	speech	speech
possession	pos-ses-sion	strictly	strict-ly
practically	prac-ti-cal-ly	successful	suc-cess-ful
preceding	pre-ced-ing	superintendent	su-per-in-tend-ent
prejudice	prej-u-dice	supersede	su-per-sede
preparation	prep-a-ra-tion	surprise	sur-prise
prevalent	prev-a-lent	suspicious	sus-pi-cious
privilege	priv-i-lege	syllable	syl-la-ble
probably	prob-a-bly	synonymous	syn-on-y-mous
procedure	pro-ce-dure	synthetic	syn-thet-ic
proceed	pro-ceed	technology	tech-nol-o-gy
processor	pro-ces-sor	temperament	tem-per-a-ment
professional	pro-fes-sion-al	temperature	tem-per-a-ture
pronunciation	pro-nun-ci-a-tion	together	to-geth-er
propaganda	prop-a-gan-da	tragedy	trag-e-dy
psychiatrist	psy-chi-a-trist	truly	tru-ly
psychological	psy-cho-log-i-cal	twelfth	twelfth
pursue	pur-sue	unanimous	u-nan-i-mous
quantity	quan-ti-ty	undoubtedly	un-doubt-ed-ly
questionnaire	ques-tion-naire	unnecessarily	un-nec-es-sar-i-ly
quizzes	quiz-zes	until	un-til
realize	re-al-ize	usually	u-su-al-ly
really	re-al-ly	various	var-i-ous
recognize	rec-og-nize	vegetable	veg-e-ta-ble
recommend	rec-om-mend	village	vil-lage
regard	re-gard	villain	vil-lain
religious	re-li-gious	Wednesday	Wednes-day
remembrance	re-mem-brance	whether	wheth-er
repetition	rep-e-ti-tion	wholly	whol-ly

Spelling

NAME _____ SCORE _____

DIRECTIONS: Each sentence contains two words from the first one-third of the spelling list. In each of these words at least one letter is missing. Write the words, correctly spelled, in the spaces at the left.

_____   1. Attend—nce at local at—letic events has been growing
_____   steadily.

_____   2. The ac—modations at the school's dorm—tory are far
_____   from lavish.

_____   3. The audi—nce was clearly dis—pointed when the sub-
_____   stitution for the star performer was announced.

_____   4. Crawford maintains that cert—n people on the member-
_____   ship com—tee of the club dislike him.

_____   5. The escapee tried desp—rately to get ac—oss the bor-
_____   der before nightfall.

_____   6. I am not comple—ly convinced that I should vote for
_____   your can—date for mayor.

_____   7. The judge ruled that our lawyer's argu—ent was not ad-
_____   mis—ble.

_____   8. I would d—cribe the applicant as a comp—tent archi-
_____   tect.

_____   9. The messenger quickly dis—peared am—ng the throng
_____   of merrymakers.

_____   10. "Let me look at my calend—r to see if I have any press-
_____   ing bus—ess for next Tuesday," she said.

DIRECTIONS: Each sentence contains three italicized words from the first one-third of the spelling list. One of the three words is misspelled. Underline the misspelled word and write it, correctly spelled, in the space at the left.

_____   1. Some teachers are *disatisfied* with the amount of *arithmetic* in the new *curriculum.*

_____   2. Clark *acquired* a distinct accent *during* his short stay in Great *Britian.*

_____   3. A company representative *conceeded* that an *awkward* employee had damaged the expensive *apparatus.*

_____   4. Jim has put his bonus to good use: He has *choosen* to buy a home *computer* and a modern *dictionary.*

_____   5. Ms. Lewis is a *conscientious, efficient* worker who has given the firm thirty years of *continious* service.

_____   6. The agent *acknowledged* that the house would be hard to sell because of its *delapidated appearance.*

_____   7. Barker's *absence definately* made a *difference* in the team's performance.

_____   8. *Apparently* the mayor's special *commission* has *accompolished* little of lasting value.

_____   9. "I have *allways appreciated* your helpful *criticism,*" said Miss Brown.

_____   10. An *acquaintance* of mine, an *amateur* photographer, has *accummulated* hundreds of pictures of sea gulls.

Spelling

NAME _____ SCORE _____

DIRECTIONS: Each sentence contains two words from the second one-third of the spelling list. In each of these words at least one letter is missing. Write the words, correctly spelled, in the spaces at the left.

_____
_____
    1. The young woman's knowl—ge of English lit—ature is most impressive.

_____
_____
    2. On the ni—th day of Feb—ary, Luke and Maria announced their engagement.

_____
_____
    3. The personnel officer told Frank that he had found some incred—ble errors in spelling and gram—r in the application letter.

_____
_____
    4. For this job advanced courses in math—atics are considered absolutely nec—sary.

_____
_____
    5. The young man's expla—ation was that his extreme lon—iness had made him desperate.

_____
_____
    6. Oc—sionally Marcia complains about her dull, boring exist—nce in the small town.

_____
_____
    7. The chairperson inter—pted the man before he could start another of his hum—rous stories.

_____
_____
    8. While the tropical storm lasted, we saw an extr—rdinary display of light—ng.

_____
_____
    9. The woman told us that she had more than fo—ty years of exp—ence as a mountain climber.

_____
_____
    10. The audience was enthus—tic, and the critics gave the play excel—nt reviews.

DIRECTIONS: Each sentence contains three italicized words from the second one-third of the spelling list. One of the three words is misspelled. Underline the misspelled word and write it, correctly spelled, in the space at the left.

_____ 1. People are gossiping about an *embarrassing occurrance* last night in the *library.*

_____ 2. According to one lawyer's *interpratation*, the college is not *liable* for an accident that happens in a *laboratory.*

_____ 3. *Guerrilla* forces continue to *harass* the *goverment* troops.

_____ 4. The debate coach said that my rebuttal, although *extreamly interesting*, was *irrelevant.*

_____ 5. Representatives of *ninty foreign* countries met to discuss the problem of *nuclear* wastes.

_____ 6. The school has spent *exorbitant* sums to provide *equiptment* for experiments with *laser* beams.

_____ 7. Your former employers report favorably on your *initiative*, your *intelligence*, and your *immagination.*

_____ 8. It was *inevitable* that the *mischievious* child would *finally* get into serious trouble.

_____ 9. *Nowadays* few people consider *marriage* a *hinderance* to a woman's career.

_____ 10. *Incidently* Senator Blank has been *influential* in matters relating to the *environment.*

EXERCISE 52
Spelling

NAME _____ SCORE _____

DIRECTIONS: Each sentence contains two words from the last one-third of the spelling list. In each of these words at least one letter is missing. Write the words, correctly spelled, in the spaces at the left.

_____   1. His friends think that Lawson is too opt—mistic about
_____   his future in pol—tics.

_____   2. It will pro—bly be at least a week unt—l you can get an
_____   appointment.

_____   3. The sup—tendent of schools has sched—led a teachers'
_____   meeting for tomorrow morning.

_____   4. Spe—ch 270 is a course required of all drama majors
_____   during their soph—ore year.

_____   5. In the shopping mall there is a new rest—rant that the
_____   food editor of the *Bugle* rec—mends highly.

_____   6. After the grueling tennis match my par—ner and I were
_____   covered with p—spiration.

_____   7. On these streets par—lel parking is permis—ble during
_____   daylight hours.

_____   8. The comedian's r—diculous pro—ciation of some words
_____   made the audience laugh.

_____   9. We students rec—nize the fact that it is indeed a pri-
_____   vil—ge to attend this concert series.

_____   10. In London we had an op—tunity to attend p—form-
_____   ances of two Shakespearean comedies.

DIRECTIONS: Each sentence contains three italicized words from the last one-third of the spelling list. One of the three words is misspelled. Underline the misspelled word and write it, correctly spelled, in the space at the left.

_____ 1. Lucy returned from the *village* store with a supply of *realy* fresh *vegetables*.

_____ 2. The word *rhetoric* is losing much of its *origional* meaning; some people now associate it with *propaganda*.

_____ 3. When arrested, the *villain* had in his *possession* a *quanity* of illicit drugs.

_____ 4. Aunt Leota *regards* dancing, tennis, and *similiar* pastimes as frivolous and time-wasting.

_____ 5. Angela *persuaded* three *proffessional* football players to take ballet lessons to improve their balance and sense of *rhythm*.

_____ 6. The police *sergeant* said that the quick action of the *psychiatrist* had averted a real *tradgedy*.

_____ 7. The office staff is planning a birthday party for Ms. Stuart's *secratary* on *Wednesday*, the *twelfth* of May.

_____ 8. We are *truly surprised* that someone of Stanton's *temperment* has survived this long as a race driver.

_____ 9. The new *procedure* for launching a *satellite* seems to be working *satisfactorly*.

_____ 10. *Usually* the vice-chairperson from the *preceeding* year is *unanimously* elected president of the club.

EXERCISE 53
Spelling Review

DIRECTIONS: A sentence may have no misspelled words, one misspelled word, or two misspelled words. Underline the misspelled words and write them, correctly spelled, in the spaces at the left.

_____
_____ 1. The governor did not exaggerate when she said that the exceptionally high temperatures of the passed month would have a disasterous effect on crops.

_____
_____ 2. The village priest announced that profits from the women's auxiliary rummage sale exceeded there most optimistic hopes.

_____
_____ 3. An acquaintance of mine, a sophomore majoring in mathematics, helped a police sergeant catch a thief in the dormatory.

_____
_____ 4. The villain had in his possession some irreplaceable equipment from a physics labratory and two dictionarys from the library.

_____
_____ 5. "I recommend that we stick together," said the guide. "If we proceed separately, someone could quiet easily loose her or his way."

_____
_____ 6. "You'll probably find this almost too incredible to believe, but I have already sold two original short stories," Mary Lou announced enthusiastically.

_____
_____ 7. Untill the boundary dispute is settled peaceably, there will be no noticeable improvement in relations between the two countries.

_____
_____ 8. "Initiative and imagination are absolutely necessary in this business," she said, "because competition is fierce, particularily durring a depression."

_____
_____ 9. The three partners usually schedule a conference every Wednesday to discuss miscellaneous problems.

_____
_____ 10. At the heighth of the argument, the commissioner made a short speech, and we immediately realized that we were being unnecessarily suspicious of each other.

DIRECTIONS: In each group of six words, one word *may* be misspelled. Underline the misspelled words and write them, correctly spelled, in the proper spaces at the left.

_____ 1. accidentally   approximately   cemetery
     dissipate   inference   psychological

_____ 2. analysis   convenient   entrepreneur
     generaly   species   whether

_____ 3. appropriate   communicate   grievious
     intercede   skies   syllable

_____ 4. basically   catagory   ceiling
     pursue   repetition   various

_____ 5. characteristic   conscious   decision
     preparation   undesirable   undoubtably

_____ 6. arctic   counterfeit   hurriedly
     irresistible   picnicking   remembrance

_____ 7. barbarious   comparatively   discipline
     neither   prejudice   questionnaire

_____ 8. consistent   curiousity   livelihood
     obedience   omission   opener

_____ 9. accompanying   bureaucracy   description
     memento   oblige   unforgettable

_____ 10. astronaut   conscience   eligible
     guarantee   representative   seige

PART V WRITING PARAGRAPHS AND ESSAYS

LESSON

1 An Overview of College Writing

Y OU WILL find that you need to do a great deal of writing in the future, both in college and in your career. If you possess highly developed writing skills, your work will be easier and your success more certain. On the other hand, it is doubtful that you can succeed in either area unless you are a good writer. In college, you will write notes and informal materials, and you will write tests, reports, and papers to submit for grades. As an engineer, as an accountant, as a computer programmer or systems analyst, you will use your writing skills to communicate your ideas and directions to others. Before you design a structure, analyze a balance sheet, or develop a program, you will need to do a tremendous amount of writing. If you develop your writing skills, your work in these areas will be easier and more effective.

Beyond such practical benefits, writing is a very effective tool for learning. Writing about a subject produces two good results: greater understanding and control of the material itself, and new connections to other facts and concepts. Writing out lecture notes and textbook materials in your own words will give you better control of those materials and will help you to connect the new materials with facts and concepts you learned earlier.

In the previous sections of this book, you examined the operating principles of the language and applied those principles to writing correct, effective sentences. Now you need to learn to combine those sentences into paragraphs, and the paragraphs into papers that will fulfill your college writing assignments.

The assignments you receive in college may be widely varied, ranging from a single paragraph narrating an event in your life to a complex research paper. Look briefly at a list of these possible assignments:

1. *Personal Essays*
- Recount an event in your life, explaining its importance.
- Discuss your position on the approaching presidential election.

2. *Essay Tests*
- Answer two of the following three questions, using well-developed paragraphs and complete sentences in your answer.

3. *Essays and Discussions*
- Explain the causes of structural unemployment in our country today.
- Discuss the work of Jonas Salk in disease prevention.

4. *Critical Papers*
- Evaluate the enclosed proposal for the construction of a new dam.
- Assess the work of the Thatcher administration in Britain.

227

5. *Persuasive or Argumentative Papers*
- Argue for or against the use of government spending to retrain displaced workers.
- Discuss the arguments against universal military training in the United States.

6. *Documented Papers*
- After thorough research into the subject, write a paper discussing the use of nuclear power in this country. Be sure to discuss the history, the current situation, and the arguments for and against continued use and further development.

This list does not include every type of assignment given in college courses, and it certainly does not include the informal writing, such as notetaking, that you will need to do in your college career. The list may look overwhelming, but fortunately you can learn one basic process and use it in writing all of the assignments you will meet in college and in your career.

The Writing Process

The process of writing a paper has two major divisions or phases, composing and editing, and each phase may be divided into specific steps. In general, in the composing phase you prepare and write out a first or rough draft. In the editing phase you convert the rough draft into a finished product by revising, correcting, and recopying.

COMPOSING

Step 1. Select or define the subject.

> BASIC QUESTION: What should I write about? Or (if the assignment is very specific): What does the assignment require me to write about?
> STRATEGY: Select the subject on the basis of these questions:
> - Are you and your reader interested in it?
> - Do you have enough knowledge to write on it? If not, can you locate enough?
> - Can you treat the subject completely within the length allotted for the assignment?

Step 2. Gather materials for possible use in the paper.

> BASIC QUESTION: What do I know about the subject?
> STRATEGY: Write down everything you can remember or can learn about the subject within the time available to you. Use this stockpile as the raw material for the paper.

Step 3. Establish a controlling statement or thesis for the paper.

> BASIC QUESTION: Exactly what can I say about this subject on the basis of what I know about it?
> STRATEGY: Write a one-sentence statement of the idea of the paper.

NOTE: This step is perhaps the most important step in the composing process, for it provides a control for the remaining steps in the development.

Step 4. Select specific items of support to include in the paper.

> BASIC QUESTION: What ideas, facts, and illustrations can I use to make the thesis completely clear to the reader?

STRATEGY: Review the stockpile of materials gathered in Step 2. Select from these materials only those ideas, facts, and illustrations that will develop and support the thesis.

Step 5. Establish an order for presenting the materials you have selected.

BASIC QUESTION: What is the most effective order for presenting the materials that I have selected?

STRATEGY: Choose from among the possible arrangements—most to least important, least to most important, chronological, or any others mentioned in the section on paragraphs (pp. 247–256)—and follow that order in writing the draft.

Step 6. Write the first draft.

BASIC QUESTION: What will the materials look like when presented in the order I have chosen?

STRATEGY: Write out a complete version of the paper, following the plan developed in the first five steps.

Step 7. Revise the rough draft.

BASIC QUESTION: What changes can I make to improve the organization and content of the draft?

STRATEGY: Follow the directions in the section on revision (pp. 270–271) and make the necessary changes in the draft.

Step 8. Correct the draft.

BASIC QUESTION: What errors in grammar and mechanics do I need to correct?

STRATEGY: Read each sentence as a unit standing alone. It should have a subject and a verb that agree in number and should form a complete, independent state.nent (Lessons 13, 21). It should contain no word or phrase that modifies more than one element contained in the sentence (Lesson 12); pronouns should be in the proper case (Lesson 23) and should agree with a clear antecedent in number and gender (Lesson 22). Verb tenses should be consistent and appropriate (Lesson 20). The choice of each preposition should conform to idiomatic use (Lesson 24). Each sentence must begin with a capital letter and end with a period, a question mark, or an exclamation point (Lesson 19). Within the sentence, commas, semicolons (Lessons 16, 17), colons, dashes, quotation marks, and apostrophes (Lesson 18) should appear as they are necessary.

Read each word as a separate unit; check its spelling and capitalization (Lessons 26–29). (Sometimes reading backward helps.) Each word should serve its appropriate use (Lesson 25).

Step 9. Write the final draft.

BASIC QUESTION: What form shall I use for the final copy of the paper?

STRATEGY: Follow the guidelines for manuscript form given by your instructor, and copy the paper neatly and carefully, making sure to include all the revisions and corrections you made on the rough draft. Proofread the final draft carefully.

This nine-step process can be followed with only minor changes for any writing assignment. Study it carefully as we apply it to various types of assignments. Make the process second nature to you, a set of habits followed anytime you write. The more you practice, the greater will be your facility in writing.

Before we begin to examine the writing process as it applies to specific projects in college writing, let's take a few moments to study the results that a professional writer can achieve using this process—or a similar one—in writing a publishable article about a personal experience.

The setting for the experience and the article is Australia; the writer is an editor of *Car and Driver*, a magazine for auto enthusiasts. The occasion is a trip across the Outback, a sparsely settled region in the interior of Australia. The author and three others are driving two cars on a 1,500-mile trip to survey Australian methods of improving auto safety. They have been driving in desolate country almost all day when, late in the afternoon, they encounter a washed-out bridge and must double back to find a new route. They have been driving fast; the detour seems to urge them to increased speed.

A DRIVE IN THE OUTBACK, WITH SECOND CHANCES
DAVID ABRAHAMSON

It took less than two seconds. The stab of oncoming headlights, a blur of looming sheetmetal in the center of the windshield, a jabbing reaction at the steering wheel and then that awful, indelible noise. And then an unearthly silence, as if nature itself knew that something irrevocable had happened and that a moment—maybe much more—was needed for the reality to be dealt with.

I have been driving fast most of the afternoon. Not really at the car's limit, but well above the posted speed. I enjoy fast driving for its own sake, and this new and isolated environment seemed to urge me on. After all, Australia's wide open spaces are exactly that, and we'd encountered less than one car an hour in either direction of the towns. And besides, Baker, my passenger, didn't seem to mind. We were in the middle of a long, sweeping righthander when suddenly the windshield was filled with another set of headlights. Coming at us, in the middle of the road, was a monstrous truck. The left front corner of the truck cab buried itself in the left front door of our car. The sound was absolutely deafening. Bits of metal and glass were everywhere. The impact ripped the watch off my wrist and the lenses out of my glasses. But I was lucky. Because it was a righthand-drive car, as the driver I was at least three feet away from the point of impact. Passenger Baker, however, was not. The true violence of the crash took place almost in his lap. Part of his seat was torn up and out

of its mount. The door and a section of the roof were battered in toward his head and left shoulder. We were both wearing lap-and-shoulder seat belts at the time. Mine saved my life. Baker's did too, but in the process broke his collarbone and badly bruised a few essential internal organs. A grisly tradeoff.

How and why had the accident happened? What exactly had been my mistake? Long after I'd returned to the United States, long after Baker had recovered from his injuries, I was still asking myself those questions. Now, almost a year later, the answers are clear. And they go far beyond any chance encounter on a strange road in a strange land, even beyond the crushing sense of remorse I felt at the time. And they tell me something about who I was and what I might be. I enjoyed driving, and a big part of that enjoyment came from taking a number of risks. Risks I thought were calculated, but in truth were not. Rather they were part of a glorious game, imbued with notions of independence, willful mobility and a heavy dose of virility. I'd had more than my share of near misses, but they merely served to prove the range of my skills at the wheel—my ability to judge relative speed and distance, the speed of my reflexes, the correctness of my kinesthetic instincts. In my car at speed, there was never any hint of my own mortality. Or of anyone else's. So the accident had to happen. Maybe not with that truck on that blind curve on the far side of the Earth, but somewhere. It has less to do with the law of averages than the laws of physics. Roads are a decidedly hostile environment, peopled with an unknown number of other drivers who are certain to do the wrong thing at the wrong time. And no amount of skill, real or imagined, can save you. Sweet reason is the only defense. Prudence, moderation and caution are not the stuff of grand illusions, unbridled exuberance and youthful panache. But they're great for survival.

And that, in the end, is what my experience boils down to. I now see, as I did not before, that my survival (and that of others who choose to ride with me) is at stake. I've never seen myself as a particularly courageous person, but I've always enjoyed sports containing an element of risk: parachuting, scuba-diving, alpine skiing and the like. Strange that something as mundane as an auto accident should, at age 30, give me my first glimpse of my own mortality. Thinking back to that evening south of Bombala, I am certain that I never want to hear that awful sound again. But I also never want to forget it.

Following the process as we have outlined it, the writer would have asked himself these questions:

1. What should I write about?

My Australian trip, or some part of it. The most memorable and important part of the trip was the terrible accident near Bombala, in which my passenger Bill Baker was injured.

2. What do I know or remember about the trip and, more specifically, about the accident?

Beginning with the plane ride from San Francisco, I can record as background material all the things we did on the flight, in Sidney, and on the trip itself. I will record in greatest detail the auto trip, focusing as closely as possible on the moments before and after the crash. I'll continue to write until I reach a statement or conclusion about that accident and its meaning to me now.

3. Exactly what can I say about this subject, the accident? What impression has it made on me?

The accident changed my view of my driving skills and the importance of those skills in preserving my safety while I drive. I never want to hear the awful sound of the crash again, but I never want to forget it, either.

4. What details, facts, illustrations, and observations can I use to make that thesis clear to my reader?

I will use visual details and facts surrounding the crash itself. I'll include the aftermath of the crash, the time while we wait to take Baker to the hospital. Finally, I'll record my thoughts on and impressions of the importance and meaning of the accident.

5. What order will most effectively present these supporting materials?

Because this piece is basically a narrative, I'll follow chronological order, but I'll use a few details of the actual crash to catch my readers' interest in the introduction.

6. What will the materials look like when I actually write out a first completed version of the article?

[You have read the final draft of the essay. The rough draft contained much more material.] I will cut out distracting material that weakens my statement.

A Few Words Before Starting

Getting started is often the most difficult part of writing. We all have a tendency to avoid the blank page and the work involved in filling it meaningfully. Writing will always be hard work, but a few preliminary exercises will help make getting started a little easier.

First: Strengthen your muscles so that you can write with ease. You would not go mountain climbing or run a marathon without getting in shape; you should not expect writing to be enjoyable unless you are in shape for it. Do the following exercises once each day:

- Sit in a place where you can watch people passing by. Writing as rapidly as possible, jot down a description of all that occurs, noting sizes, shapes, descriptions, and other visual details.
- Writing continuously, sign your name or copy other words down as many times as you can in two minutes.
- Without stopping, write everything that comes into your head when you read the following words:

submarine
photosynthesis
chocolate milkshake

The goal of these exercises is to be able to write for fifteen minutes without any discomfort and for an hour with two short breaks.

Second: Free your mind to write without constraints. The secret of developing a good stockpile of material for writing a paper is the ability to put large numbers of words on paper without being too selective about what is written down. The whole composing process depends on freedom to write; not until the editing phase should you be selective about what is written. Continue to do exercises based on the third exercise in the preceding list until you can fill two or three pages without doing much editing at all. The goal of this "free writing" is to be able to record ideas and other random notions freely, without fear or hesitation. Too many beginning writers sit and ponder, staring at the ceiling or into space, hoping that some brilliant idea will appear. Such appearances are rare. Most writers follow the pattern of John Updike, the poet and novelist, who throws away 90 percent of what he writes and rewrites the remaining 10 percent four or five times before he is satisfied.

Third: Explore Your Topic Extensively. You need to use your newly developed ability to write freely to explore all the possible aspects of your topic before you establish a thesis statement. Writing is a special way of learning about a subject because writing allows you to control ideas you have already developed, and it allows you to discover new ideas and make connections among old and new ideas. Sit with your paper and pen (or typewriter) and write about your topic. Record all that you can remember and then begin to answer questions about your topic. What is the history? When did I first learn about the topic? Why is it important? What are its important divisions? What are its causes? As you write, recording what you know and what you can learn about the topic, you will find that you can begin to formulate a specific statement about your topic. Allow the writing to develop important ideas, and use them to put your thesis statement together. Use writing to discover new ideas and to develop your thesis.

So don't wait for inspiration or good beginnings. Write what you can write as well as you can write it. If you can't think of a good way to start, start any way you can. If you can't think of exactly the right word, use a close approximation. Time and condition and the freedom to write without editing will improve your ideas; careful attention to revision and correction will improve the quality of your written expression. Practice and more practice will lead to success.

In the next section we will examine closely a very important type of college writing, the essay test.

Writing Exercises for an Overview of College Writing

1. Each day for the first two weeks of your experience in using the writing sections of this book, follow the instructions for getting in shape to write.
2. Follow the steps in the writing process illustrated with "A Drive in the Outback, with Second Chances," and write about an experience in your own life.
3. Find an example of personal writing about an experience or an attitude. Read it to locate the thesis statement or core idea (Step 3 in composing). Then outline the supporting details to show how they develop (or fail to develop) the core idea.

LESSON

2   Taking Essay Tests

E ssay tests provide an excellent opportunity to apply your writing skills to college writing assignments. Working on test taking is very practical; success on tests will improve your grades. Beyond that practical consideration, and perhaps more important, essay test answers require you to work within a very narrow subject area to produce a concise, complete written statement. These tight limitations of time and space require you to be very precise in the formulation of a topic statement and to distinguish carefully between materials essential to your answer and those that are only related to it. Finally, essay tests often require that you present your answer in a single well-developed paragraph. Paragraphs are the next step up in size from the sentence, and so studying paragraphs is a logical step in developing your writing skills. Practice in writing essay test answers will develop your ability to write successful paragraphs.

Getting Ready

The best preparation for taking any test is consistent, effective study throughout the term. In addition, however, you need special strategies for the last few days before the test to improve your chances of success.

Begin your final preparations for the test a few days in advance so that you will have ample time to study and assimilate the material. Follow these suggestions as you study.

Step 1. Make an overview or survey of the materials you have covered for the test. Look for periods, trends, theories, and general conclusions. Try to pinpoint important concepts and basic ideas in the materials. You may find it useful to consult a general encyclopedia for an overview or a summary of the subject areas to be covered by the test. If the subject is technical or complex or is part of an advanced course, consult an appropriate specialized encyclopedia or reference work in that field.

Step 2. Write a series of questions encompassing the major items that you have located. Cover broad areas of material. Try to concentrate on questions that begin with such words as *compare, trace, outline*, and *discuss*. In six to ten broad-scope questions of your own, you can cover all the possible questions that the teacher may ask. If you have covered all the material in your own questions, you will not be surprised by any questions on the exam.

Step 3. Read your outline, notes, and other materials, looking for answers to the questions you have composed. As you read and review, outline the answers, commit the outlines to memory, and use them as guides during the test. Write out answers to any questions that are difficult for you.

Step 4. Review the outlines, the materials, and the answers to your questions the afternoon before the test. Then put the whole thing aside and get a good night's rest.

Final Preparation

Just before going in to take the test:

- Eat a high-energy snack; fruit is a good choice. Coffee or tea will also help. Do some calisthenics or whatever else is necessary to make you alert.
- Get your equipment ready: pens, pencils, erasers, paper or examination booklets, and scratch paper. Take what you will need so that you will not worry about supplies once you enter the room.
- Arrive two minutes early for the test. Get yourself and your equipment arranged. Relax for a few seconds before the work begins.

Taking the Test

Your success in taking tests depends on your study habits and preparation; no student—or at least not very many students—can earn a high grade on a test without proper preparation. The section on study skills on pp. 320–322 suggests ways that will help you to organize your work and to improve your preparation for taking tests. But good preparation alone will not guarantee success. You need a strategy for taking tests, a strategy that will help you to decide which questions to answer, what order to use in answering the selected questions, and what organization to use for each question.

When you have made the best possible preparations for taking the test and are in the classroom with the test in your hands, do two things before you write:

First, read the test from start to finish, beginning with the directions. Decide which questions you know the most about. Determine the point value of each question. Answer first the questions you know the most about. Answering them first will ease you into the test, develop your confidence, and keep you from wasting time on questions you can't answer well anyway. Do first what you can do best. Use the remaining time to do the best you can on the rest of the questions.

Be sure to select the most valuable questions from among those you can answer. Don't waste time on a question of low point value when you could be answering a question with a high point value.

Always follow the directions. If options allow you to choose certain questions from a group, be sure you understand the options and make your choices based on your knowledge and on the point value of the questions. Invest your time wisely.

Second, make careful preparations before you write. Adapt the first four steps in the writing process to guide you in writing the answers.

Step 1. Identify the subject. The first step in the writing process is the selection of a subject. On a personal paper narrating an event in your life, your range of choices is wide. On a test, clearly, you have no such choice. The teacher has selected the subject for each question. Your job is to identify that subject correctly. A question that asks for a discussion of the causes of the Great Depression is not properly answered by a discussion of the characteristics of the Roaring Twenties. Make sure you answer the question that is asked.

Step 2. Review what you know about the question. Recall your outlines and notes. Bring to mind the practice answers you wrote in your review exercises. Make notes of these on a sheet of paper. Try to remember as much material as you can. List any special or technical words related to the subject.

Step 3. Decide exactly what the question asks for and what overall statement you are able to make and support in response to the question. Before you write, construct a specific statement of the idea or concept that you intend to develop in writing your answer. This point, or main idea, will come out of the materials you reviewed in Step 2.

Step 4. Carefully select supporting materials, examples, explanations, and other data that will serve to establish and clarify the main idea. You will have pulled together a considerable amount of material in your quick mental review. Not all of it will fit exactly the statement you are making; not all of it will be especially effective in your answer. Select materials that will establish and reinforce your point as effectively as possible within the constraints of time and space.

Now that you have looked at the basic steps in writing essay test answers—or any paragraph, for that matter—let us examine each of these steps in greater detail. Assume that you have read the test carefully, have selected your questions, and are now ready to start on the question you'll answer first.

Let us set up a brief example and follow it through these steps. Suppose you pick up a test and find on it a question such as this:

> Select one of the seven species of sea turtles and discuss its physical appearance, its habitat and geographic distribution, and its status in both present numbers and population trends.

Step 1 requires careful identification of the subject matter covered in the question. The sample question refers to sea turtles, not to all kinds of turtles. It also asks for a discussion of just one of the seven species of sea turtles. It asks for only three rather simple pieces of information about that species:

1. What is the physical appearance of that species?
2. In what type of habitats is the species found, and where are these habitats located?
3. How many individuals of this species are estimated to be alive, and is that number increasing or decreasing?

Only the last point is at all tricky. *Status* has in this question a somewhat specialized meaning referring to the species' survival potential based on what the estimated living population is and on whether it is increasing or decreasing worldwide. So the subject of that question is information about a particular species of sea turtle.

Step 2 is to collect material, to recall what you know about one species of sea turtle. From the textbook, your lecture notes, and a brief outside reading assignment, you remember this about sea turtles and jot down the following notes:

> Actually 7 species—only three much covered in class. One stood out because commercial importance (food & other products)—green turtle.
> Large: 3 to 6 feet from front to back over curve of upper shell (*carapace;* lower shell, *plastron*).
> Weighs 200–300 lb. average but reaches 850 lb. some specimens. Color from green-brown to near black. Scutes (bony plates) clearly marked. Head small compared to body.
> Occurs almost worldwide in warmer waters shallow enough to allow growth of sea grass turtles eat.
> Present status questionable. Not endangered because lrg. pops. in remote areas—under pressure and declining in pop. areas. Needs protection. First protective law in Caribbean, passed 1620. Used extensively for food by early sailors, who killed mainly females coming on shore to lay eggs. Now used for cosmetics and jewelry.
> Large green turtles make good zoo exhibits. W. Indian natives make soup of them.
> Nesting habits: Female beaches and lays approx. 100 eggs in shaped hole. First hatch-

lings on top of next push out sand covering them and leave. Those on bottom crawl out using sand first hatchlings displaced and crushed shells of vacated eggs as platform. 100 eggs right number—fewer places top of nest too low in hole, more requires nest too deep for last hatch to escape.

Recent increase in ecological pressure because women use more cosmetics based on turtle oil.

This quick mental review, jotted down hastily (perhaps more sketchily on an actual test than in the example), has produced enough information to allow you to move to the next step.

In Step 3 you must determine exactly what you can say in response to the question. Before you can make that determination, you must know exactly what the question directs you to do. These directions are usually given at the beginning of the question, and, although their exact wording may vary, they generally fall into one of several categories.

Instruction Words

The following list of instruction words covers most standard types of essay questions. Read these carefully; note that each type of instruction requires a different type of answer.

1. List, name, identify

These words require short-answer responses that can be written in one or two complete sentences. Do exactly what the question asks; don't try to expand the scope of the question.

> EXAMPLE: Name the presidents who served in the military prior to becoming president.

The word *identify* suggests that you ought to mention the two or three most important facts about a person or a subject area, not just any facts that come to mind. You would thus identify Eisenhower as a military commander and U.S. President, not as a West Point graduate who played golf.

2. Summarize, trace, delineate

An instruction to summarize asks that you give an overview or a capsule version of the subject.

> EXAMPLE: Summarize Senator Smith's position on tax reform.

An answer to this question would provide a three- or four-sentence statement of the main points of Smith's position.

The words *trace* and *delineate* usually ask that you describe the steps or process that brought some event to pass.

> EXAMPLE: Trace the life cycle of the monarch butterfly.

The answer requires a listing of the steps in the development of the butterfly from egg to adulthood.

3. Define

The instruction *define* usually asks that you establish the term within a class and then differentiate it from the other members of the class. "A parrot is a bird" establishes the word *parrot* in a class, and "found in the tropics and capable of reproducing human speech" is an attempt at differentiation. You should be careful to add enough elements of differentiation to eliminate other members of the class. For instance, as the myna is also a tropical bird capable of reproducing speech, you must complete your definition of *parrot* by specifying such items as size, color, and habitat.

4. Analyze, classify, outline

These command words imply a discussion of the relationship that exists between a whole and its parts.

Analyze asks that you break an idea, a concept, or a class down into its integral parts.

> EXAMPLE: Analyze the various political persuasions that exist within the Republican party.

This question asks that you look at the party and identify the various categories of political belief ranging from right to left.

Classify asks that you position parts in relation to a whole.

> EXAMPLE: Classify the following parts of an automobile as to location in engine, steering, or drive shaft:
> 1. Ball joint
> 2. Piston ring
> 3. Pinion gear

Outline requires that you break down an idea or a concept into its parts and show how the parts support and reinforce each other. Whether you arrange your sentences in the form of a whole paragraph or in a listing of main headings and subheadings, your outline must show how the idea or concept is made up of smaller parts and how these parts relate to the idea and to each other.

> EXAMPLE: Outline Senator Random's position on emission controls for automobiles.

This question requires that you state the position and its supporting points.

5. Discuss, explain, illustrate

This type of command word is probably the most general of all the possible directions for essay tests. The request here is that you expose, in detail, the idea, concept, or process in question. Single simple sentences will not suffice to answer such instructions. You must provide all pertinent information and write enough so that your readers have no questions, no gaps left in their information, when they're finished reading. Often such questions can be answered by making a statement of the idea or process and providing examples to illustrate your statements. In fact, if the instruction is *illustrate*, examples are required.

> EXAMPLE: Discuss the effect of depriving a child of physical affection in the first three years of its life.

The answer could be given by making a statement or statements of the effects and giving examples of each.

6. Compare, contrast

A question that asks you to compare, or to compare and contrast, is simply asking that you discuss the similarities and differences between two or more subjects.

> EXAMPLE: Compare the military abilities of Grant and Sherman.
> Make a comparison between Smith's plan and Jones's plan for shoring up the value of the dollar overseas.
> What are the similarities and differences between racketball and squash?

All these example questions ask you to establish categories—for example, skill in tactics, ability to motivate, and so on, as they relate to Grant and Sherman—and to explain how the subjects are alike or different in the areas you establish.

239

7. Evaluate, criticize

This type of question is probably the most difficult because it requires that you know what is correct or best or ideal and that you assess the assigned topic against that ideal. So you must know the subject *and* the ideal equally well.

EXAMPLE: Evaluate Eisenhower as a leader in foreign affairs.

The question is, then, "What are the characteristics of a leader in foreign affairs and how does Eisenhower measure up in each of these categories?"

Read each test question very carefully to determine what the teacher is asking. In order to make this determination, you must break the question into two parts: the instructions and the subject area.

Essay questions may be posed in many ways; they may have long introductions or fuzzy statements or confusing requests. But when you get the question clear in your mind, you will find two basic elements:

1. The instructions:

List
Name
Discuss
Evaluate
Etc.

2. The subject:

The qualities of Cather's prose
The reasons the Democrats won the election

Examine the subject area and the command word(s) of the question very carefully. Be sure to get both clear in your mind before you begin to write. An answer that *evaluates* will get little credit if the question says *define*. A discussion of the care and feeding of peregrine falcons will get few points if the question asks for a classification of birds of prey in North America.

Examine now the sample question presented earlier:

Select one of the seven species of sea turtles and discuss its physical appearance, its habitat and geographic distribution, and its status in both present numbers and population trends.

The direction, the instruction word, is *discuss*, which means make a statement and support it. The subject area is clear: any one of the seven species of sea turtles. The direction is clear: discuss

the physical appearance
the habitat and general distribution
the current status

You have collected information on the subject. Now determine exactly what you can say on that subject. For this sample question, your statement might read:

The green turtle is a large green-to-black sea turtle residing in warm, shallow waters all over the world; it is numerous but is declining in populated areas.

Keep the statement simple and direct. It need not state all the facts and details; indeed, it should not try to. It is designed to serve only as a guide for the development of your answer. If you follow the outline of the answer suggested by this controlling statement, you will select in Step 4 only the materials that serve to answer the question, and you will not be tempted to add irrelevant materials.

When you have completed a controlling statement for the answer, move to the next step.

Step 4 requires that you select from the collected materials those items that will develop the statement. Select specific details to explain each area within the statement. For the first section, physical appearance, your notes contain the following concrete details:

1. Size—three to six feet from front to back over the shell; average weight—200–300 pounds, record is 850 pounds.

2. Coloration—greenish brown is lightest color, almost black when splotches are close together.

3. Shape of flippers, head, tail. [Note that these items are not in the original list. New materials often come to mind during preparations.]

You can fill in the other sections by selecting from the collection of materials. Do not include any materials that do not specifically develop or illustrate the statement that controls the answer. Provide ample development, but do not pad.

In the collection of supporting materials for the sample question, the long discussion of the nesting habits and the number of eggs ordinarily laid by the green turtle does not fit into the answer. The material is interesting, it is concerned with the green turtle, but it does *not* fit any of the three categories in the question. Don't use materials simply because they relate to the general subject. Use only materials that support the answer to the specific question.

Writing the Answer

At this point you have before you on scratch paper:

1. A basic idea.

2. Supporting materials for that basic idea.

These will be useful in writing the answer, but they are not the answer. They are the *content* for the answer. The answer requires content, but it also requires form: grammatically correct, complete sentences that present the material in a logical, relevant order.

The best way to provide order for your answer is to modify your controlling statement to suggest the order that you intend to follow. This modification will help your reader to follow your answer.

A sentence combining elements of the question with a suggestion of your answer's focus offers a good beginning and adequate control:

Of the seven species of sea turtles, the green turtle is the largest and the most widely distributed, but it is nearing endangered status because it has commercial value.

Note that the sentence establishes your topic, the green turtle, and defines the aspects that you will discuss by using key words from each of those areas:

1. *Largest* leads to a physical description.

2. *Most widely distributed* leads naturally to a discussion of habitat and distribution.

3. *Nearing endangered status* opens the discussion of population size and trends.

The sentence relates your answer to the question and will keep you from wandering into irrelevancy. Try to make your first sentence as specific as possible, but be sure that you can expand on it. A statement that the green turtle is "an interesting species" is little help in controlling the answer because it does not focus on the question. You are not concerned with how interesting the species is; you are concerned with its appearance, its habitat and distribution, and its status. The entire answer to this sample question might read as follows:

> Of the seven species of sea turtles, the green turtle is the largest and the most widely distributed, but it is nearing endangered status because it has commercial value. It is a large turtle, measuring between 3 and 6 feet in length over the top of the shell and weighing on the average 200–300 pounds. The largest specimens are over 5 feet in length and weigh 800–1000 pounds. The upper shell (carapace) is light to dark brown, shaded or mottled with darker colors ranging to an almost black-green. The lower shell (plastron) is white to light yellow. The scales on the upper surface of the head are dark, and the spaces between them are yellow; on the sides of the head, the scales are brown but have a yellow margin, giving a yellow cast to the sides of the head. The shell is broad, low, and more or less heart-shaped. The green turtle inhabits most of the warm, shallow waters of the world's seas and oceans, preferring areas 10–20 feet deep where it can find good sea grass pastures for browsing. The turtles prefer areas that have many potholes, because they sleep in the holes for security. In numbers and population trends, the status of the green turtle is in doubt. It is under great pressure in highly populated areas such as the Caribbean Sea, where it is avidly hunted for food and for use in making jewelry and cosmetics. However, because it occurs in large numbers in remote areas, it is not technically an endangered species at this time. It needs better protection in populated areas so that its numbers will not decline any further.

Assignments and Exercises

The suggestions offered in this section will not improve your ability to take tests unless you practice applying them in your own work. Here are some suggested exercises to apply the principles:

1. Analyze your performance on a recent essay test and discuss the ways in which following the suggestions in this chapter might have improved your performance.
2. Assume that you are enrolled in a course in American history and must take an essay test on the Revolutionary War. The materials covered include the textbook, your lecture notes, your outside readings, and two films. Write a paragraph describing your preparations for the test.
3. As a practice test, write answers to the following questions on the chapter you have just read on essay-test taking.

- Discuss the preparations for taking a test up to the point where you enter the test room.
- Describe the process by which you would decide which questions to answer (if given options) and in which order you would answer them.
- Name and define four of the seven command-word categories often found in test questions, discussing the kinds of materials that each word requires in its answer.
- Describe the final form of the answer, including a discussion of thesis statement and development as it occurs in this chapter.

3 Writing Effective Paragraphs

The Paragraph

A paragraph is a group of sentences (or sometimes just one sentence) related to a single idea. Each paragraph begins on a new line, and its first word is indented a few spaces from the left margin. The last line of a paragraph is blank from the end of the last sentence to the right margin.

The function of a paragraph is to state and develop a single idea, usually called a **topic.** The topic is actually the subject of the paragraph, what the paragraph is about. Everything in the paragraph after the statement of the topic ought to **develop the topic.** *To develop* means to explain and define, to discuss, to illustrate and exemplify. From the reader's point of view, the content of the paragraph should provide enough information and explanation to make clear the topic of the paragraph and the function of the paragraph in the essay or the chapter.

The Topic Sentence

The first function of the paragraph is to state what it is about, to establish its topic; therefore the first rule of effective paragraph writing is as follows:

Usually, declare the topic of the paragraph early in a single sentence (called the *topic sentence*). You remember that the first sentence of our sample answer to an essay test question related the answer to the question by paraphrasing a significant part of the question. This sentence also provided direction for the answer by telling briefly what the answer would contain. Each paragraph should contain such a point of departure, a sentence that names what the paragraph is about and indicates how the paragraph will proceed. It may do so in considerable detail:

> Although the green turtle—a large, greenish-brown sea turtle inhabiting warm, shallow seas over most of the world—is not yet generally endangered, it is subject to extreme pressure in populated areas.

or rather broadly:

> The green turtle is one of the most important of the seven species of sea turtles.

Both statements name a specific topic: the green turtle. But neither sentence stops with a name. A sentence that reads

> This paragraph will be about green turtles.

is not a complete topic statement because it does not suggest the direction that the rest of the paragraph will take. Note that both the good examples are phrased so that a certain type of development must follow. The first sentence anticipates a discussion that will mention size, color, habitat, and distribution but will focus on the green turtle's chances for survival. The second sentence will develop the assertion that the species is one of the most important of the sea turtles. Note that neither example tries to embrace the whole idea of the paragraph. The topic sentence should lay the foundation for the paragraph, not say everything there is to be said.

As a general rule, make the topic sentence one of the first few sentences in the paragraph. Sometimes a paragraph has no topic sentence; occasionally the topic sentence occurs at the end of the paragraph. These exceptions are permissible, but the early topic sentence is more popular because it helps in three ways to produce an effective message:

1. It defines your job as a writer and states a manageable objective—a single topic.

2. It establishes a guide for your development of the basic idea. You must supply evidence of or support for any assertion in the topic sentence. The topic sentence is only a beginning, but it predicts a conclusion that the paragraph must reach.

3. It warns your reader what the paragraph is going to contain.

Notice how the topic sentence (italicized) in the following paragraph controls it and provides clear direction for the reader:

> Of all the inventions of the last one hundred years, *the automobile assembly line has had the most profound effect on American life*. The assembly line provided a method for building and selling automobiles at a price many could afford, thus changing the auto from a luxury item owned by the wealthy few to an everyday appliance used by almost every adult in America. Universal ownership and the use of the automobile have opened new occupations, new dimensions of mobility, and new areas of recreation to everyone. In addition, the automobile assembly line has provided a model for the mass production of television sets, washing machines, bottled drinks, and even sailboats. All these products would have been far too expensive for purchase by the average person without the introduction of assembly-line methods to lower manufacturing costs. With the advent of Henry Ford's system, all Americans could hope to possess goods once reserved for a select class, and the hope changed their lives forever.

The italicized sentence states the topic and the purpose of the paragraph: The paragraph is going to argue that the assembly line, more than any other invention, changed America's way of life. The writer is controlled by this sentence because everything in the paragraph should serve to support this argument. Readers are assisted by the sentence, for they know that they can expect examples supporting the position stated in the sentence.

Writing a good topic sentence is only the first step in writing an effective paragraph, for an effective paragraph provides complete development of the topic; that is, it tells the readers all they need to know about the topic for the purposes at hand. This principle is the second basic rule of effective paragraph writing:

Always provide complete development in each paragraph. Complete development tells the readers all that they need to understand the paragraph itself and the way the paragraph fits into the rest of the essay or chapter. Complete development does not necessarily provide all the information the reader *wants* to know; rather, the reader receives what is *needed* for understanding the internal working of the paragraph (the topic and its development) and the external connection (the relationship between the paragraph and the paper as a whole). As an illustration of that rather abstract statement, read the following paragraph, which gives a set of instructions for a familiar process:

Another skill required of a self-sufficient car owner is the ability to jump-start a car with a dead battery, a process that entails some important do's and don't's. First, make certain that the charged battery to be used is a properly grounded battery of the same voltage as the dead one. Put out all smoking material. Connect the first jumper cable to the positive terminal of each battery. Connect one end of the second cable to the negative terminal of the live battery, and then clamp the other end to some part of the engine in the car with the dead battery. DO *NOT* LINK POSITIVE AND NEGATIVE TERMINALS. DO *NOT* ATTACH THE NEGA-TIVE CABLE DIRECTLY TO THE NEGATIVE TERMINAL OF THE DEAD BATTERY. Choose a spot at least 18 inches from the dead battery. A direct con-nection is dangerous. Put the car with the live battery in neutral, rev the engine, and hold it at moderate rpm while starting the other car. Once the engine is run-ning, hold it at moderate rpm for a few seconds and disconnect the NEGATIVE cable. Then disconnect the positive cable. It is wise to take the car to a service station as soon as possible to have the battery checked and serviced if necessary.

The instructions in this paragraph are clear, and they will enable anyone to start a car with a dead battery. The curious reader, however, will have certain questions in mind after reading the paragraph:

1. What is a properly grounded battery?
2. Why is it necessary to extinguish smoking materials?
3. To what parts of the engine may one attach the negative cable? [After all, attach-ing it to the fan will have exciting results.]
4. What is the danger of making a direct connection?

Also, there are at least two important steps left out of the process:

Before connecting the two batteries,
1. Remove the caps to the cells of both batteries.
2. Check the fluid levels in the cells of both batteries.

Without these steps in the process, the car with the dead battery will start, but there is still a chance of explosion.

A paragraph that lacks material, that is not fully developed, probably won't explode. But it probably won't succeed, either. Questions raised in the mind of the reader will almost always weaken the effect of the paragraph. Sometimes the omissions are so important that the reader will miss the point or give up alto-gether in frustration. Remember the second rule for writing effective paragraphs:

Always provide complete development in each paragraph. Never leave your reader with unanswered questions about the topic.

Most of the time, you can write a well-developed paragraph by following three very simple steps:

Step 1. Make the topic statement one clear, rather brief sentence.

Step 2. Clarify and define the statement as needed.

Step 3. Illustrate or exemplify the topic statement concretely where possible.

As an example of the use of this three-step process, follow the development of a paragraph in answer to the question "What is the most important quality that you are seeking in an occupation?" The student's answer, found after much pre-liminary writing and a good bit of discussion, led to the following topic sentence:

Above all other qualities, *I want to have variety in the tasks I perform and in the locations where I work.*

CLARIFICATION
AND DEFINITION

> I know I must do the general line of work for which I'm trained, but I want to do different tasks in that work every day if possible. Repeating the same tasks day after day must be a mind-numbing experience. Our neighborhood mechanic does one tune-up after another, five days a

CLARIFICATION
AND DEFINITION

> week. A doctor friend tells me that 90 percent of her practice involves treating people ill with a virus, for which she prescribes an antibiotic against secondary infection. I want no part of that sort of humdrum work. Variety means doing a different part of a job every day, perhaps working on the beginning of one project today and the completion of another tomorrow, or working on broad concepts one day and details the next. I'd also like to work at a different job site as often as possible.

CONCRETE
EXAMPLE

> The field of architecture is one area that might suit me. I could work in drafting, and then switch to field supervision, and move from that task to developing the overall concepts of a large project. By doing this, I could vary my assignments and the locations of my work.

A revised version of such a paragraph might read this way:

TOPIC SENTENCE

> Some people want salary and others want big challenges, *but in my career I want variety, in both assignment and work location,* more than any other single quality.

CLARIFICATION
AND DEFINITION

> As much as possible, I want to do a different part of a job every day. Perhaps I could work on the beginning of one project and shift to the completion of another, or work on details for a while and then shift to broad concepts involved in planning.

CONCRETE
EXAMPLE

> For this reason architecture looks like a promising field for me. I could work in drafting and detailing, move next to on-site supervision, and then shift to developing the design concepts of a major project. I know that doing the same task in the same place would be a mind-numbing experience for me. Our family doctor says that 90 percent of her practice consists of treating patients who have a routine virus infection, for which she routinely prescribes an antibiotic against secondary infection. Our neighborhood mechanic spends all his time doing tune-ups. I want none of that humdrum sort of work. Variety is the spice of life; it is also the ingredient that makes work palatable for me.

These general guidelines will help you to provide complete development of your paragraphs:

1. Write a topic sentence.
2. Define and clarify that statement.
3. Provide concrete examples and illustrations.

In addition to these guidelines for development, there are several patterns of development that will assist you as you work on writing successful paragraphs.

Comparison/Contrast

When you are asked to compare, to contrast, or to compare and contrast two or more people, ideas, attitudes, or objects, you are being asked to examine items that fall within the same general group or class and, after this examination, to point out ways in which the items are similar and dissimilar. Common test questions read as follows:

> Compare the attitudes of General Patton and Bertrand Russell toward war and the maintenance of a standing army.
> Compare the effects of heroin and marijuana on the human body.
> Compare orange juice and lemon juice in respect to taste, vitamin C content, and usefulness in cooking.

Note that in each question there is a large class that includes the subjects of the comparison:

> Patton and Russell were both famous people who held carefully developed attitudes toward war. [If one had no attitude on war, the comparison couldn't be made.]
> Heroin and marijuana are both drugs that act on the human body.
> Orange juice and lemon juice are citrus products.

The point of comparison/contrast is that the items share certain qualities but can be separated or distinguished by other qualities that they do not share. The identification of these like and unlike qualities is the aim of comparison/contrast.

In a course in business or investments you might be asked to compare stocks and bonds as investment instruments. Begin by listing the qualities of a common stock and the qualities of a bond side by side.

A bond is	A stock is
1. an instrument used by investors.	1. an instrument used by investors.

Note how this first point in each list establishes that the two objects of comparison are members of the same large class and can therefore be compared and contrasted.

2. a certificate of indebtedness.	2. a representation of ownership of a fraction of a company.
3. a promise to repay a specific number of dollars.	3. worth the selling price on any day, whether more or less than the purchase price.
4. payable on a specified date.	4. sold anytime, but not ever payable as is a bond.
5. sold at a specific rate of interest.	5. not an interest-drawing instrument; rather, it is a share of profits.

In geology rocks can be divided into three groups:

IGNEOUS	SEDIMENTARY	METAMORPHIC
Formed when molten rock material called *magma* cools and solidifies.	Formed from deposits of older rocks or animal or plant life. Are deposited on each other and joined by pressure or natural chemicals.	Formed when old rocks change under heat or pressure. They do not divide easily into subgroups.

(continued)

IGNEOUS	SEDIMENTARY	METAMORPHIC
One type (extrusive) is forced out by pressure from within the earth, for example, a volcano erupts and spews out lava, which, if cooled quickly, becomes glassy or forms small crystals such as obsidian or pumice.	Three types: Classic—formed of older rock pieces. Chemical—formed of crystallized chemicals. Organic—formed of plant and animal remains.	

However, a detailed comparison of the three basic types of rocks is impossible in a single paragraph because of the enormous complexity of the subject. Certain qualities exist in each of the three groups—smooth surfaces, for example—but what caused the smooth surfaces in one case or another may not be particularly relevant to the factors that determine what group a rock belongs to. About all that can be dealt with in a single paragraph is a very broad comparison of the three major groups of rocks.

In the study of human anatomy, the two muscle groups—skeletal and smooth—offer a sufficient number of common points to make the exercise of comparison possible. The two groups can be compared on the basis of

	Skeletal	*Smooth*
1. Location	Attached to skeleton.	Found in blood vessels, digestive system, and internal organs.
2. Function	To move legs, arms, eyes, and so on.	To move food for digestion, contract or expand blood vessels—varies by location.
3. Structure	Long, slender fibers bundled together in parallel, contain many nuclei.	Arranged in sheets or in circular fashion, contain one nucleus.
4. Contraction	Rapid, only when stimulated by nerve; stimulus can be voluntary or involuntary.	Slow, rhythmic; cannot be controlled consciously (voluntarily); stimulated by nerves or by hormones.

It is possible to develop a paragraph of comparison/contrast in two different ways. The first pattern is clearly illustrated in the list of muscle characteristics: The qualities of both muscle groups are listed numerically in the same order. This pattern is useful if you are comparing only a limited number of characteristics. A second pattern, because it focuses the comparison point by point, provides better control of longer or more complicated topics. A paragraph comparing stocks and bonds in this way might read as follows:

Although stocks and bonds are both commonly used investment instruments, they differ in several important aspects and thus appeal to different types of investors. A bond is a certificate of indebtedness; a share of stock represents ownership of a percentage of a company. A bond involves a promise to repay a specified amount of money on a day agreed on in advance. Because it represents ownership, stock must be sold to obtain its value, and it is worth only the selling price on a given day, never a guaranteed amount. A bond earns money in the form of interest at a fixed rate, but stocks share in the profits, partial distributions of which are called *dividends*. Thus the value of a bond, if held to its date of maturity, is fixed; and the periodic interest paid by many bonds is relatively secure. A stock, on the other hand, changes its value on the basis of market conditions and its rate of return on the basis of the profitability of the company. The risk in a bond is the risk that inflation will reduce the value of its fixed number of dollars and its fixed rate of return; stocks risk a possible decline in the general market and a possible reduction of profits that might erode the sale price and the dividends. So bonds are useful where security of investment is a high priority and protection against inflation is not vital. Stocks fit an investment portfolio in which some risk is acceptable and a hedge against inflation is very important.

So in this pattern we see bonds and stocks compared in respect to the following categories:

1. The nature of the instrument itself.
2. The way the value of the instrument is established.
3. The method of earning money.
4. The relative security of the two instruments.
5. The risks inherent in each one.
6. The situations in which each might be useful as an investment.

As an exercise in comparison/contrast, you might try following each of the two patterns in writing a paragraph on the two groups of muscles described earlier.

Definition

We have all read definitions; they are the subject matter of dictionaries, which we are accustomed to using to find the meaning of an unfamiliar word. But definition, as a process, is also a useful device in writing; it can serve to establish meaning for words, concepts, and attitudes. You have often written paragraphs of definition on tests and in essays. On tests, you might find instructions such as these:

Define the *sonata-allegro form* and give examples of it in twentieth-century music.
Define *conservatism* as it is used in American politics.
Define a *boom-vang* and say how it is used in sailing.

The correct responses to such instructions are paragraphs of definition. Such paragraphs ought to follow the same rules of presentation and development that the dictionary does. Let us examine two definitions in the pattern used in dictionaries and discover how they are formed.

Basketball is a game played by two five-player teams on a rectangular court having a raised basket at each end. Points are scored by tossing a large round ball through the opponent's basket.
Football is a game played with an oval-shaped ball by two eleven-player teams defending goals at opposite ends of a rectangular field. Points are scored by carrying or throwing the ball across the opponent's goal or by kicking the ball over the crossbar of the opponent's goal post.

These two definitions concern games familiar to most of us. Notice that they both follow the same pattern:
First, they identify both words as the names of games.
Second, they specify

1. the number of teams.
2. the number of players on each team.
3. the type of playing area.

4. the way in which scoring occurs.
5. the shape of the ball.

The examples illustrate the classic pattern of definition: The first step is to classify the word within a class or group; the second step is to differentiate the word from other members of its class:

Football is a game. . . . . [Establishes in a class.]
played by two teams
of eleven players each
on a rectangular field. } [Differentiates from other games.]
Scoring occurs by crossing
  opponent's goal in a special way.

When you write a paragraph of definition, follow the same method: Classify the term, then distinguish it from other members of its class.

However, your paragraph of definition ought to offer more than just the basic points of differentiation. You should also provide illustrations, examples, and comparisons of the term being defined to terms that might be familiar to your reader. This additional information helps your reader to understand and assimilate the information that you are offering. The process is often called **extending the definition.** Examine the following paragraph defining football and note how basic definition and extension are combined to make an effective presentation:

> On any Saturday or Sunday afternoon in the fall of the year, hundreds of thousands of Americans betake themselves to stadiums, and millions more hunker down before television sets to witness the great American spectator sport, football. In simplest form, a definition of football states that it is a game played on a large field by two teams of eleven players and that scoring is accomplished by carrying or throwing an oval ball across the opponent's goal line or by kicking the ball between two uprights called *goalposts*. But such literal definition scarcely does justice to the game or to its impact on Americans. For it is more than a game or a sport; it is a happening, a spectacle, a ritual that is almost a religious experience for its devotees. The game catches them with its color: a beautiful green field surrounded by crowds dressed in a galaxy of hues, teams uniformed in the brightest shades ever to flow from the brush of deranged artists. It holds these fans with its excitement: the long pass, the touchdown run, the closing-minutes drive to victory. But above all the game seems to captivate them with its violence, with dangers vicariously experienced, with a slightly veiled aura of mayhem. This element of danger draws casual viewers and converts them into fanatic worshippers of the great American cult-sport, football.

Finally, a word of warning about constructing definitions: A fundamental rule is that a definition must not be circular. A useful definition does not define a term by using a related form of the term itself. To define the word *analgesic* by saying that it causes analgesia means nothing unless the reader knows that *analgesia* means absence or removal of pain. To define *conservatism* as a philosophy that attempts to conserve old values doesn't really add much to a reader's understanding. Thus the rule:

Do not construct circular definitions; i.e., do not use in the definition a form of the word being defined.

Analysis

Chemists analyze compounds to isolate and identify their components. Economists analyze the financial data of the nation to determine the factors contributing to recessions. Sports commentators analyze games to explain the strengths leading to a victory.

Analysis is the act of breaking down a substance or an entity into its components. It is possible to analyze a football team and to point out the various positions: ends, tackles, guards, and the rest. An army can be broken down into infantry, artillery, and engineers. A piano is made up of parts: keys, strings, sounding board, and so on.

A paragraph of analysis provides information derived from this act of breaking down into parts, usually by listing, defining, and explaining the parts of the whole in question. As an example, take the elements or characteristics that make up that rarest of animals, the good driver:

> The good driver possesses
> 1. technical competence.
> 2. physical skills.
> 3. sound judgment.
> 4. emotional stability.

A paragraph analyzing the qualities of a good driver might read this way:

> Every American over fourteen years of age wants to drive, does drive, or just stopped driving because his or her license was revoked. Not every American—in fact, only a very few Americans—can be counted in the ranks of good drivers. Good drivers must possess technical competence in the art of driving. They must know the simple steps, starting , shifting, and braking, and the highly sophisticated techniques, feathering the brakes and the power slide, for example. In addition they must possess physical skills, such as exceptional eye–hand coordination, fast reflexes, outstanding depth perception, and peripheral vision. They must also possess good judgment. What speed is safe on a rain-slick highway? How far can a person drive without succumbing to fatigue? What are the possible mistakes that the approaching driver can make? And besides the answers to these questions and the technical and physical skills listed above, good drivers possess steel nerves to cope with that potentially lethal emergency that one day will come to everyone who slips behind the wheel of a car. Only with these qualities can a person be called a good driver and be relatively sure of returning home in one piece.

A suggestion about analysis: When you divide or break down an entity into its elements, be sure that you establish parallel categories. It is not proper, in analyzing an automobile's main systems, to list

> frame
> body
> drive train
> engine
> piston ring

Although the first four items could possibly be called major systems in an automobile, piston rings are a small part of a large system, the engine, and cannot be included in a list of major systems.

The rule for analysis is
Keep categories parallel.

Process Analysis

A process paragraph is a form of analysis that examines the steps involved in an action or a sequence of actions. The most common sort of process analysis is

251

the recipe: To make a rabbit stew, first catch a rabbit, and so forth. Instructions for building stereo receivers or flying kites or cleaning ovens are all process analyses. In addition to instructions, process analysis can be used to trace the steps involved in a historical event. Such analysis would be required to answer an essay test question that begins with the words *trace* or *delineate*.

The following paragraph provides a set of instructions:

> Changing the oil and the oil filter in your car is quite a simple process, and "doing it yourself" can save several dollars every time you change the oil. First, go to an auto parts store or a discount store and buy the oil and the oil filter specified for your car. At the same time, buy an oil filter wrench, the only specialized tool necessary for this job. Don't buy these items at your gas station; prices are lower at the other stores. In addition, you will need an adjustable wrench and a pail or bucket low enough to fit under the car to catch the old oil as it drains from the crankcase. Don't lift the car on a bumper jack. Simply crawl under the car and locate the drain plug for the crankcase. From the front of the car the first thing you see underneath will be the radiator—the thing with the large hose running from the bottom. That hose runs to the engine, the next piece of equipment as you work your way back. On the bottom surface is the drain plug, usually square with a few threads visible where it screws into the oil pan. Place the pail or bucket beneath this plug. Fit the wrench to the plug by adjusting its size. Turn the plug counterclockwise until it falls out of its hole into the pail. Don't try to catch it; the oil may be hot. While the oil drains into the pail, find the oil filter on one side of the engine, usually down low. (It will look exactly like the one you bought.) Reach up (or perhaps down from the top, whichever is easier) and slip the circle of the filter wrench over it. Pull the wrench in a counterclockwise direction and take off the old filter. Put the new filter on in exactly the opposite way, tightening it clockwise by hand until it is snug. Put the drain plug back in place, tightening it firmly with the adjustable wrench. Now find the oil filter cap on the top of the engine and pour in the new oil. Tighten the filter cap firmly. Dispose of the old oil in a convenient spot of dirt and wipe your hands clean. Finally, record the mileage for this change somewhere so that you will know when the next change is due.

A process paragraph that traces a historical development might be somewhat more difficult to write than a set of instructions. Essentially, however, tracing the steps in a historical process follows the same form as instructions; the major difference is that the historical event has already occurred and the paragraph is written in the past tense. Examine the following paragraph, which traces the transformation of the computer from mainframe to microcomputer, and notice how its pattern (this happened, then that, then another thing) follows very closely the pattern of the instructions in the previous example (do this, then that, then the other thing):

> The first computers were made from vacuum tubes about as big as television tubes, and the collection of them filled up a room the size of a classroom. The tubes were inordinately sensitive to changes in temperature and humidity, and the smallest speck of dust caused them to go berserk. They were expensive to build and expensive to maintain; therefore they were operated only by highly trained technicians. Anyone who wished to use the computer was forced to deal with the people in the white lab coats, an inconvenient arrangement at best. The first step in reducing the size and increasing the reliability of the computer was the invention of transistors, small, inexpensive devices that control the flow of electricity. They are solid and durable, and, most important, they can be made very small. Scientists soon discovered that they could also be hooked together into integrated circuits known as *chips*; the chips could contain tremendous amounts of circuitry, an amount com-

parable to the wiring diagram of an office building, on a piece of silicon no bigger than your thumbnail. Finally, scientists and computer experts developed the microprocessor, the central works of a computer inscribed on a chip. Presto! The way was opened for the development of a microcomputer about the size of a bread box.

Causal Analysis

Causal analysis, as the name implies, is a discussion of the causes leading to a given outcome. On an essay test, you might be asked to explain or discuss the reasons for a lost war, a victory in an election, a depression, or the collapse of a bridge. In your life outside school, you might be called on to explain why you have selected some occupation or particular college or why you wish to drop out of school to hike the Appalachian Trail for four or five months.

Causal analysis differs from process analysis in that it does not necessarily involve a chronological sequence. Instead, it seeks the reasons for an outcome and lists them (with necessary discussion) in either ascending or descending order of importance. A process analysis concerned with the growth of inflation in the last seventy-five years might trace the fall of the dollar's value and the actions and reactions of government and consumers at intervals of ten years. On the other hand, a causal analysis on the same subject would give the reasons why the dollar has declined in value and why the reactions of government and consumers have produced progressively worse conditions. Causal analysis might also be used to explain why a course of action has been taken or ought to be taken.

It is extremely important that the United States curb inflation over the next few years. Inflation at home is reducing the value of the dollar overseas, making it very difficult for Americans to purchase products from other countries. German automobiles, even those that once were considered low-cost transportation, have increased in price dramatically in the last few years. At home, rapid price increases have made it very difficult for salary increases to keep pace with the cost of living. In spite of large pay increases over the past few years, factory workers have shown little or no gain in buying power; prices have climbed as their wages have increased, leaving them with nothing to show for a larger paycheck. Inflation has been especially hard on retired people who live on a fixed income. They receive only a set number of dollars and do not benefit from pay increases as do wage earners. But while their income has remained the same, prices have increased; thus they cannot buy the same amounts as they could previously. Unchecked inflation works a hardship on all of us, but it is especially hard on those whose income does not increase to match the increases in prices.

Causal analysis might also be used to explain the reasons why someone holds a particular position or opinion. A student explained her love of sailing as follows:

A sailboat, a broad bay, and a good breeze form perhaps the most satisfying combination in the world of sport. To be sailing before a brisk wind across an open expanse of water allows—no, requires—cooperation with the forces of nature. Working with the wind in moving the boat provides us one of the few times when we are not forced to ignore, or work against, or even overcome the natural rhythms and functions of the universe. Too much of daily life pits us against those forces; finding them on our side, aiding us in a worthwhile project, is indeed a pleasure. The boats used are in themselves very pleasant. They do not bang or clank, nor do they spout vile fumes or foul the air, suddenly explode, or cease to function altogether. Instead, they offer the soft, sliding sounds of the bow slipping through the sea, the creak of ropes and sails, and the gentle, soothing hum of the standing rigging pulled tight by the pressure of wind on sails. Most important, sailing puts

253

us in close contact, in communion, with that most basic element, the sea. The sea remains constant; winds or storms may stir the surface, but the depths are never moved. The sea always has been and always will be, or so it seems. It offers constancy and permanence in the midst of a world where flux and change are the only constants. Is it any wonder that sailing is such a delight, such a joy?

Use of Examples

One of the simplest yet most effective paragraphs states an idea and uses examples to illustrate and explain the idea. The following paragraph explains an idea by using examples:

Youth and beauty are wonderful attributes, and in combination they are a wonderful possession. But television commercials and programs extol youth and beauty to such an extreme that those not so young and less than beautiful are made to feel inferior. Cars, beer, clothes, and even lawn mowers are almost always pictured with lithe, beautiful women of tender age or well-muscled young men with luxuriant, well-groomed hair. Cosmetics are always portrayed in use by people who have almost no need of them. Beauty, and especially youthful beauty, sells goods, we surmise, and those who do not become young and beautiful after buying the car or ingesting the iron supplement are obviously unfit to share the planet with the favored ones. And the programs themselves emphasize youthful beauty. There are few homely, few truly decrepit people who play regularly in any series. Any family, and any individual, who cannot compare with those perfect people ought to be exiled from the land of the lovely. We are left to believe that only the beautiful young are acceptable.

Description and Narration

Two important orders of development remain: development by space and development by time, more commonly called *description* and *narration*. Each of these patterns involves a direction or a movement. Description requires that you move your writer's eye through a given space, picking out selected details in order to create an effect. Narration demands that you create a progression through time, providing details selected to convey a story and its impact. The success of each pattern depends on the careful selection of details of physical qualities or of action and on the vivid presentation of these details.

In *Huckleberry Finn* Mark Twain has Huck give a beautiful description of a sunrise on the Mississippi:

. . . we run nights, and laid up and hid daytimes; soon as night was most gone, we stopped navigating and tied up—nearly always in the dead water under a tow-head; and then cut young cottonwoods and willows and hid the raft with them. Then we set out the lines. Next we slid into the river and had a swim, so as to freshen up and cool off; then we set down on the sandy bottom where the water was about knee deep, and watched the daylight come. Not a sound, anywhere—perfectly still—just like the whole world was asleep, only sometimes the bull-frogs a-cluttering, maybe. The first thing to see, looking away over the water, was a kind of dull line—that was the woods on t'other side—you couldn't make nothing else out; then a pale place in the sky; then more paleness, spreading around; then the river softened up, away off, and warn't black any more, but gray; you could see little dark spots drifting along, ever so far away—trading scows, and such things; and long black streaks—rafts; sometimes you could hear a sweep screaking; or jumbled up voices, it was so still, and sound come so far; and by-and-by you could see a streak on the water which you know by the look of the streak that there's a snag there in a swift current which breaks on it and makes that streak look that way; and you see the mist curl up off the water, and the east reddens up, and the river, and you make out a log cabin in the edge of the woods, away on the bank on t'other side of the river, being a wood-yard, likely and piled by them cheats so you can throw a dog through it anywheres; then the nice breeze springs up, and comes fanning you from over there, so cool and fresh, and sweet to smell, on account of the woods and the flowers; but sometimes not that way, because they've left dead fish laying around, gars, and such, and they do get pretty rank; and next you've got the full day, and everything smiling in the sun, and the song-birds just going it!

Two qualities of this description are important to your writing. Note first the direction or movement of the unfolding picture. Beginning with the dim view of the far bank, the narrator observes traces of paleness in the sky. He then notes that the river has softened up "away off"; notice the logical progression from sky to horizon to river. After he gives details of the changing sights and sounds at river level, the mist curling up from the river focuses his attention again on the sky as the "east reddens up." Then he returns to the river and develops the picture as new details become visible in the light of morning. This movement from mid-picture to background to foreground to background to foreground follows a sensory logic, an order of increasing visibility as the sun rises and the light increases. It is important to select an order of presentation (or, as here, a logic) and to stick with the order, whether it be left-to-right, right-to-left, middle-to-left-to-right, or any other easily followed combination.

Second, Twain provides details that appeal to the senses:

Color: dull line of woods
pale sky
river changing from black to gray
dark spots and black streaks
east reddening
Sound: complete absence of sound
bullfrogs a-cluttering
sweep screaking
jumbled up voices
song birds
Smell: woods
flowers
dead fish
Motion: dark spots drifting
snag in swift current
mist curling up off the water
Touch: cooling off in water
sitting on sandy bottom of river
cool breeze springing up

Supply your reader with sensory appeal. Keep your description lively and colorful.

Twain provides us with a heart-stopping piece of narration in *Huck Finn*, the killing of the old drunk, Boggs:

So somebody started on a run. I walked down street a ways, and stopped. In about five or ten minutes, here comes Boggs again—but not on his horse. He was a-reeling across the street towards me, bareheaded, with a friend on both sides of him aholt of his arms and hurrying him along. He was quiet, and looked

255

uneasy; and he warn't hanging back any, but was doing some of the hurrying himself. Somebody sings out—"Boggs!"

I looked over there to see who said it, and it was that Colonel Sherburn. He was standing perfectly still, in the street, and had a pistol raised in his right hand—not aiming it, but holding it out with the barrel tilted up towards the sky. The same second I see a young girl coming on the run, and two men with her. Boggs and the men turned round, to see who called him, and when they see the pistol the men jumped to one side, and the pistol barrel came down slow and steady to a level—both barrels cocked. Boggs throws up both of his hands, and says, "O Lord, don't shoot!" Bang! goes the first shot, and he staggers back clawing at the air—bang goes the second one, and he tumbles backwards onto the ground, heavy and solid, with his arms spread out. That young girl screamed out, and comes rushing, and down she throws herself on her father, crying, and saying, "Oh, he's killed him, he's killed him!" The crowd closed up around them, and shouldered and jammed one another, with their necks stretched, trying to see, and people on the inside trying to shove them back, and shouting, "Back, back! give him air, give him air!"

Colonel Sherburn he tossed his pistol onto the ground, and turned around on his heels and walked off.

Again, two aspects of the narrative are important. The order is simple, straight chronology. But notice the action words. The girl comes on the run, the men jump, Boggs staggers. Few forms of the verb *to be* intrude to slow the action, and no statements of thought or emotion stop the progression. All of the impact and emotion is conveyed through action, and that use of action is the essence of good narrative.

A Final Note

Good paragraphs are not necessarily restricted to a single pattern of development. Quite often it is useful to combine patterns to produce a desired effect. The following paragraph on spider webs illustrates such a combination of patterns. The predominant device used here is analysis: The larger unit, spider webs, is broken down into three separate types or categories. But the writer uses an additional strategy; he clarifies his analysis by comparison/contrast, pointing out like and unlike details of the three kinds of spider webs:

> Three kinds of webs are constructed by web-spinning spiders. The first type is the tangled web, a shapeless helter-skelter jumble attached to some support such as the corner of a room. These webs are hung in the path of insects and serve to entangle them as they pass. The second type of web is the sheet web. This web is a flat sheet of silk strung between blades of grass or tree branches. Above this sheet is strung a sort of net, which serves to knock insects into the sheet. When an insect hits the sheet, the spider darts out and pulls it through the webbing, trapping the insect. Finally, perhaps the most beautiful of the webs, is the orb. The orb web consists of threads that extend from a center like a wheel's spokes and are connected to limbs or grass blades. All the spokes are connected by repeated circles of sticky silk, forming a kind of screen. Insects are caught in this screen and trapped by the spider.

Unity

An essential quality that you need to develop in good paragraphs is unity. A very simple rule says everything necessary to make clear the concept of unity in paragraph writing:

Handle only one idea in the paragraph. Second and subsequent ideas should be handled in separate paragraphs.

The paragraph originated as a punctuation device to separate ideas on paper and to assist readers in keeping ideas separate as they read. Introducing more than one idea in a paragraph violates the basic reason for the existence of the paragraph.

It would seem to be easy to maintain unity in a paragraph, but sometimes ideas can trick you if you don't pay close attention to your topic sentence. A student wrote this paragraph on strawberries some years ago:

> Strawberries are my favorite dessert. Scooped over ice cream or dipped in powdered sugar, they are so good they bring tears to my eyes. My uncle used to grow strawberries on his farm in New Jersey. Once, I spent the whole summer there and my cousins and I went to the carnival. . . .

Things went pretty far afield from strawberries as the paragraph continued, and you can see how one idea, "used to grow strawberries on his farm," led to a recollection of a delightful summer on that farm and opened the door to a whole new idea and a change in form from discussion to narration. "Strawberries" and "that summer on the farm" are both legitimate, interesting, and perfectly workable topics for a paragraph. But they are probably not proper for inclusion in the same paragraph. Unity demands that each topic be treated in a separate paragraph. One paragraph handling one idea equals unity.

Coherence

Another important quality that you need to develop in your paragraphs is coherence. The word *cohere* means "to stick together," "to be united." It is a term used in physics to describe the uniting of two or more similar substances within a body by the action of molecular forces. In paragraph writing, the term *coherence* is used to describe a smooth union between sentences within the paragraph. In other words, the sentences in a coherent paragraph follow one another without abrupt changes. A good paragraph reads smoothly, flowing from start to finish without choppiness to distract the reader.

The first step in establishing coherence occurs when you select a pattern for developing the paragraph. The selection of a pattern is based on the assignment that the paragraph is going to fulfill. You learned in the study of essay test answers that a question asking for discussion requires one sort of development and a question asking for comparison demands another. Review the discussions of essay tests and of paragraph patterns to keep this idea fresh in your mind.

(Note, however, that it is sometimes necessary to include more than one pattern of development in a paragraph. A narration, for example, may demand a passage of description. Don't hesitate to shift methods where a switch is useful. Do so with care, and with the possibility in mind that a new method of development might suggest the need for a new paragraph.)

The pattern you select will help to establish coherence because it produces a flow and a movement in the paragraph and because it serves as a frame for providing details of development. Select the pattern according to the demands of the assignment and follow that pattern through the whole paragraph.

The selection of development pattern is perhaps the most important step in achieving a coherent paragraph. There are, however, various other writing strategies contributing to the same end.

1. Repetition of nouns and use of reference words.

> My father asked me to dig some postholes. After I finished that, he told me the truck needed washing. It is Father's pride and joy, but I'm the one who has to do such jobs.

These three short sentences show a fairly clear pattern of development that in itself establishes coherence. There is the beginning of a story, suggesting that narration will carry the paragraph further. Events occur one after another, setting a pattern of straight chronology. But note how strongly the repeated nouns and reference words knit the sentences together:

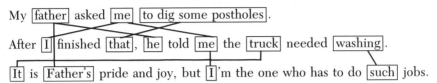

2. Use of temporal words: conjunctions and adverbs.

A series of short, abrupt sentences, although following a rigid chronological pattern, does not read as though it had coherence:

> I drove down to the corner. I stopped for a red light. A car smashed into the back of mine. I got out rubbing my neck. The driver of the other car sat behind the wheel and wept. I realized that the other driver was an elderly, gray-haired man.

The writer, sensing that something is lacking from the paragraph, might revise it this way:

> I drove down to the corner. *While* I was stopped for a red light, a car smashed into the back of mine. *As* I got out, rubbing my neck, the driver of the other car sat behind the wheel and wept. Only *then* did I realize that the other driver was an elderly, gray-haired man.

Two features of the revision have improved on the original draft. The first and most obvious is the addition of the words *while, as,* and *then* to connect the sentences by declaring the chronological sequence. Second, *while* and *as* convert short sentences into dependent clauses, thus replacing four choppy sentences with two longer ones and eliminating the jog-trot rhythm that gave the reader hiccups.

3. Use of transitional words and phrases at or near the beginning of sentences.

The coordinating conjunctions*; adverbs like *however, moreover, therefore, consequently, similarly,* and *thus;* and expressions like *on the other hand, in addition,* and *for example*—all can produce a subtle transitional effect rather like that of reference words. They force the reader to recollect the preceding material, thus making a tie between the thoughts they introduce and what has already been stated. When you read *But* at the beginning of a sentence, the author is declaring to you in loud tones, "You are to interpret the forthcoming statement as being in opposition or in contrast to what you have just read." *Moreover,* in the same place, suggests that what is coming is an addition to the last remark; *consequently* means "as a result of what I have just stated."

The ploy of cementing the parts of a paragraph together with these words and

---

* Disregard the myth that there is something wrong with starting a sentence with *and, but, for, or,* or *nor.* Do realize, however, that these words at the opening of a sentence provide a special effect and call attention to themselves and to what follows them. Don't overuse them, and be sure of your purpose when you do launch a statement with one.

phrases is used by nearly every writer. It is a perfectly good device, but unfortunately it is also a seductively easy one. The unwary writer larding sentences with *however*'s and *therefore*'s in search of elegance and poise may get into trouble with logic. "Sam drank too much on our dinner date. Consequently he threw up," may leave one wondering whether the nausea stemmed from the liquor or the date.

Exercises for Patterns for Paragraphs

1. Examine the following facts and observations:

Radial tires usually last thirty-five thousand miles.
Bias-belt tires run quietly.
Radial tires resist punctures.
Radial tires cost seventy-five dollars apiece.
Bias-belt tires maintain balance quite well.
The tread on radial tires resists skidding.
Bias-belt tires can be replaced in pairs.
Bias-belt tires are safe at most speeds.

Write a paragraph of comparison/contrast discussing the merits of these tires.
2. Write a paragraph giving directions for preparing your favorite dessert. Include every step and provide enough detail and information for a beginning cook to be able to make the dessert successfully. Check your work by preparing the dessert following your instructions.
3. Write a description of one of the buildings on your campus. Provide sufficient detail so that a person can identify the building that you are describing. Do not use the name, the location, or any identifying colors in the description.

4 Writing Longer Essays

O NCE you have mastered the steps in the writing process for paragraphs, you will need to make only a few adjustments in order to follow that same process in writing a longer essay, the sort of essay you might be assigned in a college class in biology, business, or English.

In earlier sections you have practiced writing essay tests and special paragraph arrangements; each piece of writing required the use of the writing process applied to a rather short project. In each case the process was the same. Considered as a series of questions, the process looks like the following. The first six steps are the composing or creating stage. Steps 7, 8, and 9 are the editing stage in the process.

1. What is my subject? What have I been assigned, or what do I wish to write on?

2. What do I know, what can I learn, about that subject?

3. What specific statement can I make about that subject on the basis of what I know or can learn?

4. Of all I know on the subject, what specific items will best support and illustrate that specific statement?

5. What is the best order for presenting the support and illustration?

6. What does a first attempt (draft) at writing that paper produce?

7. What changes must be made in content and organization in order to improve the draft and make it acceptable to my reader?

8. What corrections must be made in grammar, mechanics, and usage to make the paper acceptable to my reader?

9. What form must the final version take?

The same writing process works well on a structured class assignment or on an assignment in which some leeway is given on topic selection. Here is how you might develop a paper assigned in your English class.

1. Select the subject. Because this paper is a class assignment, the first step requires a look at the nature of class assignments and the problems of defining the subject and limiting it to an appropriate, manageable length.

The nature of an assignment for a paper can vary, but you will find that writing assignments usually fall into one of three categories.

1. GENERAL: Write a two-page paper on something we've covered in this course.

2. SOMEWHAT SPECIFIC: Write a two-page paper on some aspect of the novel *Huckleberry Finn*.

3. VERY DIRECTIVE: Write a two-page paper explaining why Huck Finn's experiences led him to make his final statement: "Aunt Sally's going to adopt me and sivilize me and I can't stand it. I been there before."

The first example, the general assignment, grants considerable latitude in the selection of a subject for your paper. Often this latitude will provide more of a problem than a blessing because it is necessary to find something to write about that you *and* the teacher consider interesting and worthwhile. It is of little value to write a fine paper and find that the teacher (the grader) thinks the topic so insignificant that the whole effort can't be worth more than a C. The best approach here is to review the textbook, your lecture notes, and previous tests (if any); to select from these an important content area, concept, or personality; and to use that as a starting point for your work. Be sure to choose an area that interests you, an area about which you have some knowledge and some readily accessible sources of information. Once you have made this initial selection, you have converted the type of assignment from "general" to "somewhat specific." Next, you need to restrict the area you selected or were assigned so that you can develop it fully within the assigned length of the paper. Suppose, for example, the assignment names the novel *Huckleberry Finn* as the subject for a two-page paper. Several areas are open to you:

1. Autobiographical aspects of the novel.
2. Problems of plot and structure.
3. Problems of characterization.
4. Philosophical aspects of the novel.

For the selection or restriction process, choose one of the areas and make a final selection of a topic within that area. The final selection should be fairly small in scope, something manageable within two pages. In the example of *Huckleberry Finn*, the process of restriction might look like this:

1. Philosophical aspects of the novel.
2. The relationship between individuals and society.
3. Huck Finn's attitude toward the world as he saw it.
4. Why Huck's experiences led him to say that he couldn't stand to be "sivilized."

The final version of the topic (Number 4) is probably limited enough for it to be treated adequately within the assigned length. The topic asks a single question about one person, and that question—"Why?"—can be answered: "because his experiences with civilization were unpleasant or terrifying." That statement and the unpleasant or terrifying experiences can be illustrated efficiently by the use of three or four examples. The statement of this restricted topic results in a "very directive" assignment and provides the basis for organizing and writing a two-page paper.

The process just detailed is designed to help you derive a topic that is manageable within the scope of a given assignment. There are three stages in this restriction process.

- Selection of a general subject area.
- Selection of a portion or phase of this general area to form a limited subject area.
- Final selection of a specific limited topic within the limited subject area.

Note that the way in which your teacher states the assignment dictates the starting point for your work. A general assignment requires that you go through all three stages. A somewhat specific assignment completes the first two stages for you by limiting you to a general area. You need deal only with the third stage to complete the restriction process for this assignment. A very directive assignment accomplishes all three stages and leaves you free to begin work on the organization of the paper itself.

The final version of the restricted topic is the same as that "very directive" assignment already listed:

Explain why Huck's experiences led him to make his final statement: "Aunt Sally's going to adopt me and sivilize me and I can't stand it. I been there before."

2. Gather materials. You need to establish what you know about this particular topic. What were Huck's experiences? Why did they make him want to avoid Aunt Sally's attentions? List some of the experiences he had in the "sivilized" world. Here are some possibilities:

1. The confining life at the Widow Douglas' home, and Miss Watson's efforts to teach Huck manners and religion.
2. The brutal shooting of Boggs by Colonel Sherburn, and the mob violence of the attempted lynching that was faced down by Sherburn's single-handed capacity for even greater violence.
3. The Grangerford–Shepherdson feud.
4. Huck's obvious pleasure at living outside civilization with Jim on Jackson's Island and on the raft.

Others may come to mind as you work on the paper. The immediate conclusion that you can draw from these experiences is that all of what Huck saw of civilization was unpleasant or bad or dangerous. The list of experiences leads directly to Step 3.

3. Establish a controlling statement. The thesis serves the longer essay much as the topic sentence serves the paragraph. The topic sentence states the subject of the paragraph and tells what will be said about it. The thesis statement does exactly the same thing for the longer paper. The statement controls the writer by defining the subject and what is to be said about the subject. It keeps the writer from wandering away from the subject; sometimes it is so specific that it establishes the order in which the essay will be arranged.

The thesis statement for the *Huckleberry Finn* paper is obvious:

Huck could not stand to be "sivilized" because his experiences in civilization were frightening, dangerous, or confining.

4. Select specific items of support. Keeping the thesis statement in mind, you need to select from the book experiences and observations that will clearly illustrate the conditions in civilization. All of the possible pieces of evidence listed above can be used to point out the conditions that Huck wanted to avoid. Even the pleasant experiences with Jim on Jackson's Island serve to make the bad experiences more vivid. The strange episode at the end of the book, dealing with the mock freeing of Jim, who is being held as a runaway slave at the home of Tom Sawyer's Aunt Sally, is pretty clear evidence that civilized people often act in an uncivilized fashion.

5. Establish an order of presentation. Several orders are possible, but the easiest one to follow is to take the materials in the order in which they occur in the book.

6. Write the first draft. Begin by writing an introduction and continue into the supporting paragraphs. The introduction might read this way:

At the close of the novel *Huckleberry Finn*, Huck concludes his story by saying that he intends to "light out for the Territory" because Aunt Sally intends to "sivilize" him, and he feels that he can't stand any more efforts to make him an upstanding, moral, and religious citizen. His attitude is understandable, for his experiences in society as it existed along the Mississippi were confining, unpleasant, or downright terrifying.

(We will discuss introductions again in the second example in this section.)

Continue now to the paragraphs of development. The paragraphs of development might read this way:

Huck's experiences of "home," or at the two places where he lives at the opening of the novel, are decidedly unpleasant. The home of Widow Douglas and Miss Watson tends to oppress and constrict a boy's natural energy and interests. Regular meals eaten with careful manners and polite small talk work against Huck's tendency to roam at will through the woods. Lectures on morality and religion tend to confuse him. If one can obtain his or her desires through prayer, why are folks poor, or sick, or crippled? If being good makes one blessed, why is Miss Watson so sour and seemingly unhappy? Life with Pap may be more free from the repressions of etiquette, but it also has its frightening side of drunkenness, violence, and delirium tremens. So Huck decides to leave these situations behind to look for something better.

Something better turns out to be life on the river with Jim, the runaway slave. They meet on Jackson's Island and camp there for a time. Their experiences on the island are mostly pleasant: loafing, camping, fishing, and generally hanging out, all of which suit Huck just fine. The idyll is interrupted by a snakebite (from which Jim recovers) and is ended by the threat of a search party coming out to find Jim. Jim is a slave and, by all the measures of that day, less than human, but in reality he is the only truly civilized person Huck meets in his travels. Jim loves Huck and cares for him, in spite of Huck's tendency to play cruel jokes on him. He shelters Huck from the knowledge of Pap's death and doesn't reject Huck after he discovers the hoax of Huck's dream fabrication when they have been separated in a fog. It is ironic that the only civilized person Huck meets is not considered truly human by those who regard themselves as civilized.

The other people Huck meets in his travels do very little to improve his suspicious view of the world. He and Jim happen upon some fairly terrible people as soon as they venture out on the river: slave hunters, the gamblers who are trying to kill their partner, and a nonhuman agent of civilization, a steamboat that runs them down and puts Huck back on shore. There he meets the Grangerfords, gentlemen and ladies all, living in a fine house and enjoying prosperity. The Grangerfords are aristocrats and moral churchgoing people who have only one fault: They are engaged in a murderous, generations-old feud with the Shepherdsons. One Sunday afternoon Huck witnesses an outbreak of this feud that leaves most of the people from both families dead.

Fleeing from the killing, Huck returns to the river and finds Jim. They continue down the river. Later they meet the King and the Duke, two great con artists who dupe the people in a nearby town and are eventually tarred and feathered for their efforts. During the adventures with the King and the Duke, Huck witnesses the shooting of the harmless drunk Boggs and the attempted lynching of Colonel Sherburn, the man who shot him. Taken on balance, most of Huck's experiences on shore are grim and frightening, good reasons for his lack of enthusiasm for civilization.

Even the last episode of the book does little to increase Huck's desire to live in the civilized world. Huck comes by chance on the home of Tom Sawyer's Aunt Sally and adopts Tom's identity. When Tom shows up, he is introduced as Cousin Sid. Jim is also on the plantation, being held as a runaway slave. The two boys, with Tom leading, enter an incredible plot to free Jim, although, as Tom knows but conceals, Jim has already been freed. After a series of cops-and-robber antics, the plot resolves into what looks like a happy ending. It is revealed that Jim is free, Pap is dead, and Huck's personal fortune, presumed lost, is intact. Aunt Sally offers to adopt Huck and raise him properly so that he can become a successful civilized adult. At this point Huck reviews his situation. Life in town and his misadventures on shore with the Grangerfords, the King and the Duke, Sherburn, and others suggest only bad experiences to come if he accepts Aunt Sally's offer. His time with Jim, living free and easy on the river, seems wonderfully pleasant, compared to those recollections. Little wonder, then, that he decides to "light out for the Territory."

This completes the writing process through the writing of the rough draft. The remaining steps in the process will be covered in the second example of this section.

With this review of the process fresh in your mind, follow how you might want to apply it in writing a paper of six to eight paragraphs that might be assigned in a business course.

Your class has been studying business leaders, past and present, and the assignment is to write a paper of about eight hundred words discussing the contributions of one of these leaders to American business.

1. Select the subject. Several names come to mind from the history of American business: F.W. Taylor, Thomas Watson, Douglas McGregor, Alfred Sloan, Frederick Herzberg. But perhaps the most interesting and certainly one of the most important contributors to the theory and practice of business in America is Peter F. Drucker. His contributions are famous and respected in this country and abroad, and they have been cataloged and discussed in two books published quite recently. Thus Drucker's contributions meet the criteria for selection as a subject. They are important and interesting, and information on them is readily available.

2. Gather materials. What is there to know about Peter Drucker?

He has written fifteen books and many articles on business. He was born in Vienna, Austria. Father was a college teacher in America. Drucker started career as a book-keeper and a writer. He left Germany early in WWII. Went to London and worked in a bank. Then worked for American newspapers as a British correspondent. Worked for the U.S. government during the war, then taught at two colleges, moving in 1950 to New York University, where he taught till 1970.

His first consulting job was a massive study of General Motors Corporation, a study highly critical of its management systems. From this work he wrote *The Concept of the Corporation,* a book that was the beginning of management thought in the modern sense of the word. His latest book, *Management: Tasks–Responsibilities–Practices,* is a very broad study of modern management philosophy and practices.

He continues to consult for major corporations, but he requires that the client come to him in California. He charges $1,500 a day and still manages to stay booked up far in advance.

Drucker is well known as a teacher. He taught first at NYU in a special program for active business people. He now teaches in the Claremont Graduate School in California, a position he has held since 1971. Drucker loves teaching so much that some believe he would pay to do it if necessary. He especially enjoys teaching those who are currently employed in management positions. He uses a case-study method of his own invention, not following accepted case-study methods from other colleges. His case studies are short and are not loaded with data and statistics. Instead they concentrate on analysis and on finding the right questions to ask in a given situation. Often high-level executives attend his classes for enrichment and pleasure, even though they do not need any further course work or degrees to augment their careers. His associations in the classroom often ripen into rich and enduring friendships.

Much more information could be collected about Drucker, and more probably would be needed to fill an essay of eight hundred words. But this is enough material to allow us to move to the next step.

3. Establish a controlling statement. It is clear from the information gathered about Peter Drucker that he is active in three general areas of business: He is a teacher, a consultant, and a writer. But it is important to note that the key word in the assignment is not *activity;* rather, it is *contributions.* The fact that Drucker has been active as a writer does not automatically mean that he has made a contribution to the theory and practice of American business in his writings. That remains to be determined; you must return to the information gathered in Step 2 to see what is known about his *contributions*. (NOTE: It is not uncommon to discover that writing the statement for a paper [Step 3] requires a return to the information-gathering stage [Step 2] to find additional information to use in formulating the thesis statement.)

The information already collected provides only a suggestion of Drucker's contributions: the phrase that says he wrote a book that was the "beginning of management thought in the modern sense of the word." Now the job is to collect more information directly related to that idea.

Further reading in books and articles about Peter Drucker indicates two very important areas of contribution, one theoretical and the other practical.

> In the theory of management, Drucker was the first to identify the corporation as a whole as something that needed management and that could be managed. Prior to his work, discussions of corporation management were rather fragmented, dealing with isolated problems such as accounting and materials handling. Drucker developed a theory for the operation of the entire corporation.
>
> On the practical side, Drucker developed the concept of the manager and his or her roles in the corporation, and he has written guides to the day-to-day functions of those in management. He has worked as a consultant for major corporations, and the solutions to their problems have filtered to other companies and influenced institutions such as schools and hospitals. He also did initial work on ideas that later were more fully developed by others: The "hygiene" theory of the effects of wages on motivation and the theories of motivation often labeled X and Y were initially discussed in Drucker's works, at least in concept, and were developed by other writers, Herzberg and McGregor in particular.

The addition of these ideas to the information collected provides a solid basis for working on Step 3, establishing the statement.

The nature of Drucker's contributions is now clear enough for you to try writing a statement about them. Such a statement might read:

> Peter Drucker has made both a theoretical and a practical contribution to American business.

or

> Peter Drucker was the first to develop a theory of the nature and function of the corporation, and he has made practical application of that theory to the day-to-day work of the manager through his writings and his work as a consultant. He also did initial work on concepts fully developed by others.

The second version captures most of what needs to be said, but the order is jumbled and the statement is too wordy. A better version is

> Peter Drucker developed the overall concept of the corporation, its place in society, and its operation; he also began work on specific concepts that were later developed by other men. His practical work as writer and consultant has provided direction to many managers.

You can shape that statement into a general outline for a paper and get an idea of the kinds of materials you will need to support the statement.

DRUCKER'S CONTRIBUTIONS

1. Developed theory and concept of the corporation.
2. Began work on concepts later fully developed by others.
3. Provided practical applications of those theories in writings and in consulting work.

Now you are ready to move to Step 4.

4. Select specific items of support. To develop the first point in the outline, you will need to discuss the state of management theory when Drucker began his work. Then you will need to explain how he developed his theory, where he first began to publish it, and, in general terms, what that theory of the corporation and its management is. For the second point, you need to identify the concepts that Drucker began to develop, the people who completed that development, and the name or the final form of those concepts. A discussion of his more practical books and some of the guidelines in them can be joined with a brief discussion of his work as a consultant to present the third point in the outline.

5. Establish an order of presentation. There is an order already built into the outline from the materials collected in Step 2: first, theories and concepts of the corporation as a whole, then specific theories, and then practical applications of those theories. This order also seems to arrange the contributions in descending order of importance, taking the larger, more global contributions first and moving to less important theories and practical matters next. It would be possible to reverse that order and work from least important to most important, from practical to theoretical. But such a progression does not seem to suit the materials as well as the first order, so you should present the materials in the draft in the order suggested by the outline.

6. Write the first draft. It might seem logical to begin writing a draft of a paper with the beginning, the introduction. If a clear, effective introduction comes to mind rather handily, begin with the introduction. But do not wait with pen in hand for the perfect introduction to appear on the page. Make one attempt at an introduction; if nothing comes of that first attempt, begin to write the body of the paper wherever you find the writing easiest, even if you begin with what is actually the last paragraph in the essay. Get the material written and *then* put the paper in the proper order. Write, don't wait for the inspiration.

When you do write the introduction, be sure to make it serve the two important functions of an introduction. First, and more important, an introduction must catch the interest of the reader. Second, the introduction must give the reader an idea of the direction the paper will take. This sense of direction may come from an explicit statement of the core idea or thesis of the paper, a paraphrase of the result of your work in Step 3. On the other hand, it may be given as a general identifying statement of the topic. For the paper on Peter Drucker a paraphrase of the Step 3 statement might read:

> Peter Drucker developed a philosophy of the corporation, devised specific concepts within that philosophy, and showed managers how to make a practical application of that philosophy.

Identifying the topic and making a general statement of the ideas to be covered might produce:

> Of all those who have helped to develop our ideas of the nature and workings of the corporation, Peter Drucker is among the most important.

267

With this effort to provide a sense of direction, you must also catch the reader's interest. If you have trouble thinking of methods for developing introductions, you might try one of the following strategies:

- Use a quotation or a paraphrase of a striking statement:

Peter Drucker is, in the words of C. Northcote Parkinson, "preeminent among management consultants and also among authors of books on management."

- Cite an important fact or statistic:

Prior to the writing of *The Concept of the Corporation,* the idea of the corporation as an entity that needed management did not exist. Drucker invented the corporate society.

- Recount an anecdote:

"What *is* your business?" the famous consultant asked the directors of a firm that made bottles. "Everyone knows," responded the chairman, "that we make bottles for soft drinks and other foods." "I disagree," replied the consultant to the astounded board. After a pause to let his words sink in, he continued, "Your business is not the making of bottles; you are in the packaging business." With that one question Peter Drucker, America's foremost business consultant, opened the board's eyes and provided new direction for a foundering company.

- Use a dictionary definition:

The dictionary defines a corporation as a group of individuals legally united to conduct business. Peter Drucker defines the corporation as the cornerstone of our society.

- Set up a contrast between two ideas:

The original management consultant was really an efficiency expert, timing workers on an assembly line and suggesting ways of improving their speed and productivity. Peter Drucker's work is as far removed from that practice as the supersonic transport is from the Wright brothers' first plane.

As you become a more experienced writer, you will find less and less need for those strategies. Use them now, but feel free to experiment as your confidence grows.

Always provide a conclusion for your paper. As a rule, a short sentence of summary or a restatement of the topic will suffice. The function of a conclusion for a short paper is to let the reader know that the paper has been completed, to provide a sense of "finishedness." Don't leave the reader with the impression that he or she ought to be looking for more material. Don't try to provide an extensive restatement or summary for a short paper. And be very careful that you never use the conclusion to introduce a new point or add additional information. A one-sentence conclusion should be ample for most college essays.

The first completed draft of the paper on the contributions of Peter Drucker might read this way:

Of the business people, scholars, and writers who have attempted to analyze and influence the business world of the twentieth century, none has made a greater contribution or been more interesting to observe than Peter Drucker. Drucker is a teacher, a consultant, and a writer who has drawn from each role to construct a philosophy or theoretical concept of the corporation and a workable application of the theory to actual business problems and challenges. In theory and in practice,

Drucker has been a major influence on American business for the last thirty years.

In the minds of many, Drucker is the person who almost single-handedly invented the idea of the corporation. Prior to Drucker's introduction of the idea in *The Concept of the Corporation,* the study of business management was the study of individual problems such as accounting or materials handling. Drucker changed that view and suggested that the corporation was an entity, a whole, and needed to be managed as a whole, not as a series of isolated services or problems. Much of this book, and the ideas within it, arose from a massive study of General Motors undertaken in 1943. Having examined the operation of that company in great detail, and having reported that he thought it was managed chaotically, he set about developing a unified view of the corporation and its management. He did develop such a view and, in the process, suggested that the key institution and the chief influence on the future of the Western world would be the corporation, complete with assembly lines. This view of the corporation as a whole and his realization that the corporation was a major political, social, *and* economic force have made Drucker a major contributor to the present-day theory of business.

Drucker has written extensively in the area of management and has been a leader in the development of important concepts in specific areas of management. He was a leader or at least an important forerunner of the management system commonly called *management by objectives* (MBO). He first used the term in his book *The Practice of Management* and says he first heard it used by Alfred Sloan in the 1950s. Essentially, MBO tries to focus the attention of managers on their objectives. Managers of the old school had always asked themselves, "What do I do?" Drucker turned their attention from the process to the product or objective and said that the proper question is "What do I wish to accomplish?" That principle of management is now so commonplace in business and government that it seems always to have existed. Two concepts in the area of motivation were suggested by Drucker and developed by others. The first is the now famous "hygiene" theory of compensation, which says that wages and certain other conditions of employment do not cause high morale and motivation; instead they prevent low morale and allow other positive motivators to have an impact on the workers. These *hygiene factors* do not increase motivation and production, but motivation and the accompanying higher production cannot occur without them. Drucker also was an early contributor to the theories of motivation commonly called *Theory X* and *Theory Y,* which are widely discussed by writers such as Douglas McGregor. Theory X says that people are motivated best by threat and fear, by negative or extrinsic motivation; Theory Y counters that people are better and further motivated by satisfaction of their basic needs and by appeals to their sense of participation and involvement. These ideas are well known and widely used today; Drucker was a major contributor to their early development.

But Drucker is no airy theorist incapable of practical work. He is a consultant whose services are heavily sought by industry and government. He is in such demand that he can charge $1,500 a day for his services and never lack clients. He is a consultant who does not try to provide clients with an answer to their problems. Rather, he tries to point out what the proper questions are and to help the clients find the answers. In early work with a manufacturer of glass bottles, he shocked the executive committee by asking them what business the firm was in. Silence followed the question, and then the chairman replied with a hint of anger in his voice, "We make glass bottles for soft-drink makers and others." "No," replied Drucker, "your business is not making bottles. You are in the packaging business." That answer, coming from an unusual perspective, greatly altered the executives' view of the company and its problems and led to solutions never suspected by the executive committee. Drucker constantly advises his clients to build from strength, to use the abilities that each person possesses, and to structure assignments so that no manager is forced to work long in an area where she or he is weak. Managers of the old school always looked at weaknesses and worked for their correction. Drucker said, "Forget the weaknesses. Put the person in a position where his weaknesses will not matter; use and develop the strengths of each employee."

Drucker has raised the art of consulting to new heights, making practical applications of the theories of management he developed. As a writer he has been an important contributor to the practical side of management. *The Effective Executive* is full of good advice to managers, advice useful on a day-to-day basis. His later book, *Management: Tasks–Responsibilities–Practices*, has in it long sections that are intensely practical. Even his more theoretical works have a practical bent. Arjay Miller, former president of Ford Motor Company, says that *The Concept of the Corporation* was "extremely useful in forming my judgments about what was needed at Ford. It was, by considerable margin, the most useful and pragmatic publication available and had a definite impact on the postwar organizational development within the Ford Motor Company" (*Drucker: The Man Who Invented the Corporate Society*, 1976, p. 32). Peter Drucker, philosopher, theorist, and practical authority, is, without doubt, a major figure in the history of American business and a man who helped to shape and form the corporation as we know it today.

Materials for this essay were taken from John J. Tarrant, *Drucker: The Man Who Invented the Corporate Society* (Boston: Cahners Books, Inc., 1976) and from Tony H. Bonaparte and John E. Flaherty, eds., *Peter Drucker: Contributions to Business Enterprise* (New York: New York University Press, 1970).

The completed version of the paper that comes out of Step 6 is *not*—repeat, *not*—the version of the paper that you ought to turn in. Step 6 produces a rough draft, a version suitable for revision and not much else. Think of that draft as a good start, but remember that it is still a long way from completion. Use the remaining steps of the writing process in revising your draft. Wait a day or two (if possible) between completing the draft and undertaking the revision.

7. Revise the rough draft. Read the draft all the way through twice. Then ask the following questions:

- Will the introduction interest the reader? Does it provide a sense of direction for the paper?
- Does the Step 3 statement in the introduction accurately reflect what you intend to say on the topic?
- Does the rest of the paper, does each supporting paragraph, serve to develop the statement you intend to make in the paper?
- Are the supporting points presented in the best order?
- Is there an adequate conclusion?

Read each paragraph of support very carefully.

- Is the point of support developed completely? Will readers have any questions on the point when they finish reading the paragraph? Is the paragraph *complete?*
- Is each paragraph unified? Does any paragraph treat more than one idea?
- Is each paragraph coherent? Does it read smoothly, tying the sentences together with transitional devices?

8. Correct the draft. Check the paper sentence by sentence to improve its style and to correct errors.

- Check each sentence for errors in completeness (Lesson 13), subject–verb agreement (Lesson 21), pronoun–antecedent agreement (Lesson 22), pronoun case (Lesson 23), dangling or misplaced modifiers (Lesson 12), and the use of prepositions (Lesson 24). (NOTE: As you find errors in your papers and as marked errors appear on papers returned to you, keep a record of them—either by putting a check in the appropriate lessons of this book or by marking your reference handbook. You will soon discover whether you have a tendency to repeat certain kinds of errors, and you can simplify your proofreading by checking first for these errors. In a short time, you should be able to eliminate repeat faults from your writing.)

- Check each sentence for errors in punctuation; check for missing punctuation marks *and* for unneeded marks.
- Check for errors in mechanics, capitalization, and spelling.

9. Write the final draft. Copy the paper in its final, corrected form. Be sure to observe correct margins, and to write or type neatly. If possible, make a copy of the paper before you turn it in.

PROGRESS TEST **1**
Subject and Verb; Parts of Speech (Lessons 1,2)

NAME _____ SCORE _____

DIRECTIONS: Copy the subject of the sentence on the first line at the left and the verb on the second line.

_____   1. The results of this conference will surely be beneficial.
_____

_____   2. We are reasonably sure of a sold-out house for the con-
_____   cert.

_____   3. I have many times recalled our pleasant visit.

_____   4. Never again will you encounter a sale like this one.

_____   5. Only a few of you will ride in the first bus.

_____   6. There were further delays at the Italian border.

_____   7. This will be my final offer.

_____   8. He's always been afraid of snakes.

_____   9. The first of Lapham's interviews with the prime minister
_____   took place in 1983.

_____   10. The midday meal at camp is usually ready by noon.

_____   11. Here's a copy of the afternoon program.

_____   12. The roar of the 747's engines rattled the windows.

_____   13. Two of Marcy's best friends recently moved to New
_____   York.

_____   14. Directly behind us sat a group of Rangers fans.

_____   15. The motive behind Langer's change of heart is clear to
_____   most of his friends.

_____   16. Close to the condominium is a large amusement center.

_____   17. Many of these villages had originally served as fur-trad-
_____   ing posts.

_____   18. There were still a few unoccupied seats in the rear of
_____   the auditorium.

DIRECTIONS: Each sentence contains two italicized words. In the space at the left, write one of the following numbers to identify the part of speech of each italicized word:

1. Noun	3. Verb	5. Adverb
2. Pronoun	4. Adjective	6. Preposition

_____ 1. The new administration *simplified* the enrollment *procedures.*
_____

_____ 2. *Many* engineers have commented on the *simplicity* of the device.
_____

_____ 3. These sentimental songs are an *echo* of *simpler* times.
_____

_____ 4. Mrs. Brown's young son waited *patiently outside* the grocery store.
_____

_____ 5. *Patience* is generally considered an *admirable* quality.
_____

_____ 6. These metals are *valuable* because of their *rarity.*
_____

_____ 7. A nation *rarely values* its poets over its warriors.
_____

_____ 8. Mr. Owens leaned *over* and *straightened* his son's necktie.
_____

_____ 9. The path *over* the mountain is well marked and quite *straight.*
_____

_____ 10. Following my *advice,* the police scouted the *nearby* area.
_____

_____ 11. The scout *advised* us to wait *nearby.*
_____

_____ 12. It would be *advisable* to wait until the mail *arrives.*
_____

_____ 13. *All* of us were eagerly awaiting the *arrival* of the mail.
_____

_____ 14. *Some* enthusiastic fans *swarmed* onto the playing field.
_____

_____ 15. *Some* of my neighbors voted *against* the proposal.
_____

_____ 16. I consider your behavior *quite unneighborly.*
_____

_____ 17. A *few* of her *best* photographs are in museums.
_____

_____ 18. Children *often* perform *better* without supervision.
_____

_____ 19. The *harshness* of his *voice* surprised us.
_____

_____ 20. The teacher *voiced* his objections *harshly.*
_____

Complements (Lessons 3–6)

NAME _____ SCORE _____

DIRECTIONS: Identify the italicized complement by writing one of the following abbreviations in the space before the sentence:

    S.C. (subjective complement)   I.O. (indirect object)
    D.O. (direct object)   O.C. (objective complement)

_____ 1. Too much praise can make some people *conceited*.

_____ 2. One of the native children gave *us* a shy but friendly smile.

_____ 3. What do you call your *invention*?

_____ 4. *What* do you call your invention?

_____ 5. The vicious editorial attacks caused the *candidate* real anguish.

_____ 6. Without this sympathetic guidance, Tony might have become a *dropout*.

_____ 7. How much *money* did you lose on that investment?

_____ 8. Some of the critic's comments seemed unnecessarily *unkind*.

_____ 9. Close examination revealed a tiny *flaw* in the ruby.

_____ 10. *Whom* did Senator Howe finally select for his running mate?

_____ 11. How *old* is your motorcycle?

_____ 12. We can promise *you* a relaxing stay at the beach house.

_____ 13. Darlene makes delicious *desserts*.

_____ 14. Yesterday Darlene made her *mother* an apple pie.

_____ 15. Darlene's children sometimes make their grandmother *nervous*.

_____ 16. How many *cookies* did your mother send you?

_____ 17. Jerry finally found his stray *puppy* in a neighbor's garage.

_____ 18. The agent found *us* a small but pleasant apartment.

_____ 19. We found our new neighbors quite *congenial*.

_____ 20. Uncle Joe gave *each* of his nephews one hundred shares of the stock.

_____ 21. From our altitude of forty thousand feet, Lake Tahoe looked *tiny*.

_____ 22. Do you consider the governor's statement a *bid* for reelection?

_____ 23. Dean Reynolds always has been *resistant* to new ideas.

_____ 24. Operations in this office seem particularly *chaotic* today.

_____ 25. How many *prizes* did you win?

_____ 26. Have you shown your *parents* your prizes?

_____ 27. Where do you keep your extra car *keys*?

_____ 28. Miraculously, the young children kept *quiet* during the solemn ceremony.

_____ 29. Regular, vigorous brushing will keep your dog's coat *glossy*.

_____ 30. What kind of entertainment may I offer *you*?

_____ 31. Why didn't you look up in your dictionary the exact *meaning* of the word?

_____ 32. Kamp Killkare offers the *vacationist* a variety of outdoor activities.

_____ 33. Uncle Fred left the *waiter* an insultingly low tip.

_____ 34. This incident left some of us *embarrassed*.

_____ 35. We hurriedly left the *restaurant*.

_____ 36. Susan left out *one* of the important questions on the test.

_____ 37. The disappearance of the star witness remains a *mystery*.

_____ 38. That scheme of yours sounds completely *unworkable*.

_____ 39. Why didn't someone sound the *alarm* earlier?

_____ 40. After the matinee Grandmother bought *each* of the children an ice cream sundae.

Subordinate Clauses (Lessons 8–10)

NAME _____ SCORE _____

DIRECTIONS: Each of the following sentences contains one subordinate clause. Use square brackets ([ ]) to mark the beginning and the end of each subordinate clause. Circle the subject and underline the verb of each subordinate clause. Identify the clause by writing in the space at the left one of the following:
Adv. (adverb clause)   Adj. (adjective clause)   N. (noun clause)

_____ 1. How can you concentrate while that radio is blasting in your ear?

_____ 2. Foster is, without doubt, the laziest fellow I've ever known.

_____ 3. Although the office is small, three clerks have their desks in the crowded room.

_____ 4. The passengers were told nothing except that the flight had been delayed.

_____ 5. I believe that you and I met at last year's convention.

_____ 6. If you make the right choice, you'll win a year's supply of yogurt.

_____ 7. Jim wondered if he had made the right choice.

_____ 8. The incident I refer to took place last February.

_____ 9. It is generally believed that Carstairs cannot win the nomination.

_____ 10. The security officer will show you where you should stand.

_____ 11. Turnbull hires only people whose politics are conservative.

_____ 12. Although our crew had trained vigorously, the competition was too strong for us.

_____ 13. Our star halfback still walks as if his knee bothers him.

_____ 14. The company officers must soon decide where the regional office will be established.

_____ 15. The old man would tell his wild tales to whoever would listen.

_____ 16. The old man would tell his wild tales to anyone who would listen.

_____ 17. Swanson asked the usher if there was additional seating in the balcony.

_____ 18. Unless we get some rain soon, much of the fruit crop will be lost.

_____ 19. The group then discussed a television special most of them had seen the previous evening.

_____ 20. We'll take off at daybreak provided the airport is not fogged in.

_____ 21. We would select a campsite whenever we got tired of driving.

_____ 22. In the afternoons Beth baby-sat for two youngsters whose parents both worked on the campus.

_____ 23. We'll never forget the time when our dog fell out of the canoe.

_____ 24. All of you may leave when the last test has been turned in.

_____ 25. One member of the gang told the police when the shipment would arrive.

_____ 26. In another skillet sauté the apples until they are glazed.

_____ 27. The candidate against whom Alice is running is popular with the farmers.

_____ 28. It has been determined that the accountant made several false entries in the ledger.

_____ 29. Ted's main worry is that the bank will not renew his loan.

_____ 30. Anything you say will be put in the record.

_____ 31. Whatever you say will be put in the record.

_____ 32. Did your sister sell as many tickets as you did?

_____ 33. Were I you, I'd ask for a refund.

_____ 34. Jack's only excuse was that he had misinterpreted the instructions.

_____ 35. Jerry's boss was the kind of man that children and dogs instinctively dislike.

_____ 36. The crowd made so much noise that the players couldn't hear the quarterback's signals.

_____ 37. Nearly two dozen proposals were submitted, only three of which were accepted.

_____ 38. The mechanic showed Beth how the carburetor should be adjusted.

_____ 39. Most commentators think it unlikely that the revolt will succeed.

_____ 40. Had your order arrived yesterday, we could have filled it.

Verbal Phrases (Lesson 11)

NAME _____ SCORE _____

DIRECTIONS: Each sentence contains one verbal phrase. Underline the phrase and, in the space at the left, write one of the following letters to identify the phrase:
G. (gerund phrase) P. (participial phrase) I. (infinitive phrase)

_____ 1. Delayed by the heavy traffic, we realized that we would miss the first act of the play.

_____ 2. Last weekend I did nothing except study for final exams.

_____ 3. Dean Wilkins ended his speech by telling two not very amusing stories.

_____ 4. Do you know the fellow wearing that outrageously large cowboy hat?

_____ 5. Another tactic might be to add several amendments to the revenue bill.

_____ 6. I wonder if the owner might consider lowering the price of the motorbike.

_____ 7. How do you think you would enjoy spending two weeks of rainy weather in this run-down cabin?

_____ 8. Ms. Stuart's ambition is to be appointed manager of the Milan office.

_____ 9. The witness's answers succeeded only in confusing the jury.

_____ 10. Having succeeded without the aid of a college degree, Judson distrusts most academics.

_____ 11. For thousands of people, collecting foreign and domestic stamps is a rewarding hobby.

_____ 12. We're trying to make your work easier for you.

_____ 13. Has anyone suggested lowering the admission price slightly?

_____ 14. A pamphlet containing the committee's recommendations will be available soon.

_____ 15. Can't you do something besides criticize our work?

_____ 16. On finding the window open, the watchman called the police.

_____ 17. Anyone needing transportation to or from the campus should register at the Student Union Building.

_____ 18. It's not always easy to follow one of Dr. Cook's convoluted arguments.

_____ 19. The accused woman admitted having served two earlier prison sentences.

_____ 20. The manager, troubled by these recurring rumors, ordered a thorough investigation.

DIRECTIONS: Each of the italicized words in the following sentences is used as a complement within a verbal phrase. In the first space at the left, identify the phrase by writing one of the following:

G. (gerund phrase)   P. (participial phrase)   I. (infinitive phrase)

In the second space write one of the following numbers to identify the complement:

     1. Subjective complement   3. Indirect object
     2. Direct object   4. Objective complement

_____ 1. Coach Tuttle desperately wanted to keep Phil *eligible* for basketball.
_____

_____ 2. The cottages facing the *beach* are, of course, the most expensive
_____   ones.

_____ 3. Two witnesses swore that they had heard Mr. Small offer the *guard*
_____   a bribe.

_____ 4. Being the only *son* in a large family of females has its advantages.
_____

_____ 5. Keeping the five children *amused* all afternoon will not be easy.
_____

_____ 6. I'll try to pay *you* the remaining amount before the end of the
_____   month.

_____ 7. How many *tickets* did you persuade your friends to buy?
_____

_____ 8. Your first mistake was lending your *cousin* the money for the down
_____   payment.

_____ 9. The judge would not let anyone leave the *courtroom*.
_____

_____ 10. Most people agree that cleaning a greasy *oven* is one of the most
_____   unpleasant household tasks.

_____ 11. Dora's first assignment with the consular service was in Zambia,
_____   formerly called *Northern Rhodesia.*

_____ 12. Handing *Jimmy* one of the velvet-covered menus, the waiter was
_____   clearly not amused by our behavior.

_____ 13. Mr. Thorpe stayed at home Thursday and helped his wife make
_____   green-tomato *relish.*

_____ 14. Having been declared *seaworthy,* the ship finally sailed from Hali-
_____   fax.

_____ 15. Dad can't discuss politics with his neighbor without becoming ex-
_____   tremely *agitated.*

Dangling Modifiers (Lesson 12)

NAME _____ SCORE _____

DIRECTIONS: If a sentence is correct, write *C* in the space at the left. If you find a dangling modifier, underline it and write *W* in the space at the left.

_____ 1. Having failed in three courses, the dean decided that I would be happier in business with my mother.

_____ 2. When applying for a job, your clothes should be neat and fairly conservative.

_____ 3. Having no particular talent for farming, Carol's father soon decided to move back to Chicago.

_____ 4. My life is complicated enough without falling in love.

_____ 5. Being one of the busiest streets in town, don't use Fairview Avenue for your practice driving.

_____ 6. Entering the dormitory through the sliding glass doors, a drop in temperature is immediately noticeable.

_____ 7. The leftover meat should not be put into the refrigerator without being covered.

_____ 8. The leftover meat should not be put into the refrigerator without covering it.

_____ 9. When only a year old, the family doctor took out my appendix.

_____ 10. Having earned a good salary as a lawyer, asking her new husband for spending money did not appeal to Agnes.

_____ 11. The rain having stopped, the tarpaulin was removed from the infield.

_____ 12. By drinking countless cups of black coffee to keep awake, my term paper was finally finished.

_____ 13. Instead of trying to help the bewildered freshman, he is given a mass of confusing orders and directions.

_____ 14. Before cooking the pears, they should be peeled.

_____ 15. Before cooking the pears, peel them.

_____ 16. While roaring down Aurora Avenue, already late for the interview, my mind turned over questions to ask our visitor.

_____ 17. This outline is too short to be of any real help.

_____ 18. This outline is too short to get any real help from it.

_____ 19. Greedily gnawing away at my most valuable begonia, I found a fat, repulsive slug.

_____ 20. When looking up a word, notice its spelling, its pronunciation, and its derivation.

DANGLING MODIFIERS

DIRECTIONS: Rewrite each of the following sentences twice:
      a. Change the dangler to a complete clause with subject and verb.
      b. Begin the main clause with a word that the dangler can logically modify.

1. Totaling the receipts of the rummage sale, there was a shortage of nearly forty dollars.

a.

b.

2. While taking an important test in math last Thursday, my pocket calculator went dead on me.

a.

b.

3. To be assured of getting good seats, cash should accompany the order.

a.

b.

4. Currently selling at 16.8 times estimated earnings, we consider Vortex common stock an attractive buy.

a.

b.

5. When walking on the streets and in the alleys near the waterfront, the need for an extra police patrol is obvious.

a.

b.

Sentence Building (Lessons 12–15)

NAME _____   SCORE _____

DIRECTIONS: Study these paired sentences for incompleteness, misplaced modifiers, faulty parallelism, and faulty comparisons. In the space at the left, write the letter that identifies the correct sentence.

_____   1. A. Johnson, the defensive left end, played a harder game than any man on the team.
   B. Johnson, the defensive left end, played a harder game than any other man on the team.

_____   2. A. His erratic behavior not only causing worry to his teachers but also to his parents.
   B. His erratic behavior caused worry not only to his teachers but also to his parents.

_____   3. A. The accident happened because the street light was out and the driver was careless.
   B. The accident happened because the street light was out and because of the driver's carelessness.

_____   4. A. Just as the choir started the concert, the tornado struck the auditorium and broke several windows.
   B. The tornado struck the auditorium just as the choir started the concert and broke several windows.

_____   5. A. Old-time music lovers tell us that there will never be another voice that can be compared to Caruso's.
   B. Old-time music lovers tell us that there will never be another voice that can be compared to Caruso.

_____   6. A. Every Christmas our house was more elaborately decorated than any house in our neighborhood.
   B. Every Christmas our house was more elaborately decorated than any other house in our neighborhood.

_____   7. A. We hunted all afternoon but we only shot one rabbit.
   B. We hunted all afternoon but we shot only one rabbit.

_____   8. A. Driving home from school yesterday afternoon, I saw three Chinese pheasants.
   B. Yesterday afternoon I saw three Chinese pheasants driving home from school.

_____   9. A. Gracie is of medium height, bright yellow hair, gray eyes, and moves about quickly.
   B. Gracie is of medium height, with bright yellow hair and gray eyes, and she moves about quickly.

_____   10. A. Jane could be as popular as, if not more popular than, Sarah, but people say she thinks only of her career.
   B. Jane could be as popular if not more popular than Sarah, but people say she only thinks of her career.

_____ 11. A. The architecture in this model village is original, daring, showing imagination, and sometimes it's almost fantastic.
       B. The architecture in this model village is original, daring, imagi-
native, and sometimes almost fantastic.

_____ 12. A. Going on a vacation is often more tiring than staying home.
       B. Going on a vacation often is more tiring than staying home.

_____ 13. A. His qualifications are not much different from those of most
other young college graduates.
       B. His qualifications are not much different from most other young
college graduates.

_____ 14. A. Which takes up more of your study time, chemistry or sociology?
       B. Which takes up most of your study time, chemistry or sociology?

_____ 15. A. We were able to only on Sunday nights use the home computer.
       B. We were able to use the home computer only on Sunday nights.

_____ 16. A. The weather here on the coast being much different from the
other side of the mountains.
       B. The weather here on the coast is much different from that on
the other side of the mountains.

_____ 17. A. The only way to get your work done is by putting a "study" sign
on your door and being very strict about letting anyone enter.
       B. The only way to get your work done is by putting a "study" sign
on your door and be very strict about letting anyone enter.

_____ 18. A. It is one of the most amusing pictures I saw all year, if not the
most amusing.
       B. It is one of the most amusing if not the most amusing pictures I
saw all year.

_____ 19. A. These rules must either be obeyed or you will be in serious
trouble.
       B. Either these rules must be obeyed or you will be in serious trou-
ble.

_____ 20. A. The incumbent's record on pork-barrel spending is as bad if not
worse than her predecessor.
       B. The incumbent's record on pork-barrel spending is as bad as if
not worse than her predecessor's.

Subordination (Lesson 14)

NAME _____ SCORE _____

DIRECTIONS: Change the italicized sentence to the grammatical form indicated in the parentheses and rewrite each numbered unit as one sentence.

1. *It had rained steadily for ten days.* Mud Creek flooded the valley. (adverbial clause of reason) _____
_____

2. *It had rained steadily for ten days.* Mud Creek did not flood the valley. (adverbial clause of concession) _____
_____

3. The diplomas are usually presented by Al Miller. *He is the president of the school board.* (appositive) _____
_____

4. *Mr. Miller was out of town.* Betty Allen, the secretary of the board, presented the diplomas. (absolute phrase) _____
_____

5. Be sure to apply a well-balanced fertilizer. *This will give the grass a strong root system.* (infinitive phrase) _____
_____

6. Grace made a roomy playhouse for her daughters. *She used scrap lumber left by the contractor.* (participial phrase) _____
_____

7. The Red Cross provided tents and blankets for several families. *They had been left homeless by the flood.* (adjective clause) _____
_____

8. The Red Cross provided tents and blankets for several families. *They had been left homeless by the flood.* (participial phrase) _____
_____

9. All week the boss has been riding the bus to work. *His car is in the garage for repairs.* (adverbial clause of reason) _____
_____

10. All week the boss has been riding the bus to work. *His car is in the garage for repairs.* (absolute phrase) _____
_____

SUBORDINATION

DIRECTIONS: Rewrite each of the following numbered sections as one complex sentence. In each case use the italicized subject and verb for the main clause. Use a variety of the subordinating units listed for you on the first page of Lesson 14.

1. I worked hard in the physics course for two weeks, but *I* finally *dropped* it. It was too difficult and took up too much time.

   _____

   _____

2. *Butch Larimore* likes to be unconventional. He *created* a mild sensation at the dance last night. He appeared with his head shaved clean as a billiard ball.

   _____

   _____

3. Old *Whipple* had been a seafaring man in his youth and he could tell fascinating tales, but he *failed* completely as an author.

   _____

   _____

4. Aunt Tessie called us from Toledo recently. *She reported* that she had really enjoyed her visit to our beach house. It's at Lake Crescent. The weather was not very good while we were there.

   _____

   _____

5. I finished high school in June. I couldn't find a job that I liked. *I went* back to school. I took a course in typing.

   _____

   _____

6. Some new campus parking regulations are being enforced. *I can* no longer *park* close to Bagley Hall. My office is in Bagley Hall.

   _____

   _____

7. These *jackets* have heavy woolen linings. They are also water-repellent. They *should be* popular in cold climates.

   _____

   _____

8. My old *Chevy* cost me only twelve hundred dollars. I bought it seven years ago. It was secondhand. It still *performs* well.

   _____

   _____

9. Forty-three new grade-school teachers will be needed next year. The school population has increased greatly. *I read* about it in the morning paper.

   _____

   _____

10. I finished typing the final draft of my term paper and *I was* exhausted, and so I went to bed at ten o'clock.

   _____

   _____

PROGRESS TEST 8

Commas and Semicolons (Lessons 16,17)

NAME _____ SCORE _____

DIRECTIONS: These sentences contain fifty numbered spaces. In the correspondingly numbered spaces at the left, write one of the following:

    O. (no punctuation is required)
    C. (a comma should be used)
    S. (a semicolon should be used)

_____ 1. The field was muddy, a stiff wind was blowing(1) and our

_____ 2. star player was ill(2) it's no wonder we lost the game.

_____ 3. Once inside(3) the cat lay down on the soft carpet(4)

_____ 4. and was soon fast asleep.

_____ 5. Liz told the watchman(5) that she had official business

_____ 6. at the warehouse(6) however, she was not allowed to enter.

_____ 7. After we had finished painting(7) the cook rang the dinner

_____ 8. bell(8) a mad scramble to the dining room followed.

_____ 9. The long(9) uncomfortable ride bored Donny(10) who com-

_____ 10. plained constantly to his long-suffering mother.

_____ 11. Great books are not dashed off in a hurry(11) they are

_____ 12. the products of earnest(12) patient labor.

_____ 13. No new funds have been appropriated(13) therefore the men

_____ 14. who have been hired for the project(14) will be let go.

_____ 15. At an odd(15) little Spanish tavern we had an excellent

_____ 16. lunch(16) then we started looking for lodgings.

_____ 17. At the conclusion of the performance(17) I talked with

_____ 18. one of the women(18) who had helped produce the play.

_____ 19. Dr. Bergman explained(19) that there are many kinds of

_____ 20. mushrooms(20) only a very few, however, are used as food.

_____ 21. His wife having finished washing and ironing(21) the lazy

_____ 22. man returned home(22) and resumed his television watching.

_____ 23. The flutes, oboes(23) and harp open the second movement

_____ 24. with a delicate(24) haunting melody.

_____ 25. We reached Santa Fe, the capital of New Mexico(25) just as

_____ 26. the sun sank below the low(26) brown hills to the west.

_____ 27. Ben tried not to laugh at the mild joke(27) he didn't want

_____ 28. to encourage his father-in-law(28) whose witticisms tended to be heavy and academic.

_____ 29. "Although I own a handbook, a dictionary(29) and a the-

_____ 30. saurus(30) I still find writing a difficult chore," she said.

_____ 31. The waiter favored us with a haughty(31) disdainful

_____ 32. glance(32) and quietly gathered up the menus.

_____ 33. "I'm sorry to have to tell you this(33) sir," said the

_____ 34. officer(34) "the news is a shock to you, I'm sure."

_____ 35. An interior decorator once told me(35) that this extra

_____ 36. space could be made into a pleasant(36) comfortable room.

_____ 37. The Joneses are not available for the party(37) last week

_____ 38. they closed their home(38) and left on a vacation trip.

_____ 39. Thornton is hopeful(39) that her new book will bring her

_____ 40. fame, money(40) and professional advancement.

_____ 41. While Fred was bathing(41) the dog managed to dig under the

_____ 42. fence(42) he hasn't been seen since.

_____ 43. "When we were young(43) children weren't allowed such lib-

_____ 44. erties," said Aunt Martha(44) Mr. Brown's older sister.

_____ 45. Some people think that Bert is stubborn(45) others think

_____ 46. that he is sure of himself(46) and unwilling to compromise.

_____ 47. The laboratory having lost its government funding(47) the

_____ 48. directors hope to get donations(48) and continue on a reduced bud- get.

_____ 49. Henry James(49) the American novelist, was born in New York

_____ 50. on April 15, 1843(50) he spent most of his life, however, in Europe.

Punctuation: All Marks (Lessons 16–19)

NAME _____ SCORE _____

DIRECTIONS: Each of the following numbered units contains not more than two errors in punctuation. Correct each error. Then identify the errors in each sentence by circling the right numbers in the column of figures at the left. Circle

    1. if a period is omitted or mis-used.

    2. if a comma is omitted or mis-used.

    3. if an apostrophe is omitted or misused.

    4. if quotation marks are omitted or misused.

1 2 3 4   (1) Some of us are wondering why Jackson the regular tight end, isn't in todays line-up.

1 2 3 4   (2) This doll originally belonged to my wife's maternal grandmother who carried it with her when she left Bavaria in 1896.

1 2 3 4   (3) To everybody's surprise, the visitor burst into tears, we could do nothing but sit there and wonder at the outburst.

1 2 3 4   (4) The children did as they had been told; they waited patiently until six oclock but the baby sitter did not appear.

1 2 3 4   (5) The purchase of Alaska was once called Seward's Folly, however its natural resources, especially gold, furs, fish, and oil, make the price seem insignificant.

1 2 3 4   (6) "Something funny's going on here, someone else's car is parked where our's should be," said Mark.

1 2 3 4   (7) An attendant rushed into the meeting room and announced "that someone's blue Buick in the parking lot still had it's lights on."

1 2 3 4   (8) "In heaven's name, why wasn't I told about this?" asked Mrs Thorne whose children cowered at the sound of her voice.

1 2 3 4   (9) We decided to remodel the childrens' bedrooms, and I conferred with Edith Wood who had originally designed the house.

1 2 3 4   (10) "Can't you understand," cried Susan, "that I'd be embarrassed to entertain friends in this stuffy gloomy room."

1 2 3 4   (11) "Its a good thing," said Mr. Merrick after a long, thoughtful pause, "for young people to dream noble dreams.

1 2 3 4   (12) Mr. Talbot is convinced that his daughter's teacher, Ms. Cooper does not appreciate the childs hidden talents.

DIRECTIONS: In the following sentences, circle every error in punctuation. Then, in the column of figures, circle every number that represents an error in the sentence:

1. The error involves the use of a period or a question mark.
2. There is an error in the use or omission of a comma.
3. The error involves the use of an apostrophe.
4. The error involves the use of quotation marks.

1 2 3 4   (1) "Tell me young fellow," Mr Holland said to his nephew, why I should waste my best years in retirement."

1 2 3 4   (2) The warden greeted the new inmates by saying, "It was Richard Lovelace, wasn't it, who said, 'Stone walls do not a prison make.'

1 2 3 4   (3) "I wonder how any normal person could call this an inspirational family-oriented movie," said Aunt Jane.

1 2 3 4   (4) "Its really quite simple," Lester replied, "every member of the family agreed that we'd live within our income."

1 2 3 4   (5) "See here Bronson," snapped the irate professor. "Why dont we ever get a quick answer from you."

1 2 3 4   (6) I cant see how anyone could be expected to work effectively in this hot stuffy office?

1 2 3 4   (7) "What did Myrtle mean," asked Cindy, "when she said, 'Theres going to be a real battle of wits'?"

1 2 3 4   (8) "I'm sure that Orville couldn't have broken your window Mrs Reed," said the nurse; "hes been taught never to throw rocks.

1 2 3 4   (9) Mr Blair's thesis, the product of eight year's of research, is a study of the kiwi a flightless bird that lives in New Zealand.

1 2 3 4 (10) Anyone's guess is as good as anyone else's for we have nothing but rumors to base our judgments on.

1 2 3 4 (11) The office manager, Miss. Janet Dean, reported "that too much stationery has disappeared from the stockroom."

1 2 3 4 (12) "It's really embarrassing," complained Dr Rogers. "The newspaper article quoted me as saying, 'The patient's purse is weak' when I really said, 'The patient's pulse is weak.' "

Punctuation: All Marks (Lessons 16–19)

NAME _____ SCORE _____

DIRECTIONS: The following sentences contain fifty numbered spots between words or beneath words. (The number is beneath the word when the punctuation problem involves the use of an apostrophe in that word.) In the correspondingly numbered spaces at the left, write *C* if the punctuation is correct or *W* if it is incorrect.

1. _____
2. _____
3. _____
4. _____
5. _____
6. _____
7. _____
8. _____
9. _____
10. _____
11. _____
12. _____
13. _____
14. _____
15. _____
16. _____
17. _____
18. _____
19. _____
20. _____
21. _____
22. _____
23. _____
24. _____

(1) "Don't you think you're too young to be riding such a vicious¹ unmanageable horse," asked the cashier.²

(2) If you can't get off² work in time to get to the committee meeting;³ I can appoint someone to sit in for you.⁴

(3) The decrease in population is due to several things: the closing⁵ of the paper factory, the alarmingly small salmon catch and the⁶ decline in tourism.

(4) The decrease in population is due to: the closing of the paper⁷ factory, the alarmingly small salmon catch, and the decline in⁸ tourism.

(5) At five oclock⁹ the men returned to the cabin; their¹⁰ fishing trip having been unproductive.

(6) I doubt that Eliot will ever become a really good teacher, he's¹¹ too nervous, too dogmatic, and too impatient.¹²

(7) "Can anyone tell me," asked Virginia, "why a lovely delicate¹³ flower should have an ugly name like *scabiosa.*"¹⁴

(8) Samson, the third baseman, threw down his glove, and¹⁵ screamed that the runner hadnt¹⁶ touched the base.

(9) I wonder who the man is who's¹⁷ talking so intently with our hostess?¹⁸

(10) To receive a prize, you should send ten box tops to the following address;¹⁹ Box 372, Burton, Iowa 50112.²⁰

(11) Shortly after eleven thirty²¹ convicts assembled in the dining hall²² and announced that they would not eat.

(12) "At these neighborhood events," complained Mother, "everyone else's kids seem to behave better than our's."²³ ²⁴

291

25. _____ (13) Having made an impressive record in high-school football,
26. _____   basketball, and track; Stevick has been offered scholarships
                from several colleges.

27. _____ (14) Our meetings are scheduled to begin at 9 A.M. but it's usually
28. _____   half an hour later before we start.

29. _____ (15) The pilot finally stopped the taxiing plane; firefighters then
30. _____   quickly sprayed foam on the engine and the passengers exited
                through the rear stairway.

31. _____ (16) A rusted broken-down old car was bought by a farmer, whose
32. _____   son needed transportation to school.

33. _____ (17) A sleek imported car was bought by our county assessor, who
34. _____   is planning to run for governor.

35. _____ (18) "Your theme would be improved, I think," said Miss. Tate, "if
36. _____   you would use fewer *and*'s to join your clauses."

37. _____ (19) When I have been working hard, and need some activity to
38. _____   make me forget my daily problems; I read a mystery novel.

39. _____ (20) Because Thelma's new neighbors, the Jones's, don't have a
40. _____   telephone yet, she is letting them use her's.

41. _____ (21) "Really Mrs. Lewis, you shouldn't have asked me to sing," said
42. _____   Maud, who just happened to have her music portfolio with her.

43. _____ (22) She is a spry, alert septuagenarian but she admits that she can't
44. _____   always recall her grandchildrens' names.

45. _____ (23) The outer office is a cold sterile room; the only noninstitutional
46. _____   touch being a few decals on the windows.

47. _____ (24) "They didn't win the game, we handed it to them with our
48. _____   mistakes," said Coach Shaw whose contract has not been re-
                newed.

49. _____ (25) To make this rich dessert, you will need: dark chocolate,
50. _____   honey, unsalted butter, sugar, and chopped pecans.

PROGRESS TEST **11**
Verbs (Lessons 20, 21)

NAME _____ SCORE _____

DIRECTIONS: Study these sentences for (1) the correct form of a principal part and (2) the correct subject–verb agreement. Underline every incorrect verb and write the correct form in the space at the left. Some sentences may be correct. No sentence contains more than two incorrect verb forms.

_____ 1. Fred shouldn't have wore that outfit to the wedding;
_____   neither the yellow socks nor the red tie were appropri-
                    ate.
_____ 2. Last month Pete begun an advertising campaign with
_____   the slogan "Come to Pete's Car Lot—The difference in
                    savings are staggering."
_____ 3. Ironically, the release of some eight thousand pages of
_____   hitherto restricted documents have proved to be a
                    boomerang.
_____ 4. "I been told that in that unhappy country one out of
_____   every thirty people are addicted to some drug," said the
                    lecturer.
_____ 5. The only time human hands touch the berries are when
_____   they are picked and put into a wash before being flash-
                    frozen.
_____ 6. The price of basic foods and medicines are higher now
_____   than they were when I begun to support myself.
_____ 7. Shortly after breakfast one of the young campers come
_____   running into the office and said that she had been stung
                    by a bee.
_____ 8. Setting right there in plain sight on my neighbor's table
_____   was several of the items he had stolen from me.
_____ 9. One of the main causes for the strikes were the wore-
_____   out condition of the equipment.
_____ 10. I've given the matter much thought and have become
_____   convinced that neither Frank nor Jack is qualified for the
                    job.
_____ 11. I already seen Dr. Cutler, but where is Mrs. Cutler and
_____   their daughter Betsy?
_____ 12. Don't your nephew ever get tired of just laying around
_____   the house and watching television?
_____ 13. The manager, no less than the treasurer, is responsible
_____   for seeing that bills are payed on time.
_____ 14. We should have gone to the library to study; there's too
_____   many disturbances here at home.
_____ 15. A youngster who has been brought up with many sisters
_____   and brothers don't have many chances to be selfish.
_____ 16. Now that the company has become so large, each one of
_____   the seven managers have well-defined duties.

17. The financial officer of the college has often spoke of this problem; she says that the stock will be sold when a gain on existing holdings seem likely.

18. Eddie has grown tired of studying; he now admits that the only part of college life that interests him is the athletic contests.

19. "I could have swore that yesterday there was at least two dozen cookies in that jar," said Mother.

20. Scientists have long known that the high acidity of the sulfuric acid particles affect people living near the foundry.

21. I had just lain down for a short nap when my neighbor come running over to announce that a blizzard was on its way.

22. The memorial is a bronze plaque on which is carved the names of local residents who have fell in battle.

23. Neither time nor money were spared when this community center was built.

24. The taxi driver, along with two slightly injured passengers, were setting on the curb waiting for the ambulance.

25. Usually there's three or four of Jason's mongrel dogs laying on the rough boards near the stove.

26. The fact that your clock radio was broke and you slept till ten don't convince me that you should be given a make-up test.

27. "Please let me rest; I've eaten four burgers and drunk five glasses of milk," moaned Phil as he lay down on the cot.

28. Every one of the people who were chosen in the lottery drawing have been notified.

29. Has either of you two girls ever swum from the camp dock to Lookout Point across the lake?

30. The fact that, strictly speaking, you haven't broke any law don't make your behavior acceptable.

Pronouns (Lessons 22,23)

NAME _____ SCORE _____

DIRECTIONS: Study the following sentences for poorly used pronouns. Look for wrong case forms, misspelled possessives, and vague or inexact reference. Circle each incorrect pronoun. In the space at the left of each pair of sentences, write the letter that identifies the correct sentence.

_____ 1. A. The promotion went to Fred Lawson, not I, in spite of the fact that I'd been with the firm longer than him.
B. The promotion went to Fred Lawson, not me, in spite of the fact that I'd been with the firm longer than he.

_____ 2. A. We were surprised that neither Lucas nor Ferris was able to meet her sales quota.
B. Neither Lucas nor Ferris was able to meet their sales quota, which surprised us.

_____ 3. A. Most of us women in the shipping department were bitterly disappointed when we learned who the new supervisor will be.
B. Most of we women in the shipping department were bitterly disappointed when we learned whom the new supervisor will be.

_____ 4. A. Next we stopped at the assessor's office, where they told my wife and I that our property would be reassessed.
B. Next we stopped at the assessor's office, where my wife and I were told that our property would be reassessed.

_____ 5. A. For some of we middle-aged guys, any vacation should offer a chance to improve your golf game.
B. For some of us middle-aged guys, any vacation should offer a chance to improve our golf game.

_____ 6. A. According to the morning broadcast, police arrested a tenant who they say left a burning mattress in the hall.
B. It said on the morning broadcast that police arrested a tenant whom they say left a burning mattress in the hall.

_____ 7. A. Luke told his younger brother that he should diet and take off at least twenty pounds.
B. Luke told his younger brother, "I should diet and take off at least twenty pounds."

_____ 8. A. I let Janet use my motorcycle today; hers is in the shop having its semiannual refurbishing.
B. I let Janet use my motorcycle today; her's is in the shop having it's semiannual refurbishing.

_____ 9. A. In his deposition Wilcox named fifteen people who he claimed committed criminal acts while in office.
B. In his deposition Wilcox named fifteen people whom he claimed committed criminal acts while in office.

_____ 10. A. I stood in line for an hour, and then I was told that one had to have his membership card before he could vote.
B. I stood in line for an hour, and then they told me that you had to have your membership card before you could vote.

_____ 11. A. Mike told Roger and I that a car has to be over thirty years old before you can call it a true antique.

               B. Mike told Roger and me that a car has to be over thirty years old before it can be called a true antique.

_____ 12. A. The tackle was made by Wexler, whom, as we told you earlier in the broadcast, has a very sore back.

               B. The tackle was made by Wexler, who, as we told you earlier in the broadcast, has a very sore back.

_____ 13. A. "Just between you and I," Gary said to Ben, "the responsibility for the misunderstanding is your's, not mine."

               B. "Just between you and me," Gary said to Ben, "the responsibility for the misunderstanding is yours, not mine."

_____ 14. A. We were surprised that neither Wadsworth nor Stewart added her endorsement to the petition.

               B. Neither Wadsworth nor Stewart added their endorsement to the petition, which surprised us.

_____ 15. A. Aunt Lydia's ailments seem more painful than anyone else's, and she'll describe them vividly to whoever will listen.

               B. Aunt Lydia's ailments seem more painful than anyone elses, and she'll describe them vividly to whomever will listen.

_____ 16. A. My neighbor is an avid bird-watcher, and he is trying to get my wife and I interested in it.

               B. My neighbor is an avid bird-watcher, and he is trying to get my wife and me interested in bird-watching.

_____ 17. A. If one values their reputation, they should not associate with Benson, who, if rumors are correct, the FBI is watching.

               B. One who values his or her reputation should not associate with Benson, whom, if rumors are correct, the FBI is watching.

_____ 18. A. And whom among we five candidates do you think will get more votes than me?

               B. And who among us five candidates do you think will get more votes than I?

_____ 19. A. According to this bulletin, all graduate students must have paid their fees by October 15.

               B. It says here in this bulletin that every graduate student must have paid their fees by October 15.

_____ 20. A. Another tourist whom we chatted with in Abilene told us that there were minor floods farther west.

               B. Another tourist who we chatted with in Abilene told us that they were having minor floods farther west.

Modifiers; Appropriate Use (Lessons 24,25)

NAME _____ SCORE _____

DIRECTIONS: Choose the preferred form from within the parentheses and copy it in the space at the left.

_____
_____
1. You could (have, of) finished the chores if you had worked (steady, steadily) till sundown.

_____
_____
2. The grade on your theme was lowered (because of, due to) six words that were spelled (incorrect, incorrectly).

_____
_____
3. (Let's, Let's us) budget our time so that we can finish this boring work (faster, more faster) than usual.

_____
_____
4. Two pedestrians were hurt (real, very) (bad, badly) in the accident.

_____
_____
5. My sister and I took the same test; mine received the (better, best) grade because I made (fewer, less) mistakes.

_____
_____
6. This coffee tastes so (bad, badly) that I (can hardly, can't hardly) drink it.

_____
_____
7. After his first day of work on the loading dock, Ben was (plenty, very) tired, and he slept (good, well) that night.

_____
_____
8. "(Where, Where at) did you buy (them, those) beautiful earrings?" asked Ms. Sumner.

_____
_____
9. Joan (aggravated, annoyed) her parents by driving (a lot, much) faster than they told her to.

_____
_____
10. The superintendent seems (real, really) (enthused, enthusiastic) about the new reading program.

_____
_____
11. The lawyers (believed, figured) that the prisoner behaved so (strange, strangely) because he had been drugged.

_____
_____
12. The teacher told us that we are (suppose, supposed) to pronounce words (distinct, distinctly) when we make the recording.

_____
_____
13. I have no doubt (but what, that), of the two job offers, the one from the auto repair shop is the (more, most) attractive.

_____
_____
14. Coach Allen is (sure, surely) unhappy about the large (amount, number) of injuries his team has suffered recently.

_____
_____
15. The old man was (awful, very) angry when the driver would not let him get (off, off of) the bus in the middle of the block.

_____
_____
16. "In those days your mother and I (use to, used to) go dancing (regular, regularly) at the old Trianon Hall," said Dad.

_____
_____
17. "(Leave, Let) us not forget that medical costs have risen (considerable, considerably) since then," concluded Dr. Wright.

_____
_____
18. We (had ought to, should) be proud that our team did so (good, well) in the regional tournament.

_____
_____
19. The children had to stay (inside, inside of) the tent because rain fell (steady, steadily) all day.

_____
_____
20. "This (type, type of) computer is the kind you should buy, (irregardless, regardless) of the price," said the sales representative.

_____
_____
21. I think that (this, this here) oil painting would look (good, well) on your living room wall.

_____
_____
22. The typhoon developed so (sudden, suddenly) that the residents of the island (could scarcely, couldn't scarcely) prepare for it.

_____
_____
23. "(Try and, Try to) make the new worker feel at home; he's (real, very) eager to do a good job," said the boss.

_____
_____
24. Bob (sure, surely) was surprised to find out how (easy, easily) the boat handled after it was repaired.

_____
_____
25. Larry admitted that he was (kind of, rather) surprised when he learned how (good, well) he had done on the final examination.

Usage (Lessons 20–25)

NAME _____ SCORE _____

DIRECTIONS: Each sentence contains two italicized expressions. If you think an expression is correct for serious writing, write *C* in the space at the left. If you think an expression is inappropriate, write a correct form in the space.

_____
_____ 1. The new witness was *sworn* in, and he pointed out two suspects *whom* he claimed had helped him rob the bank.

_____
_____ 2. *Due to* the heavy traffic, we *couldn't scarcely* get to the other side of the street.

_____
_____ 3. "If you know of some other person who is more experienced than *I*, send *them* to Washington in my place," replied the beleaguered lawmaker.

_____
_____ 4. The housemother divided the housekeeping chores *among* ten of *us* freshmen.

_____
_____ 5. It may be that the reason your son is not cooperating is *because* taking part in vigorous body-contact sports *don't* appeal to him.

_____
_____ 6. Ted was soaking wet when he *come* home from work yesterday; he should have *wore* his raincoat.

_____
_____ 7. "*Is* any one of your pipe wrenches large enough to fit *this here* pipe?" my neighbor asked me.

_____
_____ 8. Just between you and *I*, I was so tired that I could have *lain* down on those rough boards and been asleep in two minutes.

_____
_____ 9. The number of people wanting tickets for the extra concerts *were* a pleasant surprise to *we* board members.

_____
_____ 10. "I feel *like* I've been *setting* in this old truck for half my life," complained the driver as he wearily descended from the cab.

_____
_____ 11. *Has* either of the two senior vice-presidents of your firm *begun* to think about retirement yet?

_____
_____ 12. Because our tardiness had been *due to* the icy roads, all of *us* latecomers were given excuses.

_____ 13. I feel certain, Betty, that *somewheres* in this great land
_____   of *our's* there is a politician who can be trusted.

_____ 14. Anyone who drives as *recklessly* as you should be sure
_____   that *their* insurance is in order.

_____ 15. *Who* do you think will be assigned to room with you and
_____   *me* next semester?

_____ 16. We were told that the sale of season tickets for our foot-
_____   ball games this year *have* declined *considerable*.

_____ 17. It's a miracle that anyone could have *swum* through
_____   those rock-strewn rapids without seriously injuring
                     themself.

_____ 18. I wish I could make pies that taste as *good* as *your's*
_____   always do.

_____ 19. There was a large purse *laying* on the table, but none of
_____   us knew *who's* it was.

_____ 20. "Has Jim *begun* to let his hair return to *it's* natural
_____   color?" asked Virginia.

_____ 21. Mr. Knox boasts to *whoever* will listen about how *good*
_____   he has done in the stock market.

_____ 22. The clerk gave Dad and *I* a pamphlet containing infor-
_____   mation in *regards* to the state fishing regulations.

_____ 23. It was a long *ways* back to the ski lodge, and I was
_____   nearly *froze* when we arrived.

_____ 24. Experienced old-timers like you and *I* know *who* the
_____   real troublemakers in the union are.

_____ 25. *There's* still three new members to be *chosen* for the
_____   nominating committee.

Spelling (Lessons 26,27)

NAME _____ SCORE _____

DIRECTIONS: Choose the correctly spelled form from within the parentheses and copy it in the space at the left.

_____
_____
1. If you work at the post office during the holiday, (your, you're) not going to have any (leisure, liesure) time.

_____
_____
2. The (affects, effects) of the freezing weather are (noticable, noticeable) if you travel on the unimproved rural roads.

_____
_____
3. Passing this test with a high grade is (quiet, quite) an (acheivement, acheivment, achievement, achievment).

_____
_____
4. Professor Lapham's research has (shone, shown) that the disease is not (incurable, incureable).

_____
_____
5. These (incidence, incidents), along with a few other (regretable, regrettable) events, forced Jason to resign.

_____
_____
6. We all admit that she's beautiful, but she's so (conceited, concieted) that she is rapidly (loosing, losing) her friends.

_____
_____
7. The (principal, principle) of our school promised that the culprits would be punished for their (outrageous, outragous) behavior.

_____
_____
8. The old king's (rain, reign, rein) ended when invaders from the North laid (seige, siege) to his castle.

_____
_____
9. These singers are relatively unknown here, but I'm told that (their, there, they're) quite (fameous, famous) in the South.

_____
_____
10. His uncle is a (financeir, financier) (who's, whose) reputation is far from spotless.

_____
_____
11. Mrs. Lowry maintains that certain TV programs make her children (to, too, two) (excitable, exciteable).

_____
_____
12. Sue did not explain her choice, saying only that it was a matter of (personal, personnel) (preference, preferrence).

13. Many people consider San Felipe a (desirable, desire-able) place to live because of (its, it's) mild climate.

14. "I rarely (receive, recieve) social notes on such garish hotel (stationary, stationery)," said Ms. Arbuthnot.

15. The frightened girl secretly (past, passed) a note to the alert bank (casheir, cashier).

16. With (admirable, admireable) courage the teacher rang the alarm and then (lead, led) the children out of the building.

17. Mr. Lamson's three young (neices, nieces) followed him into the (dining, dinning) room.

18. With great (presence, presents) of mind, the officer (sheilded, shielded) the children from the falling rocks.

19. "I'd like to (complement, compliment) the cook on the delicious (desert, dessert) we were served," said Senator Fowler.

20. "Back in the (sixties, sixtys), when I was in school, we had to work harder for grades (than, then) you kids now do," he boasted.

21. Both Jenkins and Booth want the job; in all (likelihood, liklihood) the (later, latter) will get it.

22. "The richly decorated (altar, alter) of the church is a thing of almost (unbeleivable, unbeleiveable, unbeliev-able, unbelieveable) beauty," said Jane.

23. "We cannot, of (coarse, course), guarantee that the high (yeild, yield) on the stock will continue," said the broker.

24. I (advice, advise) you to buy really (servicable, service-able) tires before you attempt this trip.

25. Mr. Beach is not (all together, altogether) happy about (retireing, retiring) next year.

Spelling (Lessons 26–29)

NAME _____ SCORE _____

DIRECTIONS: Each sentence contains two words with letters missing. Write the words, correctly spelled, in the spaces at the left.

_____
_____

1. I'm embar——sed when I fail to reco——ize someone whom I've met before.

_____
_____

2. Our weather in January and Feb——ary is maddeningly chang——ble.

_____
_____

3. The op——rtunity to travel in South America made the job offer particu——ly attractive.

_____
_____

4. In his letter Coach Hoskins emph——sized the fact that he would prob——ly retire within a year.

_____
_____

5. I would have pref——red a more int——sting topic for my term paper.

_____
_____

6. After earning n——ty quarter hours of credit, a sop—— more officially becomes a junior.

_____
_____

7. We cert——nly enjoyed our tour of Great Brit——n.

_____
_____

8. The elderly man was trying desp——tely to work his way ac——s the crowded, busy street.

_____
_____

9. In your letter you d——cribed accurately the barely adequate ac——modations of the inn.

_____
_____

10. Don't attempt to repair your damaged comput——r; that's a job for a prof——sional.

303

DIRECTIONS: A sentence may be correct, it may have one misspelled word, or it may have two misspelled words. Underline every incorrectly spelled word and write it, correctly spelled, in a space at the left of the sentence.

1. This term I usualy spend Wednesday evenings in the reference library.

2. The eminent psychiatrist gave some excellent advice to the disappointed student.

3. The candidate was wholly unaware of the grievious effect produced by his speach.

4. Generally I am able to find a usable dictionary in the dormatory.

5. Leroy felt awkward and self-conscious during his first conference with the marriage counselor.

6. It's my belief that our sergeant doesn't always really appreciate my conscientious efforts.

7. Those of you who's scheduals are not yet complete should see your home-room teacher immediately.

8. "Your interpretation of this peice of literature shows real immagination," said Ms. Tuttle.

9. Quite naturally, some of our more mischievious students take advantage of our gentle school principal.

10. There is little likelihood of a repitition of last year's disasterous flood.

Spelling (Lessons 26–29)

NAME _____ SCORE _____

DIRECTIONS: Each sentence contains two words with letters missing. Write the words, correctly spelled, in the spaces at the left.

_____
_____

1. The accused man adm——ted having once had the microfilm in his pos——sion.

_____
_____

2. I'd hardly call a peanut butter san——ch and a cup of watery veg——ble soup a lavish lunch.

_____
_____

3. Carstens will plunge headlong into an argu——nt, even though he has little know——ge of the subject.

_____
_____

4. Incident——y, I wish you wouldn't inter——pt me when I am telling a story.

_____
_____

5. It is indeed a priv——ge to be asked to serve on your advisory com——tee.

_____
_____

6. The attendance officer told Gary that his excuse was n———ther convincing nor orig——nal.

_____
_____

7. Most local brokers are extre——ly opt——mistic about the company's prospects.

_____
_____

8. Marylou's grades in geography and arith——tic improved notic——bly the next semester.

_____
_____

9. A few people in the aud——nce laughed at my unusual pron——ciation of the polysyllabic medical terms.

_____
_____

10. The owner of the rest——rant told us that we would have to wait unt——l ten o'clock to be served.

DIRECTIONS: A sentence may be correct, it may have one misspelled word, or it may have two misspelled words. Underline every incorrectly spelled word and write it, correctly spelled, in a space at the left of the sentence.

_____
_____
1. The consultant adviced us to increase the insurance coverage on the irreplaceable equiptment in the laboratory.

_____
_____
2. Do you think it appropriate for a famous astronaut to make money reccommending a new product for the relief of headaches?

_____
_____
3. Some of our most competent teachers have resigned, and classroom discipline has almost compleatly dissappeared.

_____
_____
4. My outside work program, totaling approximately fourty hours a week, leaves little time for athletics and other pastimes.

_____
_____
5. It surprised me to find amoung my friends several who are enthusiastic about working in politics and local government.

_____
_____
6. I truly believe that my business partner would serve satisfactorily as club secretary.

_____
_____
7. On the eighth and ninth of next month, our superintendent will be attending a conference on new scientific proceedures.

_____
_____
8. Publications similiar to this pamphlet, full of propaganda, will undoubtedly appear before election day.

_____
_____
9. Brent often tells us about humerous, sometimes ridiculous, experiences he had when he taught the twelfth grade in the village school.

_____
_____
10. The personnel officer acknowledged that he was dissatisfied with the new questionnaire.

Plurals and Capitals (Lesson 28)

NAME _____ SCORE _____

DIRECTIONS: Write the plural form or forms of each of the following words. When in doubt, consult your dictionary. If two forms are given, write both of them.

1. cemetery _____ _____

2. circus _____ _____

3. crisis _____ _____

4. dodo _____ _____

5. donkey _____ _____

6. Eskimo _____ _____

7. fowl _____ _____

8. Frenchman _____ _____

9. grandchild _____ _____

10. grotto _____ _____

11. gulf _____ _____

12. hypothesis _____ _____

13. louse _____ _____

14. mongoose _____ _____

15. oasis _____ _____

16. ox _____ _____

17. roomful _____ _____

18. son-in-law _____ _____

19. swine _____ _____

20. syllabus _____ _____

21. tableau _____ _____

22. tax _____ _____

23. Thomas _____ _____

24. wharf _____ _____

25. wolf _____ _____

PLURALS AND CAPITALS

DIRECTIONS: The following sentences contain forty numbered words. If a word is correctly capitalized, write *C* in the space with the corresponding number. If a word should not be capitalized, write *W* in the space.

1. _____ 2. _____   (1) My French teacher, Professor Quinn, spent last
                          ₁   ₂

3. _____ 4. _____   Summer traveling in the Far East with another
                          ₃   ₄   ₅

5. _____ 6. _____   College Professor.
                          ₆   ₇

7. _____ 8. _____   (2) Four miles South of town there was a colony of
                                       ₈

9. _____ 10. _____   Mennonites who had originally come from the
                          ₉

11. _____ 12. _____   East before the Spanish-American War.
                          ₁₀   ₁₁   ₁₂   ₁₃

13. _____ 14. _____   (3) The Anderson Memorial Library is located on the
                                ₁₄   ₁₅   ₁₆

15. _____ 16. _____   first street West of Market Street.
                          ₁₇   ₁₈

17. _____ 18. _____   (4) If I remember correctly, one of my Aunts had just
                                                          ₁₉

19. _____ 20. _____   sent Mother a copy of Edith Wharton's *A Son At*
                          ₂₀   ₂₁ ₂₂ ₂₃

21. _____ 22. _____   *The Front.*
                          ₂₄   ₂₅

23. _____ 24. _____   (5) We hope to spend Thanksgiving Day in California
                                             ₂₆   ₂₇

25. _____ 26. _____   with Aunt Effie.
                              ₂₈

27. _____ 28. _____   (6) Our buildings are predominantly Gothic in style,
                                                      ₂₉

29. _____ 30. _____   although Meyer Hall and some of the new
                                  ₃₀

31. _____ 32. _____   Engineering units are modern.
                          ₃₁

33. _____ 34. _____   (7) All Freshmen at Clearwater College take a re-
                                ₃₂   ₃₃

35. _____ 36. _____   quired course, General Studies 100; their elective
                                        ₃₄   ₃₅

37. _____ 38. _____   courses are chiefly in English, Mathematics,
                                                  ₃₆   ₃₇

39. _____ 40. _____   Physics, Chemistry, and German.
                          ₃₈   ₃₉   ₄₀

General Review

NAME _____ SCORE _____

DIRECTIONS: Identify each italicized unit by writing one of the following numbers in the space at the left:

    1. Noun clause   3. Adverb clause   5. Participial phrase
    2. Adjective clause   4. Gerund phrase

_____ 1. Have you finally finished *reading the instructional booklet?*

_____ 2. The letter informed me *that I had won a lottery prize.*

_____ 3. The prize *that I won* amounted to only twenty dollars.

_____ 4. I should be happy *that I won even a small prize.*

_____ 5. Do you know the man *standing beside the governor?*

_____ 6. *Appearing in public with the governor* is good publicity.

_____ 7. *If I were you,* I'd start looking for another job.

_____ 8. Take notes on everything *Dr. Lemon says.*

_____ 9. Take notes on *whatever Dr. Lemon says.*

_____ 10. There's a strange car *parked in my neighbor's driveway.*

DIRECTIONS: Underline every incorrect expression and write a correct form in the space at the left.

_____ 1. Don't it impress you that six of us freshmen scored high in the test?

_____ 2. Lenny lay on the cot until most all of the other dormitory residents had left.

_____ 3. Wasn't it he who suggested that the reward be divided equally between you and I?

_____ 4. Matthew, along with two friends, are skiing today.

_____ 5. He's an excellent student whom most of us think will have a brilliant career.

_____ 6. Bernie is taller than me, but I can run faster than he.

_____ 7. The older of their two sons is plenty enthusiastic about becoming an astronaut.

_____ 8. Lucy hit the golf ball well, but now there's a tree between she and the green.

_____ 9. Has either of your parents visited you at camp?

_____ 10. The range of your interests and experiences amaze me.

DIRECTIONS: In the column of figures before each sentence circle each number that represents an error in the sentence. Use these numbers:

    1. Wrong punctuation
    2. Dangling or misplaced modifier

    3. Error in agreement of subject and verb
    4. Error in case or number of pronoun

1 2 3 4   (1) Glancing at the clock, the man told us that usually the supervisor or his assistant arrive by six oclock.

1 2 3 4   (2) "There's only four or five other people who I'd trust with this information," said old Dr Stanton.

1 2 3 4   (3) Leaving the gym and assembling by the pool, the instructor asked how many of we freshmen could swim?

1 2 3 4   (4) "The prize should have gone to you, not I," said Sally Osborn who did not, however, sound very convincing.

1 2 3 4   (5) Going over the books with our accountant, its quite likely that the company is having it's best year.

1 2 3 4   (6) Every woman who signed up for our exercise and diet course will say that they got their moneys worth.

1 2 3 4   (7) Being a school holiday, our youngest child, together with two of his pals, were racing around the house all day.

1 2 3 4   (8) "The prospect of another week at this damp campground don't thrill me," said Mother who prefers life in town.

1 2 3 4   (9) Was either of the two electricians able to before meal time repair your stove.

1 2 3 4   (10) Mr. Bradshaw was a true philanthropist, he always seemed ready to offer a helping hand to whomever was in need.

DIRECTIONS: Underline each misspelled word and write it, correctly spelled, in the space at the left.

_____   1. The audience was becoming really annoyed by the unnecessary interruptions of the preformance.

_____   2. Durring February we rarely go picnicking because of the extremely changeable weather.

_____   3. The sergeant's advise to me was that dining in any eating place in the village could be disastrous.

_____   4. The speaker emphasized the fact that our candidate has fourty years of experience in politics.

_____   5. The new secretary was embarrassed because she had made a grievous error in her first business letter.

_____   6. The equipment necessary for an excellent athletic program is gradually being accumulated.

_____   7. Each member of the committee acknowledged that my speech had been appropriate for the occassion.

_____   8. On the ninth day of February, represenatives of several companies will hold a conference here.

_____   9. I always appreciate the personal courtesies shone me when I visit this restaurant.

_____   10. Murmuring some rediculous answer, the awkward young man hurriedly left the room.

General Review

DIRECTIONS: Underline every incorrect expression and write the correct form in the space before the sentence.

_____ 1. You shouldn't of lain in the hot sun all day.

_____ 2. There's still a few odd jobs for us to do today.

_____ 3. Let's us promise to keep this news just between you and me.

_____ 4. A man whom I barely knew came in and set down beside me.

_____ 5. Most of the horses swam across the stream, but two of them drownded.

_____ 6. Our team played real good in the second half.

_____ 7. Jan is three years older than me, but she looks younger.

_____ 8. I'm sure I left the keys somewheres in this desk.

_____ 9. After dinner Lucas begun to tell Bob and me about his trip to Tibet.

_____ 10. If you were me, you'd also feel bad about what happened.

DIRECTIONS: If you find an error in punctuation, circle the error and write W before the sentence. If the sentence is correctly punctuated, write C in the space.

_____ 1. As you may have suspected the boy's motives were not made clear to his family.

_____ 2. "You know where the dean's office is, dont you," asked Ned.

_____ 3. Miss. Kane will probably wonder why she wasn't invited?

_____ 4. This sofa is too wide, we cant get it up our narrow staircase.

_____ 5. "Merciful heavens Ben, whats happened to you?" said Vera.

_____ 6. The concert featured works by: Brahms, Ravel and Debussy.

_____ 7. "And now, good friends, it's time to adjourn," announced Dr. Lambert.

_____ 8. While painting Jeff stumbled on the top step, and spilled nearly a quart of paint.

_____ 9. Michael, his eyes full of tears, asked if we would forgive him.

_____ 10. "Remember, madam," said the clerk, "that the responsibility is your's, not mine."

DIRECTIONS: If you find a misspelled word, underline it and write it correctly at the left. (Consider an omitted or misused apostrophe a punctuation error, not a spelling error.) In the column of figures at the left, circle the numbers that identify the errors in the sentence:

  1. Dangling or misplaced modifier
  2. Error in case or number of pronoun
  3. Error in subject–verb agreement
  4. Error in punctuation

_____ 1 2 3 4
1. Leaving the new highway just beyond Bellville, our progress was slower, we had to procede carefully because of the flooding in the area.

_____ 1 2 3 4
2. To our suprise, the principal of the school said, "Neither of these jackets are mine, mine only has one pocket."

_____ 1 2 3 4
3. One of the members of the Committee on Natural Resources were late for the meeting, her taxi had broken down during the four-oclock traffic rush.

_____ 1 2 3 4
4. "And whom may I say is calling," said Mr. Dunn's secretary, who had recently taken a speach course at a local business college.

_____ 1 2 3 4
5. "The performance of our offensive line and defensive backs have been, to put it mildly, less than impressive," said Coach Loew whose job is in peril.

_____ 1 2 3 4
6. The manager encouraged Tim and I when she said, "Either one of you are eligible for the job in the laboratory, you will both be interviewed soon."

_____ 1 2 3 4
7. Don't it seem rather odd that every one of the trainees except you and I were given excellent reccommendations.

_____ 1 2 3 4
8. "You either adhere to the closing-time rules or your restaurant is in danger of loosing it's permit," the officer announced.

_____ 1 2 3 4
9. After driving accross the state line, the roads will be in bad condition; the harsh winter and sudden thaw having damaged the pavement.

_____ 1 2 3 4
10. A few of we housewives in the village have been doing Mrs Alworthy's daily shopping since breaking her ankle.

_____ 1 2 3 4
11. To enroll in Literature 472, a student either must be in the honors program or have their application approved by Professor Hart who teaches the course.

_____ 1 2 3 4
12. Most of us farmers are dissatisfied with the work of the maintainance crews, there's still some bad chuckholes on our county roads.

APPENDIX A STUDY SKILLS: BASIC TOOLS FOR COLLEGE WORK

T HE ABILITY to write well is a great advantage to a college student. But there are other skills that you should master early in your college career. Using the dictionary, outlining, paraphrasing, and summarizing written material will be necessary almost from the first day of class. Managing your time is extremely important for success in college. The following sections will serve as an introduction to these very important skills.

Use of the Dictionary

You will soon find that a desk dictionary is as necessary to your writing as pen and paper. A good one is worth every cent of its cost; don't economize on a paperback pocket version and expect it to serve you adequately. Your instructor will probably recommend any of the following:

The American Heritage Dictionary, Second College Edition
The Random House College Dictionary, Revised Edition
Webster's Ninth New Collegiate Dictionary
Webster's New World Dictionary of the American Language, Second College Edition

Make your dictionary earn its price. Use it. Keep it near you when you study or write. It's a trove of information and will tell you much more than the mere meanings of words. Before you begin to use your dictionary, look inside the covers to see what is printed on the endpapers. It may be something you'll want to refer to often. Browse through the first few pages—especially those that explain the dictionary's system of pronunciation symbols, indication of preferred spellings and pronunciations, treatment of alphabetical order, usage notes, arrangement of multiple meanings, and notation for parts of speech. Then turn to the back pages. Does the dictionary have separate listings for geographic and biographical names? Does it give tables of weights and measures, rules for punctuation and mechanics? If you know what extra content your dictionary holds, you may be able to save yourself time, bother, and even cold cash when the need arises for some odd little fact.

1. Spelling. The dictionary will, of course, give the correct spelling of a word—sometimes two correct spellings, of which the first entry is usually the more widely used spelling. Can you look up the spelling of a word in the dictionary if you can't spell the word to begin with? Yes, almost always. Words like *phobia, pneumatic, rhyme, xylophone,* and a few others in which the first or second letter is the doubtful point may give trouble, but one or two searches under likely combinations will usually turn up the answer.

cat·a·logue also cat·a·log (kăt'l-ôg', -ŏg') —*n.* **1. a.** A systematized list, usually in alphabetical order, often with descriptions of the listed items. **b.** A publication, such as a book, containing such a list. **2.** A card catalog. —*tr. & intr.v.* -logued, -logu·ing, -logues also -loged, -log·ing, -logs. To list in or make a catalogue. [ME *cathaloge* < OFr. *catalogue* < LLat. *catalogus*, enumeration < Gk. *catalogos* < *kata-legein*, to list : *kata-* (intensive) + *legein*, to count.] —**cat′a·loqu′er, cat′a·log′er** *n.*

2. Pronunciation. Before you can use your dictionary effectively, you must learn its symbols for primary and secondary accent marks, for division of syllables, and for use of a hyphen when a word is to be broken at the end of a line.

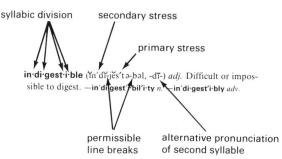

syllabic division   secondary stress

primary stress

in·di·gest·i·ble (ĭn′dĭ-jĕs′tə-bəl, -dī-) *adj.* Difficult or impossible to digest. —**in′di·gest′i·bil′i·ty** *n.* —**in′di·gest′i·bly** *adv.*

permissible   alternative pronunciation
line breaks   of second syllable

The American Heritage Dictionary

The presence of more than one pronunciation means that different people in different parts of the country pronounce the word differently. It does not mean that one is right and the other wrong.

Look up the pronunciations of the following:

1. acclimate	4. decadent	7. exquisite	10. pianist
2. adult	5. desperado	8. neither	11. processes
3. Caribbean	6. drama	9. pejorative	12. sonorous

3. Plurals. If you are not sure about the correct plural of a noun, your dictionary will settle the question.

cur·ric·u·lum (kə rik′yə ləm) *n.*, *pl.* **-u·la** (-lə), **-u·lums** [L., lit., a running, course, race, career < *currere*, to run: see CURRENT] **1.** a fixed series of studies required, as in a college, for graduation, qualification in a major field of study, etc. **2.** all of the courses, collectively, offered in a school, college, etc., or in a particular subject —**cur·ric′u·lar** *adj.*
‡**curriculum vi·tae** (vīt′ē; vē′tī, wē′-) *pl.* **cur·ric′u·la** (-lə) **vi′tae** [L., course of life] a summary of one's personal history and professional qualifications, as that submitted by a job applicant; résumé

Look up the correct plurals of the following:

1. adieu	4. bus	7. genus	10. radius
2. appendix	5. crocus	8. mother-in-law	11. solo
3. beau	6. cupful	9. ox	12. species

4. Capitalization. Problems of capitalization may also be referred to your dictionary. You know, of course, that proper nouns—that is, names of persons and places—are capitalized. You know that common nouns are not capitalized. But often the real question is whether a noun is used in its proper sense or its common sense. With the help of your dictionary, try to determine whether the italicized words in the following sentences should be capitalized:

1. She ordered *french fries* with her steak.
2. This should be set up in *roman* type.
3. Many students do not understand *roman* numerals.
4. Later in life he was attracted to the *christian* religion.
5. He brought back some very fine *china* from *china*.

5. Principal parts of verbs. If you are not sure whether to say, "His coat was laying on the bed" or "His coat was lying on the bed," whether to say, "My sister growed," or "My sister grew," the dictionary will help you.

> **grow** (grō), *v.*, **grew, grown, grow·ing.** —*v.i.* **1.** to increase by natural development, as any living organism or part by assimilation of nutriment. **2.** to arise or issue as a natural development: *Our friendship grew from common interests.* **3.** to increase gradually in size, amount, etc.; expand: *The influence of this group has grown over the last two decades.* **4.** to become gradually attached or united by or as by growth: *The branches of the trees grew together.* **5.** to come to be, or become, by degrees: *to grow old.* —*v.t.* **6.** to cause to grow: *He grows corn.* **7.** to allow to grow: *to grow a beard.* **8.** to cover with a growth (used in the passive): *a field grown with corn.* **9. grow into, a.** to become large enough for. **b.** to become mature or experienced enough for. **10. grow on** or **upon, a.** to increase in influence or effect: *An uneasy feeling grew upon him.* **b.** to become fixed gradually in one's mind or affections: *a village by the sea that grows on one.* **11. grow out of, a.** to become too large or mature for; outgrow. **b.** to originate in; develop from. **12. grow up, a.** to be or become fully grown. **b.** to come into existence; arise. [ME *grow(en)*, OE *grōwan*; c. D *groeien*, OHG *grouwan*, Icel *grōa*] —**grow′a·ble,** *adj.* —**Syn. 1.** develop, multiply, swell, enlarge, expand, extend. **2.** originate. **3.** wax. **6.** raise. —**Ant. 1.** decrease. **3.** wane.

The Random House College Dictionary, Revised Edition, Copyright © 1984 by Random House, Inc. Reprinted by permission.

As *grew* is given because *grow* is an irregular verb and does not form the past by adding *ed*, clearly, "My sister *grew*" is the correct choice. Note that *grow* is identified as both *v.i.* and *v.t.*, that is, as an intransitive verb and a transitive one. An intransitive verb does not act on an object; a transitive verb does. Now look up *lay* and *lie* in the dictionary. Why is "His coat was *lying* on the bed" the better sentence?

You should know the principal parts of the following troublesome verbs:

1. bring	5. do	9. hang
2. burst	6. drag	10. pay
3. buy	7. drown	11. shine
4. dive	8. eat	12. take

6. Meaning. Many words, some of them very ordinary words, have a variety of meanings. The dictionary lists and separates all the definitions and gives their applications.

> **rush**[1] (rush), *v.i.* **1.** to move, act, or progress with speed, impetuosity, or violence. **2.** to dash, esp. to dash forward for an attack or onslaught. **3.** to appear, go, pass, etc., rapidly or suddenly. —*v.t.* **4.** to perform, accomplish, or finish with speed, impetuosity, or violence: *He rushed the work.* **5.** to carry or convey with haste. **6.** to cause to move, act, or progress quickly; hurry. **7.** to attack suddenly and violently; charge. **8.** to overcome or capture (a person, place, etc.). **9.** *Informal.* to court intensively; woo. **10.** to entertain (a prospective fraternity or sorority member) before making bids for membership. **11.** *Football.* **a.** to carry (the ball) forward across the line of scrimmage: *The home team rushed the ball a total of 145 yards.* **b.** to carry the ball (a distance) forward from the line of scrimmage: *The home team rushed 145 yards.* **c.** (of a defensive team member) to attempt to force a way quickly into the backfield in pursuit of (the back in possession of the ball). —*n.* **12.** the act of rushing; a rapid, impetuous, or violent onward movement. **13.** a hostile attack. **14.** an eager rushing of numbers of persons to some region to be occupied or exploited: *the gold rush to California.* **15.** a sudden appearance or access: *a rush of blood to his face.* **16.** hurried activity; busy haste: *the rush of city life.* **17.** a hurried state, as from pressure of affairs. **18.** press of work, business, traffic, etc., requiring extraordinary effort or haste. **19.** *Football.* **a.** an attempt to carry or instance of carrying the ball across the line of scrimmage. **b.** the act or an instance of rushing the offensive back in possession of the ball. **20.** *U.S.* a scrim-

mage held as a form of sport between classes or bodies of students in colleges. **21.** Usually, **rushes.** *Motion Pictures.* the first prints made after shooting a scene or scenes. **22.** *Informal.* a series of lavish attentions paid a girl by a suitor. —*adj.* **23.** requiring or done in haste. **24.** characterized by excessive business, work, traffic, etc. [ME *rusche(n)* < AF *russh(er), russ(er),* c. OF *re(h)usser, re(h)user, ruser* << LL *recūsāre,* to push back < L: to refuse. See RECUSANT] —**rush′ing·ly,** *adv.*
—**Syn. 1.** hasten, run. RUSH, HURRY, SPEED imply swiftness of movement. RUSH implies haste and sometimes violence in motion through some distance: *to rush to the store.* HURRY suggests a sense of strain or agitation, a breathless rushing to get to a definite place by a certain time: *to hurry to an appointment.* SPEED means to go fast, usually by means of some type of transportation, and with some smoothness of motion: *to speed to a nearby city.* —**Ant. 16.** sloth, lethargy.
rush² (rush), *n.* **1.** any grasslike herb of the genus *Juncus,* having pithy or hollow stems, found in wet or marshy places. **2.** any plant of the family *Junaceae.* **3.** a stem of such a plant, used for making chair bottoms, mats, baskets, etc. **4.** something of little or no value; trifle. [ME *rusch, risch,* OE *rysc, risc;* c. D, obs. G *Rusch*] —**rush′like′,** *adj.*
Rush (rush), *n.* **Benjamin,** 1745–1813, U.S. physician and political leader: author of medical treatises.

Random House College Dictionary

7. Appropriate use. A certain word, either in all of its uses or in some of its special meanings, is effective if it is appropriate to the occasion, the purpose, the time, and the place of its use. By means of usage labels, such as *Slang, Colloq., Dial., Archaic, Obs., Illit.,* a dictionary tries to indicate that a certain word has a restricted appropriateness. (Note that dictionaries may vary in their application of these labels.)

Examine this selection from *Webster's New World Dictionary,* in which you will find several words marked *Slang* and three marked *Colloq.* Some dictionaries use *Substandard* for *Slang* and *Informal* for *Colloq.* Words marked *Colloq.* are more appropriate in informal than in formal situations, especially in informal spoken language. Words without any usage label are usually appropriate at all times, on every occasion, in every situation.

good·y¹ (-ē) *n., pl.* **good′ies** [Colloq.] **1.** something considered very good to eat, as a piece of candy ☆**2.** *same as* GOODY-GOODY —*adj.* [Colloq.] *same as* GOODY-GOODY —*interj.* a child's exclamation of approval or delight
good·y² (-ē) *n., pl.* **good′ies** [< GOODWIFE] [Archaic] a woman, esp. an old woman or housewife, of lowly social status: used as a title with the surname
Good·year (good′yir′), **Charles** 1800–60; U.S. inventor: originated the process for vulcanizing rubber
good·y-good·y (good′ē good′ē) *adj.* [redupl. of GOODY¹] [Colloq.] moral or pious in an affected or canting way —☆*n.* [Colloq.] a goody-goody person
☆**goo·ey** (gōō′ē) *adj.* **goo′i·er, goo′i·est** [GOO + -EY] [Slang] **1.** sticky, as glue **2.** sticky and sweet **3.** overly sentimental
goof (gōōf) *n.* [prob. < dial. *goff* < Fr. *goffe,* stupid < It. *goffo*] [Slang] **1.** a stupid, silly, or credulous person **2.** a mistake; blunder —*vi.* [Slang] **1.** to make a mistake; blunder, fail, etc. **2.** to waste time, shirk one's duties, etc. (usually with *off* or *around*)
☆**goof·ball** (-bôl′) *n.* [GOOF + BALL¹] [Slang] a barbiturate, or sometimes a stimulant drug, tranquilizer, etc., esp. when used nonmedically: also **goof ball**
goof-off (-ôf′) *n.* [Slang] a person who wastes time, neglects his duties, or avoids work; shirker
goof·y (-ē) *adj.* **goof′i·er, goof′i·est** [Slang] like or characteristic of a goof; stupid and silly —**goof′i·ly** *adv.* —**goof′i·ness** *n.*

Webster's New World Dictionary

Where the labels *Slang, Colloq.,* and so on are inapplicable, a dictionary may give, at the end of the entry, a short paragraph or two of usage information. (For this purpose *American Heritage* makes use of a panel of consultants.)

dec·i·mate (děs′ə-māt′) *tr.v.* **-mat·ed, -mat·ing, -mates. 1.** To destroy or kill a large part of. **2.** To select by lot and kill one in every ten of. [Lat. *decimare, decimat-* < *decimus,* tenth < *decem,* ten.] —**dec′i·ma′tion** *n.*

Usage: *Decimate* originally meant to kill every tenth person, a punishment sometimes inflicted by Roman commanders. The meaning has been extended to include the destruction of any large proportion of a group: *Famine decimated the population.* The Usage Panel accepts this extension but considers that *decimate* should not be used to describe the destruction of a single person, or an entire group, or any specified percentage other than one-tenth; avoid a sentence such as *The famine decimated 37 per cent of the population.*

The American Heritage Dictionary

en·thuse \in-'th(y)üz\ *vb* en·thused; en·thus·ing [back-formation fr. *enthusiasm*] *vt* (1827) 1 : to make enthusiastic 2 : to express with enthusiasm ~ *vi* : to show enthusiasm ⟨a splendid performance, and I was *enthusing* over it —Julian Huxley⟩
  usage *Enthuse* is apparently American in origin, although the earliest known example of its use occurs in a letter written in 1827 by a young Scotsman who spent about two years in the Pacific Northwest. It has been disapproved since about 1870. Current evidence shows it to be flourishing nonetheless, esp. in journalistic prose on both sides of the Atlantic.

By permission. From Webster's Ninth New Collegiate Dictionary. Copyright © 1984 Merriam-Webster Inc., publisher of the Merriam-Webster® dictionaries.

Look up each of the italicized words in the following sentences:

1. The game was delayed by a long *rhubarb* at the plate.
2. Out of the argument he got a black eye that was a *lulu*.
3. The batter called the umpire a *windbag*.
4. "*Forsooth*," cried the umpire, "do not try to *flimflam* me."
5. "You are a *braw laddie*," he retorted, "but I may cast you into *yon loblolly*."
6. Butch had enough *bread* to hire a *mouthpiece* who kept him out of the *pokey*.

8. Synonyms and antonyms. Although it is impossible for a dictionary to give differentiated synonyms for every word it contains, it does group relatively common words that have similar definitions to demonstrate particular qualities and various shades of meaning. Often, it also gives words of opposite meaning (antonyms) as an aid to distinction. (See, for example, the entry for *rush* on page 315.)

mon·strous \'män(t)-strəs\ *adj* (15c) 1 *obs* : STRANGE, UNNATURAL 2 : having extraordinary often overwhelming size : GIGANTIC 3 a : having the qualities or appearance of a monster b *obs* : teeming with monsters 4 a : extraordinarily ugly or vicious : HORRIBLE b : shockingly wrong or ridiculous 5 : deviating greatly from the natural form or character : ABNORMAL 6 : very great — used as an intensive — mon·strous·ly *adv* — mon·strous·ness *n*
  syn MONSTROUS, PRODIGIOUS, TREMENDOUS, STUPENDOUS mean extremely impressive. MONSTROUS implies a departure from the normal (as in size, form, or character) and often carries suggestions of deformity, ugliness, or fabulousness ⟨the imagination turbid with *monstrous* fancies and misshapen dreams —Oscar Wilde⟩ PRODIGIOUS suggests a marvelousness exceeding belief, usu. in something felt as going far beyond a previous maximum (as of goodness, greatness, intensity, or size) ⟨made a *prodigious* effort and rolled the stone aside⟩ ⟨men have always reverenced *prodigious* inborn gifts —C. W. Eliot⟩ TREMENDOUS may imply a power to terrify or inspire awe ⟨the spell and *tremendous* incantation of the thought of death —L. P. Smith⟩ but in more general and much weakened use it means little more than very large or great or intense ⟨success gave him *tremendous* satisfaction⟩ STUPENDOUS implies a power to stun or astound, usu. because of size, numbers, complexity, or greatness beyond one's power to describe ⟨all are but parts of one *stupendous* whole, whose body Nature is, and God the soul —Alexander Pope⟩

Webster's Ninth New Collegiate Dictionary

Note in the example that each synonym is illustrated by a quotation. Not all dictionaries provide this particularly helpful feature.

You can use synonyms in two ways to improve your writing. The first use simply prevents repetition. The same word used again and again may look more important to the message than it really is; it may also make the message dull. The second use of synonyms, possibly the crucial one, is the matter of precision, of discovering just the right word for the sense. By the "right" word we mean no more than a word apt or suitable in its context. There are bookish or literary words that may be suitable in some formal contexts, in serious books. There are simple and homely words that are right in more informal writing. The distinctions between them are learned slowly, it is true, and all we can do here is give a few examples:

BOOKISH WORDS	SIMPLE WORDS
impecunious	poor
opulent	rich, wealthy
discoursed	talked, spoke
dolorous	sad, painful, mournful
emolument	pay, wages, salary, fee
sustenance	support, food

9. Denotation and connotation. A dictionary definition will establish the meaning of a word, but that definition does not necessarily include all the information about meaning that you need to use the word. In *The Random House College Dictionary* the first definition given for the adjective *fat* is "having too much adipose [fatty] tissue. . . . " For a listing of synonyms, the reader is referred to the entry for *stout*, where we find this: "STOUT, FAT, PLUMP imply corpulence of body." Definitions such as "having too much adipose tissue" and "corpulence of body," stated in cold, factual, almost clinical analysis, are the *denotative* meanings of the words. A stout man, a plump man, and a fat man are all overweight. But although *stout*, *fat*, and *plump* share the same denotative meaning, the words are not always interchangeable. They have different emotional weights, different associations with the pleasant and the unpleasant; they express different degrees of positive and negative attitude or appeal. This emotional implication of a word is its *connotation*. A stout man is a fat man who gives an impression of solidity, strength, health, and vigor; *stout* thus has a positive connotation. A plump man is fat, but in a sense of the ridiculous, as though it were more a question of his being too short for his girth than of his being too broad for his height. *Plump* applied to a woman, on the other hand, is usually a term of approval, implying that the excess adipose tissue is tastefully distributed. The different uses may reflect the sexism of a male-dominated language, but they are also matters of connotation, of emotional values added to words by the uses to which the words are customarily put.

Study the following list of words, referring to a dictionary as necessary. Which words are usually positive or neutral by connotation? Which negative? Which words have similar denotative meanings?

1. articulate	6. demure	11. liberal	16. proud
2. blunt	7. eloquent	12. officious	17. prudish
3. candid	8. fussy	13. particular	18. reject
4. credulous	9. garrulous	14. profligate	19. trusting
5. decline (refuse)	10. haughty	15. prolix	20. zealous

10. Derivations of words. Your dictionary will tell you the derivation or source of any word. Although there is some danger in assuming that the original meaning of a word is still its exact meaning (meanings change, you know, through long use), quite often a knowledge of the source and the original meaning of a word can illuminate it for you and give it a vividness of meaning that you will never forget. Did you know that *salary* comes from the Latin *salarium*, which meant the money given to Roman soldiers to buy salt with? Or that *tribulation* comes from a Latin word meaning a threshing sledge? Hence a man afflicted with tribulation is like a man beaten with the swinging clubs used to pound out grain on a threshing floor. Or consider *recalcitrant*. A recalcitrant child is an obstinate child. But if you look up the original meaning of the word, you find that the child is really "kicking back," like a mule.

The following words have interesting histories. Look them up in your dictionary.

1. bowery	4. carouse	7. laser	10. sabotage
2. boycott	5. curfew	8. nice	11. tawdry
3. carnival	6. hussy	9. panic	12. terrier

11. Persons and places. The most convenient source of information about persons and places is your dictionary. It is true that the information you get there is condensed, but in most cases it is enough to set you on the right track. As a means of finding out where proper names are listed, you might look up some of the names in the following list. Remember that some dictionaries have a special section for geographic names and another for names of persons, whereas others list everything in the regular vocabulary.

1. Boucicault	3. Cassandra	5. Galen	7. Mount Kosciusko
2. Casanova	4. Corday	6. Ganges	8. Poseidon

12. Miscellaneous information. Finally, the dictionary contains in easily accessible form a large amount of miscellaneous information about science, geography, biography, history, mythology, and so forth. Test this statement by looking up the following:

1. Who usually lives at 10 Downing Street?
2. What were the former names of Zimbabwe, Sri Lanka, and Namibia?
3. What is Mrs. Malaprop noted for?
4. Give an example of a spoonerism.
5. Why is *cheeseburger* a totally illogical name?
6. What sort of person would shed crocodile tears?
7. Where is Liechtenstein? What is its capital?
8. What is the most notable characteristic of a Manx cat?
9. If you bought a litre of petrol, what would you get, and how much?
10. Look up the four italicized words and then explain the meaning of this sentence: The word *radar* is unusual, perhaps even *unique*, in that it is both an *acronym* and a *palindrome*.

Paraphrasing

You will also find it useful to be able to paraphrase short passages that are particularly important or particularly difficult to read. A paraphrase is a rewriting of the original version in your own words—almost a translation. It simplifies, but does not necessarily shorten, the passage. Read the following technical passage on the description and purpose of an automobile turbocharger:

Basically turbocharging is a system for increasing engine horsepower by using the exhaust gases to drive a turbine connected by a shaft to a compressor which pumps the fuel/air mixture into the engine. With an increase in engine speed, this compressor forces a greater volume of mixture into the combustion chambers, producing more power. During the cruising or light-load conditions, the turbocharger is essentially quiescent and the volume of mixture ingested is about the same as with any normally aspirated engine. The primary benefit of turbocharging, then, is that a fuel efficient small-displacement engine can have increased performance with little or no sacrifice in fuel economy (*Road and Track*, February 1978, p. 88).

Two words require immediate definition before any other efforts at simplification can begin:

1. *turbine:* a machine that has a rotor (a system of rotating airfoils) driven by the pressure of moving water, gases, or air. [Sometimes even dictionaries are no help. Picture a set of blades mounted around a shaft, much as the paddles of a water wheel are arranged. These blades—the rotor—are mounted inside a chamber, and water, gas, or even air moving at high speed flows through the chamber and turns the rotor by pressing on the blades.]

2. *compressor:* a pump or other machine for reducing the volume and increasing the pressure of gases. [Again the dictionary is not a great help. This part of the turbocharger pushes more gas–air mixture into the combustion chamber than would enter under ordinary pressure.]

NOTE: These two definitions offer a classic example of the problems facing a beginner in any field: The dictionary definitions are given in words too technical for a beginner to grasp, forcing the beginner to seek further definitions in the dictionary or to find a person both willing and able to explain the term in simple words. Asking for help from a teacher or a knowledgeable student is the easiest way out of the difficulty.

With these definitions in hand, try the passage in its existing order, making it simpler by substituting simpler words wherever possible.

A turbocharger is a device mounted on an automobile engine to increase the power of the engine. It uses exhaust gases to turn a wheel mounted on a shaft (turbine), which then turns another wheel or pump and forces the fuel–air mixture into the cylinders under pressure. Thus more fuel enters than ordinary pressure would bring in; more fuel mixture produces greater power. At low engine speed the device doesn't turn very fast, and the cylinders receive about as much mixture as they would through an ordinary carburetor. At high speed the compressor greatly increases the efficiency with which the engine uses the fuel–air mixture. The result is that a small engine can produce good performance without sacrificing fuel economy.

Sometimes it is equally useful to shorten a passage and make the basic idea easier to remember. A summary of that same paragraph on the turbocharger might read:

A turbocharger is a compressor driven by a rotor turned by exhaust gases. The compressor forces fuel–air mixture into the cylinders under greater than normal pressure, providing more fuel–air mixture for each detonation; thus the power of a small engine can be increased without a loss of economy.

This new version cuts the number of words in the passage by half and simplifies the wording somewhat. The shorter version ought to prove more manageable during study or review.

Outlining and Taking Notes

As you study, you will need to outline some of the materials you read in order to get an overall view of their scope and direction. Reading, outlining, and taking notes from a chapter of a textbook are not exceptionally difficult, but they constitute a very important skill.

Begin by reading the chapter through once rather quickly, trying to catch the general subject and the direction that the author is taking. Then read the chapter a second time, paying close attention to detail. In this second reading you should look up any words that are unclear to you. Paraphrase short passages that are especially difficult for you to read. This is the time to get complete control of the chapter.

On the third reading, locate the major divisions of the chapter. Note the headings, usually printed in contrasting type; they often indicate major divisions in a chapter. If you do not find headings within the chapter, search the introductory paragraphs for clues or statements that will help you to pick out the major divisions. Quite often the introduction contains some statement of the thesis of the chapter or provides enough direction so that you can find the major divisions.

If the chapter has no headings and the introduction does not offer enough direction to enable you to find the major divisions, work through the chapter paragraph by paragraph, writing a one-sentence summary for each paragraph. Read these sentences and try to group them into topics. If you are able to divide these topics into groups, summarize the ideas in each group and use those summaries as the headings in your chapter outline.

In addition to outlining the chapter, you should take other notes that will give you a complete picture of its content. Write down all the important dates. List the names of people, ideas, and events that figure in the chapter; later on, write out a brief identification of each item in the list. Take from the chapter illustrations and examples that might help to develop an answer on a test or a portion of a paper. Record quotations that seem to state an idea or a concept with exceptional clarity. With an outline and a thorough collection of notes such as these suggested, you should be able to master the material in a chapter without much difficulty.

Planning Your Time and Your Work

Some students do a bare minimum of work during the term and then cram massive amounts of studying into the last few days. Because such cramming requires that you ingest large and potentially harmful doses of coffee, amphetamines, and other stimulants, and because material learned quickly is forgotten quickly, a system of regular, manageable doses of work has much to recommend it.

Such a system of regular work is a necessity for success in college. The time spent in class in a college course is significantly shorter than the class time of a high-school course. New students sometimes fool themselves into believing that this shorter class time means that college is less work than high school. Nothing could be more likely to lead to failure. Many people believe that the average college student ought to spend *at least* an hour in outside work for every hour of class time in a college course. So in a three-credit course you should do three hours of preparation each week. And note that *one hour* is the *minimum* time for an average student. If you wish to make more than an average grade, or if you find a course difficult, you must spend more than the minimum time in outside preparation. Here are a few suggestions that might make your time allotted to preparation more productive:

1. Schedule study (and work, if you have a job) at regular times during the day. Provide enough time to keep up with your course work without cram sessions every two or three weeks to catch up. Allot your time so that the classes

needing greater effort will receive extra time. Remember to schedule time regularly for working on long-term assignments and for library work. A large project will be easier and more beneficial if you do it in a number of short sessions than if you cram all the work into one or two marathon sessions.

2. Review your lecture and discussion notes immediately after the class or just before the next session. Consolidate and organize the notes while the material is fresh in your mind.

3. Do outside reading and writing assignments when they are assigned so that work outside the class will relate closely to the lectures and discussions in the class. Use class work and outside preparation to reinforce each other.

4. Work regularly rather than in fits and starts. Your mind needs time to understand new material and to develop new ideas. It does these tasks best in smaller units of time and materials. Trying to pressure-pack four or five weeks of material into a single day's cramming for a test is a very inefficient way to use your time and your mind. The same amount of time, spread out over several weeks, will yield far better results—more learning and better grades—with less strain on you.

5. Work neatly and carefully. Keep your notes and other materials in neat, well-organized folders. Time spent in the regular care and maintenance of these materials will allow you to study productively when test time finally arrives, without the frustration of searching for lost materials and of deciphering unreadable notes.

Regular work, performed with consistent high quality and meticulous care, is the only guarantee of success in college. Good work habits, developed at the beginning of your college career, will pay dividends from the start. It is impossible to emphasize too much the importance of working regularly, as opposed to letting matters slide and trying to catch up in agonized bursts of effort later in the term. A ten-hour project will always take ten hours to complete successfully. You will put in the time one way or another, but ten hours spent in five two-hour sessions will produce far better results than ten hours spent in a single marathon session. Invest your time wisely.

DIAGNOSTIC TEST: *Punctuation*

NAME _____ SCORE _____

DIRECTIONS: In the space at the left of each pair of sentences, write the letter that identifies the correctly punctuated sentence.

_____ 1. A. "Whenever I try to study my class notes are almost unreadable," complained Ruth, "I must be more careful about my handwriting."
B. "Whenever I try to study, my class notes are almost unreadable," complained Ruth; "I must be more careful about my handwriting."

_____ 2. A. Some of the stockholders are now wondering if the company has overextended itself by buying the two new ships.
B. Some of the stockholders are now wondering, if the company has overextended itself by buying the two new ships?

_____ 3. A. Although the Perkinses live less than a block away from us, we hardly feel that we know them well.
B. Although the Perkins's live less than a block away from us; we hardly feel that we know them well.

_____ 4. A. The following notice recently appeared on the bulletin board; "The editors of this years Senior yearbook have decided to dispense with the so-called humor section."
B. The following notice recently appeared on the bulletin board: "The editors of this year's Senior yearbook have decided to dispense with the so-called humor section."

_____ 5. A. I scraped the mud and mashed insects from the windshield and Norma sadly inspected the crumpled, rear fender.
B. I scraped the mud and mashed insects from the windshield, and Norma sadly inspected the crumpled rear fender.

_____ 6. A. After they had cleaned the kitchen, put the children to bed, and locked the front door, Pete and Jane looked forward to a quiet, peaceful evening.
B. After they had cleaned the kitchen, put the children to bed and locked the front door; Pete and Jane looked forward to a quiet peaceful evening.

_____ 7. A. Some neighbors asked questions about Jim's strange friends but Mother told them that it was nobodys concern except our family's.
B. Some neighbors asked questions about Jim's strange friends, but Mother told them that it was nobody's concern except our family's.

_____ 8. A. "Tryouts for the class play have been completed," Miss. Lowe, the drama coach, announced, "this year we are blessed with almost too much talent."

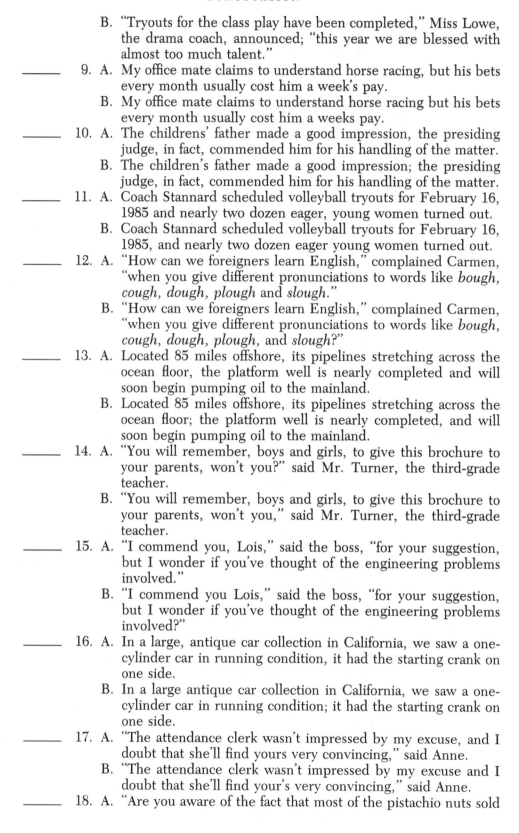

B. "Tryouts for the class play have been completed," Miss Lowe, the drama coach, announced; "this year we are blessed with almost too much talent."

_____ 9. A. My office mate claims to understand horse racing, but his bets every month usually cost him a week's pay.

B. My office mate claims to understand horse racing but his bets every month usually cost him a weeks pay.

_____ 10. A. The childrens' father made a good impression, the presiding judge, in fact, commended him for his handling of the matter.

B. The children's father made a good impression; the presiding judge, in fact, commended him for his handling of the matter.

_____ 11. A. Coach Stannard scheduled volleyball tryouts for February 16, 1985 and nearly two dozen eager, young women turned out.

B. Coach Stannard scheduled volleyball tryouts for February 16, 1985, and nearly two dozen eager young women turned out.

_____ 12. A. "How can we foreigners learn English," complained Carmen, "when you give different pronunciations to words like *bough, cough, dough, plough* and *slough*."

B. "How can we foreigners learn English," complained Carmen, "when you give different pronunciations to words like *bough, cough, dough, plough,* and *slough*?"

_____ 13. A. Located 85 miles offshore, its pipelines stretching across the ocean floor, the platform well is nearly completed and will soon begin pumping oil to the mainland.

B. Located 85 miles offshore, its pipelines stretching across the ocean floor; the platform well is nearly completed, and will soon begin pumping oil to the mainland.

_____ 14. A. "You will remember, boys and girls, to give this brochure to your parents, won't you?" said Mr. Turner, the third-grade teacher.

B. "You will remember, boys and girls, to give this brochure to your parents, won't you," said Mr. Turner, the third-grade teacher.

_____ 15. A. "I commend you, Lois," said the boss, "for your suggestion, but I wonder if you've thought of the engineering problems involved."

B. "I commend you Lois," said the boss, "for your suggestion, but I wonder if you've thought of the engineering problems involved?"

_____ 16. A. In a large, antique car collection in California, we saw a one-cylinder car in running condition, it had the starting crank on one side.

B. In a large antique car collection in California, we saw a one-cylinder car in running condition; it had the starting crank on one side.

_____ 17. A. "The attendance clerk wasn't impressed by my excuse, and I doubt that she'll find yours very convincing," said Anne.

B. "The attendance clerk wasn't impressed by my excuse and I doubt that she'll find your's very convincing," said Anne.

_____ 18. A. "Are you aware of the fact that most of the pistachio nuts sold here, are imported from Greece and Turkey," asked Dr. Ash who is a storehouse of trivia.

    B. "Are you aware of the fact that most of the pistachio nuts sold here are imported from Greece and Turkey?" asked Dr. Ash, who is a storehouse of trivia.

_____ 19. A. The auto age for America really began in 1908 when Henry Ford, the son of a farmer, produced his Model T which was black, reliable and cheap.

    B. The auto age for America really began in 1908, when Henry Ford, the son of a farmer, produced his Model T, which was black, reliable, and cheap.

_____ 20. A. The manager smiled faintly and said, "It seems a shame, doesn't it, that a football player of Jake's ability must retire just because someone's spreading ugly rumors?"

    B. The manager smiled faintly and said, "It seems a shame, doesn't it, that a football player of Jake's ability must retire just because someones spreading ugly rumors."

_____ 21. A. It was four o'clock of a chilly, damp September afternoon, and the beach was deserted except for two bored lifeguards.

    B. It was four oclock of a chilly, damp, September afternoon and the beach was deserted except for two bored lifeguards.

_____ 22. A. My daughter pulled on her gloves and started to snip off the wilted blossoms, her expression revealing her complete lack of interest in gardening.

    B. My daughter pulled on her gloves, and started to snip off the wilted blossoms; her expression revealing her complete lack of interest in gardening.

_____ 23. A. Some of the electrical equipment failed, for nearly twenty hour's the explorers had no radio contact with the base.

    B. Some of the electrical equipment failed; for nearly twenty hours the explorers had no radio contact with the base.

_____ 24. A. If theres one thing today's students don't need; it's more critical, admonitory, or threatening advice hurled at them by long-nosed sanctimonious adults.

    B. If there's one thing today's students don't need, it's more critical, admonitory, or threatening advice hurled at them by long-nosed, sanctimonious adults.

_____ 25. A. "A team that won't be beaten can't be beaten," shouted Coach Miller, who had a seemingly endless supply of clichés.

    B. "A team that wont be beaten can't be beaten," shouted Coach Miller who had a seemingly endless supply of clichés.

DIAGNOSTIC TEST: *Spelling*

NAME _____ SCORE _____

DIRECTIONS: Each of the following sentences contains three italicized words, one of which is misspelled. Underline each misspelled word and write it, correctly spelled, in the space at the left.

_____ 1. "There are limitations on the length, breadth, and *heighth* of packages we ship, and the weight must not *exceed forty* pounds," the agent said.

_____ 2. My present was a box of fancy *stationery;* I was *dissappointed* that I didn't *receive* something more practical.

_____ 3. The food served at this rural inn is *becoming fameous* throughout Great *Britain.*

_____ 4. Lathrop sought the *advise* of an *eminent psychiatrist.*

_____ 5. This may sound *unbelievable* to you, but our city *library* has been struck three times by *lightening.*

_____ 6. Jerry is *dissatisfied* with his new *schedual* because it does not allow him time for studying *during* the afternoons.

_____ 7. In his *sophmore* year Gerald took a course in *speech* and two courses in *literature.*

_____ 8. The play had *it's* first *performance* in Hartford last *February.*

_____ 9. "An *acquaintance* of mine *reccommended* your *restaurant* to me," said Mrs. Watkins to the receptionist.

_____ 10. The applicant attempted to flatter the interviewer by saying, "You are *undoubtably knowledgeable* about the latest *technology* in our field."

_____ 11. "Your *humorous* remarks were not *appropriate* for a serious *occasion* such as this one," said the chairperson.

_____ 12. I admit that my new dog behaved *deploreably* last *Wednesday* at *obedience* school.

_____ 13. The data we get from these *questionnaires* could have an *effect* on next year's hiring *proceedures.*

_____ 14. *Reference* to a *dictionary* could have quickly settled the *arguement* the two of you were having.

_____ 15. We must all *recognize* the fact that tourism is the *principle* source of income in our quaint *village*.

_____ 16. Yesterday one of the arrested men *lead* the police officers to the place where the *equipment* stolen from the *laboratory* had been hidden.

_____ 17. A *goverment* spokesperson announced that the new *satellite* will provide weather forecasters with *indispensable* data.

_____ 18. The coach happily announced a *noticeable improvement* in batting averages, *especialy* in those of our outfielders.

_____ 19. A serious accident on the highway caused us to *loose approximately ninety* minutes of valuable time.

_____ 20. A senior *pardner* of the firm *conceded* that further meetings would very likely be *necessary*.

_____ 21. "This *pamphlet* is full of the most *rediculous propaganda* I've ever read," shouted the incumbent.

_____ 22. "*Neither* of these two small countries could withstand a long *seige*," replied *Sergeant* Lewis.

_____ 23. As he presented Enid with the award, the *superintendent* said, "Here is a young person *who's courageous* fight has inspired all of us."

_____ 24. When arrested, Edgar had in his *possession* a large *quanity* of *counterfeit* money.

_____ 25. "Serving on this *committee* has been a *priviledge* and a wonderful *experience*," said the retiring chairperson.

DIAGNOSTIC TEST: *Usage*

DIRECTIONS: In the space at the left, copy from within the parentheses the form that would be appropriate in serious writing.

_____ 1. Bert was surprised to learn that everyone in the class except Maria and (he, him) had to take another test.

_____ 2. The thief apparently had crept through the broken ventilator grill and had (laid, lain) quietly in the storeroom until nightfall.

_____ 3. Mary Ellen wasn't at the park yesterday; it hardly could have been (she, her) who tore your scarf.

_____ 4. Anyone selected for the acting presidency must prepare (himself or herself, themself, themselves) for a short and thankless term of office.

_____ 5. The reason I'm looking so pale is (because, that) my sunlamp needs repairing.

_____ 6. Some fellow who had occupied the room before I arrived had left some of (his, their) old clothes in the closet.

_____ 7. I wish someone on the school paper would write an editorial in (regard, regards) to the noise in the library reading room.

_____ 8. Just between you and (I, me), Luke shouldn't expect to get off with only a lecture from the judge.

_____ 9. You're convinced now, aren't you, that you (hadn't ought to, shouldn't) leave your garage unlocked?

_____ 10. My sister once studied the alto saxophone but never played it (good, well) enough to be chosen for the school band.

_____ 11. The robbers, (whoever, whomever) they were, must have known exactly when the workers would be paid.

_____ 12. The school's new program must be effective, for there (has, have) been surprisingly few complaints from parents.

_____ 13. Not many jobs are available, (because, being that) the government has curtailed operations at the navy yard.

_____ 14. After speaking into the microphone, Laura played back the tape and commented on how (different, differently) her voice sounded.

_____ 15. "Vote for (whoever, whomever) you think is the best candidate," answered Anita's father.

_____ 16. In a political campaign every candidate makes promises that (they know, he or she knows) cannot possibly be kept.

_____ 17. Also included in the packet (is, are) a travel guide, some special trip tips, and two exceptional bonus prizes.

_____   18. Someone should have told (we, us) ushers that the main door had not been unlocked.

_____   19. Do you know who the woman is who is (setting, sitting) at the head table next to the guest speaker?

_____   20. As everyone knows, neither DDT nor any other insecticide (has, have) the ability to distinguish between good and bad insects.

_____   21. If the helicopter pilot had not dropped blankets to the men stranded on the ice floe, they probably would have (froze, frozen) to death.

_____   22. After a few months Carrie (began, begun) to have doubts about her nephew's ability to manage her investments.

_____   23. No one could have been more surprised than (I, me) to learn of your recent marriage.

_____   24. The gratification resulting from working on the school newspaper and other publications (outweighs, outweigh) the demands on one's time.

_____   25. After a person has sat for five hours in the blazing sunlight listening to this kind of music, (he or she feels, they feel) numb and beaten.

DIAGNOSTIC TEST: *Sentence Structure*

NAME _____ SCORE _____

DIRECTIONS: Study these paired sentences for incompleteness, dangling or misplaced modifiers, faulty parallelism, and faulty comparisons. In the space at the left, write the letter that identifies the correct sentence.

_____ 1. A. The cotton crop this year, we all hope, will be much better than last years.
B. The cotton crop this year, we all hope, will be much better than last year's.

_____ 2. A. Because we are the parents of five active children, our washing machine is running much of the time.
B. Being the parents of five active children, our washing machine is running much of the time.

_____ 3. A. Searching the area carefully, we finally found the tunnel entrance, expertly covered by underbrush and which the other searchers had overlooked.
B. Searching the area carefully, we finally found the tunnel entrance, which had been expertly covered by underbrush and which the other searchers had overlooked.

_____ 4. A. The group's intention, surely a noble one, to constantly and relentlessly encourage the protection of the environment.
B. The group's intention, surely a noble one, is to encourage constantly and relentlessly the protection of the environment.

_____ 5. A. Believing me to be a better public speaker than anyone else in the class, my parents told all the relatives that I would be the valedictorian.
B. Being a better public speaker than anyone in the class, my parents told all the relatives that I would be the valedictorian.

_____ 6. A. Malaysia and other countries proved incapable of sheltering or unwilling to shelter all of the refugees.
B. Malaysia and other countries proved incapable or unwilling to shelter all of the refugees.

_____ 7. A. "I neither intend to withdraw from the race nor to in any degree stop pointing out my opponent's shortcomings," Ms. Hawley replied.
B. "I intend neither to withdraw from the race nor in any degree to stop pointing out my opponent's shortcomings," Ms. Hawley replied.

_____ 8. A. When seen from a distance, the white cliffs seem to resemble icebergs.
B. When seen from a distance, one might think that the white cliffs were icebergs.

_____ 9. A. This popular young actor lives high in the Hollywood hills in a small apartment decorated with posters of auto races and bullfights.
B. This popular young actor lives in a small apartment decorated with posters of auto races and bullfights high in the Hollywood hills.

331

_____ 10. A. The relatively small amount of flood water has not and probably won't cause any major damage.
B. The relatively small amount of flood water has not caused and probably won't cause any major damage.

_____ 11. A. When we replaced the wooden shingles with a composition roof, the insurance company agreed to lower our annual premium quite considerably.
B. By replacing the wooden shingles with a composition roof, the insurance company agreed to quite considerably lower our annual premium.

_____ 12. A. Commissioner Reed stated that our downtown streets are as clean, if not cleaner than, other cities.
B. Commissioner Reed stated that our downtown streets are as clean as, if not cleaner than, those of other cities.

_____ 13. A. I already have a full enough schedule of work today without being asked to listen to you practice your speech.
B. I already have a full enough schedule of work today without asking me to listen to you practice your speech.

_____ 14. A. The reason for our moving being that the security system at Elmhurst Manor is more modern than the old apartment.
B. The reason for our moving is that the security system at Elmhurst Manor is more modern than that at the old apartment.

_____ 15. A. Sylvia Andrews is a self-sufficient and talented person who, since her husband died, has supported herself and her family tutoring students in mathematics.
B. Sylvia Andrews, a self-sufficient and talented person who has supported herself and her family since her husband died tutoring students in mathematics.

_____ 16. A. My mother's paternal grandmother was one of the very few, if not the only, woman to study veterinary medicine in the early 1900's.
B. My mother's paternal grandmother was one of the very few women, if not the only woman, to study veterinary medicine in the early 1900's.

_____ 17. A. You must either return these books to the library or pay a substantial fine.
B. Either you must return these books to the library or pay a substantial fine.

_____ 18. A. I hope that the yield from these tax-free bonds will be equal to, if not more than, the yield from your stocks.
B. I hope that the yield from these tax-free bonds will be equal, if not more than, your stocks.

_____ 19. A. Albert's plan being to, as soon as he receives his inheritance, retire to some remote island in the South Seas.
B. Albert's plan is to retire to some remote island in the South Seas as soon as he receives his inheritance.

_____ 20. A. You will be given preferred seating only if you have donated at least two hundred dollars to the Opera Guild.
B. You will only be given preferred seating if you have donated at least two hundred dollars to the Opera Guild.

_____ 21. A. Ellen hopes that her tax-deductible contributions this year will be equal to, if not more than, last year's.

   B. Ellen hopes that her tax-deductible contributions this year will be equal, if not more than, last year.

_____ 22. A. Pietro maintains that most people in his country are easygoing, warmhearted, friends to Americans, and having a tolerance for the ideas and ways of foreigners.

   B. Pietro maintains that most people in his country are easygoing and warmhearted, are friends to Americans, and have a tolerance for the ideas and ways of foreigners.

_____ 23. A. Fairhaven has one of the largest airports in the state, if not the largest.

   B. Fairhaven has one of the largest, if not the largest, airport in the state.

_____ 24. A. While just getting nicely adjusted to high-school life, my family moved again, this time to Baltimore.

   B. While I was just getting nicely adjusted to high-school life, my family moved again, this time to Baltimore.

_____ 25. A. Quickly totaling the bills, imagine my dismay on discovering that I nearly owed my entire month's salary.

   B. Quickly totaling the bills, I was dismayed to discover that I owed nearly my entire month's salary.